Salem Witchcraft: Accident or Arson?

Volume 4 in the "Salem Witchcraft" Series

Enders Anthony Robinson

Professor Emeritus of Applied Geophysics in the
Maurice Ewing and J. Lamar Worzel Chair
Columbia University in the City of New York

Goose Pond Press

Available from Amazon.com and other retail outlets

Front cover: Samuel Wardwell, when it was his turn, spoke to the people claiming his innocence. The executioner, smoking, stood beside him. Smoke blew into Wardwell's face and interrupted his words. The afflicted girls chanted, "The Devil hinders Wardwell with smoke."

Copyright © 2019

by

Enders A. Robinson

All Rights Reserved Worldwide

Goose Pond Press

In reading Authors, when you find
Bright passages that strike your mind—
And which perchance you may have reason
To think of at another season—
Be not contented with the sight
But take it down in black and white.

(From a notebook kept by my great aunt Hanna Wardwell)

Contents

Preface

In 1672, my ancestor Samuel Wardwell, carpenter, moved from Salem to Andover. The wealthy Adam Hawkes, ancestor of Presidents John Adams and John Quincy Adams, died soon thereafter, leaving his beautiful 21-year old widow Sarah Hawkes a small fortune in money and land. In his book *The House of the Seven Gables*, Nathaniel Hawthorne wrote: "Her eyes fell upon the carpenter, clad in a green woolen jacket, a pair of loose breeches, open at the knees, and with a long pocket for his rule, the end of which protruded. A glow of artistic approval brightened over her face; she was struck with admiration—which she made no attempt to conceal—of the remarkable comeliness, strength and energy of his figure." Samuel Wardwell married Sarah Hawkes and their family prospered.

Twenty years later, in July 1692, Samuel Wardwell prophesied his own death. On August 15, 1692, Samuel Wardwell was arrested for witchcraft and imprisoned in Salem. He initially made a confession, but later denied it saying, "I belied myself. It is all one. I know I shall die for it whether I admit it or not." In Salem on September 22, 1692, Samuel Wardwell, carpenter, aged 49, was executed for the crime of witchcraft. In the words of Nathaniel Hawthorne (op. cit.): "He was one of the martyrs to that terrible delusion, which should teach us that the influential classes are fully liable to all the passionate error that has ever characterized the maddest mob. Clergymen, judges, statesmen—the wisest, calmest, holiest persons of their day—stood in the inner circle round about the gallows, loudest to applaud the work of blood."

Marion Starkey, in her book *The Devil in Massachusetts*, wrote: "Samuel Wardwell of Andover stood his trial, heard his sentence, and suffered it without once going back to his former story, his confession. What was it that guided Wardwell now? Was it the Devil, or was it perhaps an angel of God, and if the latter, who were the sinners, who the murderers?"

Chapter 1. Introduction

Confession of William Barker

My ancestor William Barker Sr. was one of the very few of the arrested witches in 1692 who managed to escape from prison. His confession (Massachusetts Archives, Vol. 135 No. 39) warns of a dangerous conspiracy of witches. Barker's confession reads as follows:

> 29 August 1692. Coram Major Gidney, Mr. Hathorne, Mr. Corwin, Captain Higginson.
> William Barker of Andover's examination & confession.
> He confesses he has been in the snare of the devil three years. That the devil first appeared to him like a black man and perceived he had a cloven foot. That the devil demanded of him to give up himself soul & body unto him, which he promised to do. He said he had a great family; the world went hard with him and was willing to pay every man his own. And the devil told him he would pay all his debts and he should live comfortably. He confesses he has afflicted Sprague, Foster and Martin, his three accusers. That he did sign the devils book with blood brought to him in a thing like an Inkhorn that he dipped his fingers therein and made a blot in the book, which was a confirmation of the Covenant with the devil.
>
> He confesses he was at a meeting of witches at Salem Village where he judges there were about a hundred of them. That the meeting was upon a green piece of ground near the minister's house. He said they met there to destroy that place by reason of the peoples being divided & their differing with their ministers. Satan's design was to set up his own worship, abolish all the churches in the land, to fall next upon Salem and so go through the country. He says the devil promised that all his people should live bravely, that all persons should be equal; that there should be no day of resurrection or of judgement, and neither punishment nor shame for sin. He says there was a Sacrament at

> that meeting, there was also bread & wine. Mr. Burse was a ringleader in that meeting and name several persons that were there at the meeting. It was proposed at the meeting to make as many witches as they could. And they were all by Mr. Burse and the black man exhorted to pull down the Kingdom of Christ and set up the kingdom of the devil. He said he knew Mr. George Burroughs and Goody Howe to be such persons. And that he heard a trumpet sounded at the meeting and thinks it was Burse that did it. The sound is heard many miles off, and then they all come one after another. In the spring of the year the witches came from Connecticut to afflict at Salem Village, but now they have left it off. And that he has been informed by some of the grandees that there are about 307 witches in the country. He says the witches are much disturbed with the afflicted persons because they are discovered by them. They curse the judges because their Society is brought under. They would have the afflicted persons counted as witches but he thinks the afflicted persons are innocent & that they do God good service. And that he has not known or heard of one innocent person taken up & put in prison. He says he is heartily sorry for what he has done and for hurting the afflicted persons his accusers, prays their forgiveness, desires prayers for himself, promises to renounce the devil and all his works. And then he could take them all by the hand without any harm by his eye or any otherwise.—
> 5 September 1692. The above Said is the Truth as witness my hand. (signed by William Barker)

William Barker Sr. had critical foresight in knowing exactly what the governing hierarchy wanted to hear. His confession gave a forewarning of Satan's plan to abolish all the churches and cautioned that there were 307 witches in the country. If it were not for the reality of the situation which involved deep suffering of innocent people, this confession of William Barker Sr. would certainly stand as a minor masterpiece in witchcraft lore. Recall that the word "bravely" in the seventeenth century has the same meaning as the word "splendidly" today. William Barker claimed that

> "The devil promised that all his people should live splendidly, that all persons should be equal; that there should be no day of resurrection or of judgement, and neither punishment nor shame for sin."

Was Willian Barker prophetic? Today, the word "sin" is carefully avoided. However, in 1692, punishment and shame for sin were paramount.

The spark that lit the fire

In February 1692 in Salem Village, Betty Parris, aged 9, and her cousin Abigail Williams, aged 11, began to have fits that were regarded as beyond the power of natural disease. They were the daughter and niece of Rev. Samuel Parris. The girls screamed, threw things about the room, uttered strange sounds, crawled under furniture, and contorted themselves into peculiar positions. Other girls and women began to exhibit similar behaviors. This group was called the afflicted circle. The afflicted circle complained of being pinched, pricked with pins, and otherwise tortured. It was believed that the afflicted were bewitched. Who were the witches? A witch hunt began.

Ann Putnam Jr., aged 12, was the leading member of the afflicted circle. In the time period from February 1692 to the end of the witch hunt, the afflicted circle accused many people of being witches. The Salem witch trials were carried out by two courts: (1) The Court of Oyer and Terminer which held meetings in the period from June 2, 1692 to September 17, 1692 and (2) The Superior Court which held meetings in the period from January 1693 to May 1693. The legal process involved four steps.

> (1) When an afflicted person accused someone of being a witch, the parent or guardian would file a written complaint. If the authorities accepted the complaint, then an arrest warrant would be issued. The accused person would be arrested and examined. The word "faction" as used here designates a small group (within a town) that is antagonistic or self-seeking. Except for a few special cases, the authorities only accepted complaints initially

from a **Salem Village faction of accusers** and later from an **Andover faction of accusers**. In other words, the accusers were not a random sample of men in Essex County. Instead the accusers were lumped together into two small factions (Salem Village and Andover). Because the Salem Village faction of accusers was made up of members of the extended family of Thomas Putnam, it is alternatively called the **Putnam faction**.

(2) If the examination gave sufficient damning evidence (which it did, except for one case), the accused witch would be sent to prison waiting for an indictment and a grand jury hearing.

(3) If the grand jury found the evidence sufficient (which it did for all cases brought to it), there would be a jury trial (aka the witch trial).

(4) If jury found the accused guilty (which it did for all that came to trial), the convicted witch would be sentenced to death by hanging. Fortunately the sentence was carried out only in nineteen cases. It could have been much more if courageous people had not acted.

The afflicted girls were involved in each of the four steps.

(1) Their sufferings were described in the written complaints.
(2) They demonstrated their sufferings in the examinations.
(3) Their sufferings were evidence presented to the grand jury.
(4) They demonstrated their sufferings before the justices in the witch trials.

The episode of Salem witchcraft took place over a period from February 1692 to May 1693. Worst of all, some of the afflicted girls would be present at the hangings, which were gruesome. The ministers present at the hangings (notable Rev, Cotton Mather and Rev. Nicholas Noyes) mocked the ones who died.

Many current academic books on the Salem Witch Trials regard the involvement of the afflicted girls not as an ordeal, but as a triumph. The reason is that afflicted girls held center stage, a magnificent reversal of gender roles. In colonial days, girls and young women lacked social and legal power. However, the afflicted girls had overcome such barriers. They directed the course of action for the entire witch hunt. As a matter of fact, no government official ever questioned the validity of anything that an afflicted girl said or did. The afflicted girls were exalted in the examinations and in the trials. The height of authority, the magistrates, believed the afflicted girls. No other group has ever been treated with such respect.

Yet there is another interpretation, however unpopular. There was no reversal of gender roles at all. The afflicted girls were a casualty of the witchcraft proceedings as much as those whom they accused. That the afflicted suffered is of central importance. It was not the witches who hurt them; rather, it was their own parents and guardians. At the deepest level, the girls were afflicted by the manipulations of those they most trusted. To a greater degree than any other group, the girls were victims of deceit. Because their elders were the offenders, the afflicted girls had no place to turn for counsel or help. When the tragic play-act was finished, each girl was left with cruel markings on her spirit which, whether subtle or obvious, were unlikely to heal.

The following is from an article by Rebecca Beatrice Brooks available at `https://historyofmassachusetts.org/ann-putnam-jr`

> "In 1991, Enders A. Robinson published *The Devil Discovered: Salem Witchcraft, 1692*, which introduces to the Salem episode a conspiracy theory on a far grander scale than previously suggested by any scholar. According to Robinson, Thomas Putnam and Samuel Parris formed a circle of local men who decided to take advantage of the testimony of the afflicted children and eliminate the opposing faction in the Salem Village Church. Among the leaders of this conspiracy who were responsible for instigating the witchcraft accusations he listed Reverend Samuel Parris, Sergeant Thomas Putnam, Dr. William

> Griggs, Deacon Edward Putnam, Captain Jonathan Walcott, Constable Jonathan Putnam, and Lieutenant Nathaniel Ingersoll. These ringleaders were assisted by an outer circle of co-conspirators including Thomas Putnam's two uncles, John Putnam, Sr., and Nathaniel Putnam, his cousin Edward Putnam, Joseph Houlton, Thomas Preston, and Joseph Hutchinson. These men were less involved yet helpful when accusations and testimony were needed. Robinson alleged that what tied these conspirators together were bonds of kinship and friendship. Their goal was merely to reassert power over the families and forces that had gradually assumed control of Salem Village, seeking vengeance against those suspected of wrongdoing or what they deemed to be undesirable elements. In this task, they were ably assisted by their female children, servants, and relatives, including Mary Walcott, Sarah Churchill, Ann Putnam, Jr., Ann Putnam, Sr., Mary Warren, Susannah Sheldon, and Elizabeth Booth – in short, the majority of the 'afflicted girls.'"

Ann Putnam Jr. (aged 12) and Mary Walcott, (aged 17) were the most prominent members of the Salem Village afflicted circle. In July 1692, they were invited to the town of Andover on horse. In Andover, Joseph Ballard's wife was deathly sick. It was thought that the sickness was due to witchcraft. The girls confirmed that diagnosis. The girls were taken to sickbeds in other Andover homes. In every case, the girls said that the cause was witchcraft. The article by Rebecca Beatrice Brooks (op cit.) continues:

> "Of the 62 people Ann Putnam Jr. accused and testified against during the Salem Witch Trials, 17 were executed: Bridget Bishop (June 10), George Burroughs (August 19), Martha Carrier (August 19), Martha Corey (September 22), Mary Easty (September 22), Sarah Good (July 19), Elizabeth Howe (July 19), George Jacobs Sr. (August 19), Susannah Martin (July 19), Rebecca Nurse (July 19), Alice Parker (September 22), John Proctor (August 19), Anne Pudeator (September 22), Wilmot Reed (September 22), Margaret Scott (September 22, 1692), Sarah Wildes (July 19),

> John Willard (August 19). Like the other afflicted girls, not much is known about Ann's life after the Salem Witch Trials ended. What historians do know is that Ann's parents died suddenly in 1699, leaving Ann to raise her seven remaining siblings by herself, whose ages ranged from seven months to 16 years."

The responsibility of causing 62 arrests and 17 executions must have been a heavy burden for a pre-teen girl to carry. The events were not in the abstract. She watched the accused taken to prison and she watched the convicted die. Ann Putnam Jr. never married and remained in Salem Village the rest of her life. In 1706, when Ann Putnam Jr. wanted to join the Salem Village Church, she first had to confess any wrongdoings in her past. Ann Putnam Jr.'s apology reads as follows (Rebecca Beatrice Brooks, op cit.):

> "I desire to be humbled before God for that sad and humbling providence that befell my father's family in the year about 1692; that I, then being in my childhood, should, by such a providence of God, be made an instrument for the accusing of several persons of a grievous crime, whereby their lives were taken away from them, whom now I have just grounds and good reason to believe they were innocent persons; and that it was a great delusion of Satan that deceived me in that sad time, whereby I justly fear I have been instrumental, with others, though ignorantly and unwittingly, to bring upon myself and this land the guilt of innocent blood; though what was said or done by me against any person I can truly and uprightly say, before God and man, I did it not out of any anger, malice, or ill-will to any person, for I had no such thing against one of them; but what I did was ignorantly, being deluded by Satan. And particularly, as I was a chief instrument of accusing of Goodwife Nurse and her two sisters, I desire to lie in the dust, and to be humbled for it, in that I was a cause, with others, of so sad a calamity to them and their families; for which cause I desire to lie in the dust, and earnestly beg forgiveness of God, and from all those unto whom I have

> given just cause of sorrow and offence, whose relations were taken away or accused.

Ann Putnam Jr. was the only one of the afflicted girls to make such a confession. The confession of Ann Putnam Jr. in 1706 was an honest attempt to express her remorse and at the same time free herself from her parents' web of deceit. Seven years earlier, in 1699, her parents had died within fifteen days of each other.[1] Hopefully Ann never realized that her parents had used her as a tool for their own evil purposes. Ann Putnam Jr never married. She died in 1716 at the age of thirty-seven.

Ann Putnam Jr. was not the only afflicted girl to become a responsible adult. Elizabeth Booth married at age eighteen during the witch hunt. In 1695, Mary Walcott, almost twenty, married Isaac Farrer of Woburn and raised six children. After the Salem tragedy was over Mercy Lewis went to Greenland (not the ice-bound island, but a small hamlet with the same name in New Hampshire), where her aunt, Mary (Lewis) Lewis was living. In 1696, Elizabeth Booth's sister, Alice, who had participated as an afflicted girl, married at age eighteen. In 1709, at the age of thirty-seven, Sarah Churchill married a weaver in Berwick, Maine. In 1710 Elizabeth (Betty) Parris, age twenty-seven, married Benjamin Barnes in Concord, Massachusetts. That these afflicted girls found the strength to grow beyond their damaging early experiences and become contributing members of their communities was a remarkable achievement.

Accused of witchcraft

Let us now turn to the people who were accused of witchcraft. We never can completely grasp the anguish and terrors that they experienced. Their government leaders were their enemies, responsible for their suffering. Trapped and tormented, the accused, like the afflicted, had nowhere to turn. The accused witches were scorned. According to their ministers, the accused could not turn even to God, because, as witches, they were deserving only of punishment. The

[1] Thomas Putnam died at age forty-six on May 24, 1699. His wife, Ann Putnam Sr. died, at age thirty-seven, on June 8, 1699.

church members who were accused were excommunicated and spurned by the very congregations that were supposed to provide solace and protection in time of crisis. The 169 people accused of being witches are:

Charged	Name of accused, Age, Town	Fate after Arrest
November 1691	1. Martha (Barrett) Sparks, Chelmsford. Committed by Lieut. Gov. Thomas Danforth as a prelude to the Salem witchcraft affair.	Imprisoned more than a year; released on bail December 6, 1692
ARREST PHASE OF SALEM VILLAGE WITCH HUNT		
Feb. 29, 1692	2. Sarah (Solart) Poole Good, 38, Salem Village	Imprisoned; condemned June 30; executed July 29
Feb. 29	3. Suckling child of Sarah Good, Salem Village	Died in prison in April 1692 from cold and hunger
Feb. 29	4. Sarah (Warren) Prince Osborne, 50, Salem Village	Imprisoned 9 weeks; died in prison May 10
Feb. 29	5. Tituba, Salem Village	Imprisoned 13 months; sold to slavery in 1693
Mar. 19	6. Martha (mnu) Rich Corey, 65, Salem Village	Imprisoned; condemned Sept. 9; executed Sept. 22
Mar. 23	7. Rebecca (Towne) Nurse, 70, Salem Village	Imprisoned; condemned June 30, executed July 19
Mar. 23	8. Dorothy (aka Dorcas) Good, 4, Salem Village	Imprisoned almost 9 months; released on bail Dec. 10
Mar. 29	9. Rachel (Haffield) Clinton, 63, Salem Village	Imprisoned in Ipswich
Apr. 4	10. Sarah (Towne) Bridges Cloyce, 51, Salem Village	Imprisoned; cleared Jan. 3, 1693
Apr. 4	11. Elizabeth (Bassett) Proctor, 41, Salem Farms	Imprisoned; condemned Aug. 5; reprieved for pregnancy; released in 1693
Apr. 11	12. John Proctor, 60, Salem Farms	Imprisoned; condemned Aug. 5; executed Aug. 19
Apr. 18	13. Giles Corey, 80, Salem Village	Pressed to death, Sept. 19
Apr. 18	14. Bridget (Playfer) Wasselbe Oliver Bishop, 60, Salem Town	Imprisoned; condemned June 2; executed June 10

Apr. 18	15. Abigail Hobbs, 22, Topsfield	Imprisoned; condemned Sept. 17; reprieved; released Apr. 1693 after 12 months imprisonment
Apr. 18	16. Mary Warren, 20, Salem Village	Briefly imprisoned; released as an afflicted person
Apr. 21	17. William Hobbs, 50, Topsfield	Released 1693
Apr. 21	18. Deliverance (mnu) Hobbs	Imprisoned 12 months; Released Apr. 1693
Apr. 21	19. Nehemiah Abbot, Jr., 29, Topsfield	Released at preliminary examination, the only such case
Apr. 21	20. Mary (Towne) Easty, 51, Salem Village	Imprisoned; condemned Sept. 9; executed Sept. 22
Apr. 21	21. Sarah (Averill) Wildes, 65, Topsfield	Imprisoned; condemned June 30; executed July 19
Apr. 21	22. Edward Bishop, Jr., 44, Salem Village	Imprisoned, escaped
Apr. 21	23. Sarah (Wildes) Bishop, 41, Salem Village	Imprisoned, escaped
Apr. 21	24. Mary Black, slave, Salem Village	Imprisoned 8 months; cleared by proclamation Jan. 11
Apr. 21	25. Mary (Hollingsworth) English, 40, Salem Town	Imprisoned at least 6 weeks; escaped
Apr. 27	26. Thomas Dyer, Ipswich	Imprisoned
Apr. 28	Samuel Passanauton (an Indian)	Imprisoned
unknown	27. Female slave of Mrs. Thatcher, Boston	Imprisoned
unknown	28. Mary Cox	Imprisoned; record of irons ordered for her
Apr. 30	29. Philip English, 41, Salem Town	Imprisoned but escaped
Apr. 30	30. Lydia (mnu) Dustin, 65, Reading	Imprisoned; found not guilty Jan. 31, 1693; held in prison for fees; died in prison Mar. 10, 1693
Apr. 30	31. Susannah (North) Martin, 66, Amesbury	Imprisoned; condemned June 30; executed July 19
Apr. 30	32. Dorcas (Galley) Hoar, 60, Beverly	Imprisoned; condemned Sept. 9; reprieved; released 1693

Apr. 30	33. Sarah Morrell, 14, Beverly	Imprisoned 35 weeks; "tried and cleared" Jan. 1693
Apr. 30	34. Rev. George Burroughs, 41, Wells, Maine	Imprisoned; condemned Aug. 5; executed Aug. 19
May 7	35. Sarah Dustin, 39, Reading	Imprisoned; found not guilty Feb. 1, 1693; held in prison for fees; released March 23, 1693
May 8	36. Bethia (Pearson) Carter, 47, Woburn	Imprisoned; released on bail Dec. 8
May 8	37. Bethia Carter, Jr., 21, Woburn	Fled before arrest
May 8	38. Ann (mnu) Farrar Sears, 71, Woburn	Imprisoned; released on bail Dec. 3
May 10	39. George Jacobs, Sr., 76, Salem Town	Imprisoned; condemned Aug. 5; executed Aug. 19
May 10	40. Margaret Jacobs, 16, Salem Town	Imprisoned; released on bail in December; found not guilty Jan. 3, 1693
May 10	41. John Willard, 33, Salem Village	Imprisoned; condemned Aug. 5; executed Aug. 19
May 12	42. Alice (mnu) Parker, Salem Town	Imprisoned; condemned Sept. 9; executed Sept. 22
May 12	43. Ann (mnu) Greenslade Pudeator, 65, Salem Town	Imprisoned; condemned Sept. 9; executed Sept. 22
May 13	44. Abigail Somes, 37, Salem Town	Imprisoned; cleared Jan. 6, 1693
May 13	45. Thomas Hardy, Great Island, NH	
May 14	46. Daniel Andrew, 48, Salem Village	Fled before arrest
May 14	47. George Jacobs, Jr., 50, Salem Village	Fled before arrest
May 14	48. Rebecca (Andrew) Frost Jacobs, 46, Salem Village	Imprisoned 6 months; found not guilty on Jan. 3, 1693
May 14	49. Sarah (Smith) Buckley, 70, Salem Village	Imprisoned over 8 months; found not guilty on Jan. 4, 1693
May 14	50. Mary (Buckley) Whittredge, 27, Salem Village	Imprisoned over 8 months; found not guilty on Jan. 4, 1693
May 14	51. Elizabeth (Hutchinson) Hart, 65, Lynn	Imprisoned 7 months; cleared January 1693

May 14	52. Thomas Farrar, Sr., 75, Lynn	Imprisoned 7 months; cleared by proclamation Jan. 12, 1693
May 14	53. Elizabeth Colson, 15, Reading	Fled; captured Sept. 14 and imprisoned
May 15	54. Mehitabel (Brabrook) Downing, 40, Ipswich	Imprisoned at Ipswich prison
May 18	55. Dr. Roger Toothaker, 58, Billerica	Imprisoned; died in prison June 16
May 21	56. Sarah Proctor, 15, Salem Farms	Imprisoned
May 21	57. Sarah (Hood) Bassett, 35, Lynn	Imprisoned; cleared on Jan. 3, 1693
May 21	58. Susannah (mnu) Roots, 70, Beverly	Imprisoned
May 23	59.Benjamin Proctor, 33, Salem Farms	Imprisoned "several months."
May 23	60. Mary (Bassett) De Rich, 35, Salem Village	Imprisoned about 6 months
May 23	61. Sarah (mnu) Pease, Salem Town	Imprisoned
May 28	62. Elizabeth (Walker) Cary, 42, Charlestown	Imprisoned; escaped
May 28	63. Capt. John Alden Jr., 69, Boston	Imprisoned; house arrest 15 weeks; escaped; cleared by proclamation Apr. 25, 1693
May 28	64. Capt. John Floyd, 55, Malden	Imprisoned
May 28	65. Elizabeth (mnu) Betts Fosdick, 32, Malden	Imprisoned
May 28	66. Wilmot (mnu) Redd, 55, Marblehead	Imprisoned; condemned Sept. 17; executed Sept. 22
May 28	67. Sarah (mnu) Davis Rice, 61, Reading	Imprisoned
May 28	William Proctor, 17, Salem Farms	Imprisoned; cleared Jan. 1693
May 28	68. Elizabeth (Jackson) Howe, 54, Topsfield	Imprisoned; condemned June 30; executed July 19
May 28	69. Arthur Abbot, 53, Topsfield	Imprisoned
May 28	70. Martha (Allen) Carrier, 38, Andover	Imprisoned; condemned Aug. 5; executed Aug. 19
May 28	71. Mary (Allen) Toothaker, 47, Billerica	Imprisoned; found not guilty Feb. 1, 1693
May 28	72. Margaret Toothaker, 9, Billerica	Imprisoned

June 2	73. Elizabeth (Carrington) Paine, 53, Charlestown	Imprisoned
June 1	74. Sarah Churchill, 20, Salem Village	Briefly imprisoned; then released as an afflicted person
June 4	75. Mary (Leach) Ireson, 32, Lynn	Imprisoned
June 4	76. Job Tookey, 27, Beverly	Imprisoned; found not guilty on Jan. 5, 1693
June 6	77. Ann (Higginson) Dolliver, 29, Gloucester	Imprisoned
June 28	78. Mary (Perkins) Bradbury, 75, Salisbury	Imprisoned; condemned Sept. 9; escaped
July 1	79. Margaret (mnu) Hawkes, Salem Town	Imprisoned
July 1	80. Candy, female slave, Salem Town	Imprisoned; found not guilty on Jan. 6, 1693
c. July 15	81. Elizabeth Scargen	Imprisoned
c. July 15	82. child of Elizabeth Scargen	Imprisoned; died in prison
ARREST PHASE OF ANDOVER WITCH HUNT		
July 15, 1692	83. Ann (mnu) Foster, 72, Andover	Imprisoned; condemned Sept. 17; reprieved; died in prison Dec. 1692
July 19	84. Mary (Foster) Lacey, 40, Andover	Imprisoned; condemned Sept. 17; reprieved; pardoned in 1693
July 19	85. Mary Lacey, Jr., 18, Andover	Imprisoned 10 weeks; released on bail Oct. 6; found not guilty Jan. 13, 1693
July 21	86. Richard Carrier, 18, Andover	Imprisoned; released on bail mid October
July 21	87. Andrew Carrier, 15, Andover	Imprisoned; released on bail mid October
July 22	88. Martha (Toothaker) Emerson, 24, Haverhill	Imprisoned; cleared Jan. 12, 1693
July 28	89. Mary (Tyler) Post Bridges, 48, Andover	Imprisoned; found not guilty Jan. 12, 1693
July 30	90.Hannah (mnu) Tyler Brumidge, 60, Haverhill	Imprisoned in Ipswich prison; cleared Jan. 1693

July 30	91.Mary (Green) Green, 34, Haverhill	Imprisoned in Ipswich prison; released on bail, Dec. 16
c. Aug. 1	92. Rebecca (Blake) Eames, 51, Boxford	Imprisoned; condemned Sept. 17; reprieved; released Mar. 1693 after 7 months in prison
Aug. 2	93. Mary Post, 28, Andover	Imprisoned; condemned Jan. 12, 1693; reprieved; released April 1693 after more than 8 months in prison
Aug. 3	94. Mary (Johnson) Davis Clarke, 53, Haverhill	Imprisoned in Ipswich prison
Aug. 5	95. Margaret (Stevenson) Scott, 72, Beverly	Imprisoned; condemned Sept. 17; executed Sept. 22
c. Aug. 9	96. Daniel Eames, 29, Boxford	Imprisoned
c. Aug. 10	97. Thomas Carrier, Jr., 10, Andover	Imprisoned; Released on bail Oct. 6
c. Aug. 10	98. Sarah Carrier, 7, Andover	Imprisoned; Released on bail Oct. 6
Aug. 10	99. Elizabeth Johnson Jr., 22, Andover	Imprisoned; condemned Jan. 12, 1693; reprieved; imprisoned 6 months; released Feb. 1693
Aug. 11	100. Abigail (Dane) Faulkner, 40, Andover	Imprisoned; condemned Sept. 17; reprieved for pregnancy; released about Dec. 8
c. Aug. 15	101. Samuel Wardwell, 49, Andover	Imprisoned; condemned Sept. 17; executed Sept. 22
c. Aug. 15	102. Edward Farrington, 30, Andover	Imprisoned
c. Aug. 15	103. Sarah Parker, 22, Andover	Imprisoned 17 weeks; released on bail about Dec. 12
Aug. 18	104. Frances (mnu) Hutchins, 75, Haverhill	Imprisoned; released on bail Dec. 21
Aug. 18	105. Ruth Wilford, 17, Haverhill	Imprisoned
Aug. 25	106. Susannah Post, 31, Andover	Imprisoned; found not guilty May 10, 1693
Aug. 25	107. Hannah Post, 26, Boxford	Imprisoned; found not guilty Jan. 12, 1693

Aug. 25	108. Sarah Bridges, 17, Andover	Imprisoned 6 weeks; released on bail about October 6; found not guilty Jan. 12, 1693
Aug. 25	109.Mary Bridges, Jr., 13, Andover	Imprisoned; released on bail October 15; found not guilty May 12, 1693
Aug. 25	110. Mary Barker, 13, Andover	Imprisoned 6 weeks; released on bail about Oct. 10; found not guilty May 10, 1693
Aug. 25	111. William Barker, Sr., 46, Andover	Imprisoned; escaped
Aug. 25	112. Mary (Osgood) Marston, 27, Andover	Imprisoned; released on bail Dec. 20; found not guilty Jan. 12, 1693
Aug. 25	113. John Jackson, Sr., 50, Rowley	Imprisoned
Aug. 25	114. John Jackson, Jr., 22, Rowley	Imprisoned
Aug. 25	115. John Howard, 48, Rowley	Imprisoned
Aug. 29	116. Elizabeth (Dane) Johnson, 51, Andover	Imprisoned 5 months; found not guilty Jan. 7, 1693
Aug. 29	117.Abigail Johnson, 10, Andover	Imprisoned 5 weeks; released on bail Oct. 6
Aug. 30	118. Stephen Johnson, 13, Andover	Imprisoned 5 weeks, released on bail Oct. 6
Sept. 1	119. William Barker, Jr., 14, Andover	Imprisoned 6 weeks; released on bail about Oct. 10; found not guilty May 10, 1693
Sept. 1	120. Sarah (Hooper) Hawkes Wardwell, 42, Andover	Imprisoned; condemned Jan. 10, 1693; reprieved; released spring 1693
Sept. 1	121. Rebecca Wardwell, nearly a year old, Andover	Imprisoned with mother
Sept. 1	122. Sarah Hawkes, 21, Andover	Imprisoned 5 months; found not guilty Jan. 10, 1693
Sept. 1	123. Mercy Wardwell, 18, Andover	Imprisoned; found not guilty Jan. 10, 1693
Sept. 1	124. Mary (Ayer) Parker, 55, Andover	Imprisoned; condemned Sept. 17; executed Sept. 22
Sept. 3	125. Elizabeth (Austin) Dicer, Gloucester	Imprisoned in Ipswich prison

Sept. 3	126. Margaret (mnu) Prince, 62, Gloucester	Imprisoned in Ipswich prison
Sept. 5	127. Mary (Dustin) Colson, 41, Reading	Imprisoned; released Mar. 2, 1693
Sept. 5	128. Jane (mnu) Lilly, 48, Reading	Imprisoned; released on bail Dec. 8; cleared Feb. 3, 1693
Sept. 5	129. Mary (Harrington) Taylor, 40, Reading	Imprisoned; found not guilty Feb. 1, 1693
Sept. 5	130. Joseph Emons, Manchester	Imprisoned
Sept. 5	131. Nicholas Frost, Portland, N.H.	
Sept. 7	132. Deliverance (Haseltine) Dane, 37, Andover	Imprisoned 13 weeks; released about Dec. 8
Sept. 7	133. Rebecca (Aslet) Johnson, 40, Andover	Imprisoned 13 weeks; released on bail about Dec. 8; case dismissed Jan. 7, 1693
Sept. 7	134. Rebecca Johnson, Jr., 17, Andover	Imprisoned 13 weeks; released on bail about Dec. 8
Sept. 7	135. Mary (Clement) Osgood, 55, Andover	Imprisoned 15 weeks; released on bail Dec. 20; found not guilty Jan. 12, 1693
Sept. 7	136. Eunice (Potter) Frye, 51, Andover	Imprisoned 15 weeks; released on bail Dec. 20; found not guilty May 10, 1693
Sept. 7	137. Sarah (Lord) Wilson, 44, Andover	Imprisoned 15 weeks; released on bail about Dec. 20; cleared May 1693
Sept. 7	138. Sarah Wilson, Jr., 14, Andover	Imprisoned 6 weeks; released on bail about Oct. 15; cleared May 1693
Sept. 7	139. Abigail (Wheeler) Barker, 36, Andover	Imprisoned 18 weeks; found not guilty Jan. 6, 1693
Sept. 7	140.Mary (Lovett) Tyler, 40, Andover	Imprisoned; found not guilty Jan. 7, 1693
Sept. 7	141. Hannah Tyler, 14, Andover	Imprisoned; released on bail about Oct. 15; found not guilty Jan. 5, 1693

Sept. 7	142. Joanna Tyler, 11, Andover	Imprisoned; released on bail about Oct. 6; cleared May 1693
Sept. 7	143. Martha Tyler, 11, Andover	Imprisoned; released on bail about Oct. 6; cleared May 1693
Sept. 7	144. Abigail Faulkner, Jr., 9, Andover	Imprisoned 1 month; released on bail Oct. 6; cleared by proclamation May 1693
Sept. 7	145. Dorothy Faulkner, 12, Andover	Imprisoned 1 month; released on bail Oct. 6; cleared by proclamation May 1693
Sept. 7	146. John Sadie, Jr., 13, Andover	Imprisoned
Sept. 7	147. Joseph Draper, 21, Andover	Imprisoned
Sept. 7	148. Henry Salter, 65, Andover	No record of further legal action
Sept. 7	149. Male slave of Nathaniel Dane, Andover	Imprisoned 8 weeks
ARREST PHASE OF RESIDUAL ACCUSATIONS		
Sept. 10, 1692	150. Hannah (mnu) Carroll, Salem Town	Imprisoned
Sept. 10	151. Sarah (Davis) Cole, 42, Salem Town	Imprisoned; released on bail Jan. 14, 1693; cleared May 1693
Sept. 13	152.Joanna (mnu) Brabrook Penny, 72, Gloucester	Imprisoned in Ipswich
Oct. 1	153. Sarah (Aslet) Cole, 30, Lynn	Imprisoned; found not guilty Feb. 1, 1693; returned to prison for fees; released Mar. 23, 1693
Early Oct. 1692	154. Phoebe (Wildes) Day, 39, Gloucester	Imprisoned at Ipswich
Early Oct. 1692	155. Mary (Prince) Rowe, 34, Gloucester	Imprisoned at Ipswich
Early Oct. 1692	156. Rachel (Varney) Cooke Langton Vinson, 62, Gloucester	Imprisoned at Ipswich
Nov. 5	157.Rebecca (Dolliver) Dike, 41, Gloucester	Imprisoned
Nov. 5	158. James Dike, infant, few weeks old, Gloucester	Imprisoned with mother

Nov. 5	159. Esther (Dutch) Elwell, 53, Gloucester	Imprisoned
Nov. 5	160. Abigail Rowe, 15, Gloucester	Imprisoned
Unknown	161. John Durrant, 44, Billerica	Died in Cambridge prison Oct. 27, 1693
Unknown	162. Henry Somers	Imprisoned at Cambridge
Unknown	163. Edward Wooland	Imprisoned at Salem
Unknown	164-168. Four or five men	Imprisoned at Ipswich
Unknown	169. Mary Watkins, a young white woman unable to pay her prison fees	Imprisoned, sold as a slave after August 11, 1693

As the above table shows, there were about 169 people officially accused of witchcraft. Of this number twenty were executed, who all stood by their declarations of innocence to the end. These twenty deliberately chose to die rather than to sign a false confession. They lost their lives because they followed the way of truth. The names of the twenty are:

Hanged on June 10, 1692	1. Bridget Bishop.
Hanged on July 19, 1692	2. Rebecca Nurse 3. Elizabeth Howe 4. Sarah Good, 5. Sarah Wilds 6. Susannah Martin.
Hanged on Aug. 19, 1692	7. Rev. George Burroughs 8. John Proctor 9. John Willard 10. George Jacobs Sr. 11. Martha Carrier
Pressed to death on Sept. 19, 1692	12. Giles Corey
Hanged on Sept. 22, 1692	13. Martha Corey 14. Mary Easty 15. Alice Parker 16. Ann Pudeator 17. Margaret Scott 18. Wilmot Redd 19. Mary Parker Sr. 20. Samuel Wardwell

In addition to the twenty who were executed, there are at least eight who died in prison, bringing the total number of deaths to twenty-eight. The eight people are

21. Sarah Good's nursing infant died in prison in May 1692.
22. Sarah Osborne died in prison on May 10, 1692.
23. Dr. Roger Toothaker died in prison on June 16, 1692.
24. Elizabeth Scargen's child died in prison after four months' confinement.
25. Ann Foster, sentenced to death, died in prison in December 1692.
26. Lydia Dustin, found innocent by trial by jury, but not released, died in Cambridge prison on March 10, 1693.
27. Rebecca Chamberlain died in Cambridge prison.
28. John Durrant died in Cambridge prison.

The Salem tragedy was a witch hunt on a grand scale; it was like a massive firestorm. It cannot be dismissed simply as mindless mass hysteria. The age of rationality already had reached America's shores. Innocent citizens, either as individuals or as members of extended families, suffered from legally authorized deadly attacks. The afflicted girls were utilized to engage in hysterical outbursts in order to deliver patently false testimony. People were invited into the courtroom to give the most brazen slander against the accused. Thomas Hutchinson[2] in his book published in 1768, came to this conclusion about the Salem witchcraft tragedy.

> "A little attention must force conviction that the whole was a scheme of fraud and imposture." [3]

The Salem episode can be explained as a government-sponsored event, born of deceit and fed by envy and pride. Who were the authorities responsible for the deception of ferreting out agents of Satan? Rev.

---

[2] Thomas Hutchinson (1711–1780) became the royal governor of colonial Massachusetts in 1769. He had access to original records, many of which are no longer extant.

[3] *The History of the Colony and Province of Massachusetts-Bay*. London, 1768. Reprint. 3 vols. Cambridge, MA, 1936. 2:47

Cotton Mather would be the foremost religious authority. Because of his morbid fascination with the diabolical and his cravings for power, he contributed greatly to the fueling of the flames of witchcraft in 1692. Instead of fighting a military war with the French and the Indians, Cotton Mather preferred the safer position of crusader in an imaginary war with the Devil. He saw the episode as one in which the powers of darkness preyed on the unregenerate condition of mankind. He pressed the fantasy that New England was threatened by a conspiracy of witches. By calculated action or by deliberate neglect, Cotton Mather used his position to offer tacit if not outright encouragement to the witch trials. He was blinded to a bitter truth; namely, the real threat was never Satan, but rather the glimmers of enlightened thinking among plain citizens.

However, culpability does not lie just with Cotton Mather and other religious leaders. The sordid business was carried out at two levels. At the tactical level, ten men in Salem Village were the members of the Salem Village accuser faction (aka Putnam faction).[4] Thomas Putnam is the most conspicuous in this group. Later a similar faction was formed in Andover. The power of these two accuser factions resided in higher authority.

At the strategic level, the old-guard Puritans granted the authority under which the factions operated. The old guard believed in strict adherence to Calvinist doctrine. The waned none of Anglican, Baptist, or Quaker doctrine. The old guard members were the councilors, magistrates, judges, and high military officers who ruled the colony. Only the old guard had sufficient authority to sanction the atrocities of the witch hunt. The beginning of 1692 saw the old guard running a colonial government that soon would be replaced by a royal

[4] In earlier writings we used the term conspiracy (i.e., a group of "conspirators") instead of the word "faction." The word "conspiracy" implies a secret agreement among several people usually involving criminality. Although the faction made frequent use of treachery, in the strict sense the faction was not criminal because it operated within the law. Indeed, the faction was sanctioned and respected by high government figures.

government. The colonial government was exclusively made up of the old guard Puritans. Under the new royal charter, the Puritans would lose their monopoly. The old guard harbored a deep-seated fear and hatred of the new royal charter which, among other things, promised democracy and freedom of religion.

At the beginning of 1692 the old guard was in mental turmoil. The desperately wanted to maintain their control under the new charter. And then they received the news about witchcraft in Salem Village. It was the spark that lit the fire. Essex County magistrates Jonathan Corwin and John Hathorne issued arrest warrants for the three women accused. Their action set the fire ablaze.

At this point, other old guard members could have put the fire out. In other American colonies, the extinguishing of such fires occurred time and again. Not so in Massachusetts. The old guard eagerly accepted the outmoded doctrines preached by Cotton Mather and subtly encouraged superstition and prejudice. They were willing to pervert the legal system into a judicial massacre. They urged forward the witchcraft persecutions in a desperate attempt to retain their power. Ultimate responsibility for the Salem disaster of 1692, therefore, must be laid on the Puritan government itself.

The most prominent names in the old guard were those of John Hathorne and William Stoughton. None of the other magistrates or judges was more fanatical than these two. John Hathorne, in carrying out most of the preliminary examinations, was especially abusive. Later, the transcripts of these examinations were used as evidence in the grand jury inquests and in the trials. William Stoughton, as chief justice in the witchcraft trials, was the main culprit, callous and ruthless.

The most effective contemporary voices raised by citizens against the Salem witch trials were those of Thomas Brattle and Robert Calef. Thomas Brattle gave his findings in his letter of October 8, 1692. He attacked the proceedings so incisively that his letter was an important factor in ending the witchcraft trials. In May 1693, all of the suspected witches still in jail were released. Cotton Mather refused to accept the ruling as final. He continued his campaign to warn New England of the dangers it faced from the forces of Satan. His fanaticism was so extreme that he could well have succeeded in reviving the witch hunt. However, he was countered by material that Robert Calef had painstakingly compiled. By 1698 Cotton Mather had become seriously alarmed. In his diary he wrote that:

> "There is a sort of Sadducee [i.e., Robert Calef] in this town, a man [some words in the manuscript have been carefully obliterated at this point] ... whom no reason will divert from his malicious purposes. This man, out of enmity to me for my publicly asserting such truths about the existence and influence of the Invisible World, has often abused me with venomous reproaches, and most palpable injuries."

Because of pressure from Cotton Mather and his father Increase Mather, no printer in New England would publish Robert Calef's manuscript. Robert Calef, undeterred, sent it to England, where it was printed in 1700 with the title *More Wonders of the Invisible World*. This book provided an antidote to the poison of Cotton Mather's *The Wonders of the Invisible World*. In spite of their efforts, Cotton Mather and Increase Mather were unable to suppress its sale throughout New England. The cold, hard logic of the Robert Calef spoke for itself. The official records of witchcraft cases were written in the formal abstract and purified language of lawyers, government officials, or theologians. Robert Calef was the first one to write the human side of the witchcraft tragedy.

On December 28, 1700 Cotton Mather wrote, "Calef's book sets the people in a mighty ferment." As president of Harvard College, Increase Mather ordered the wicked book to be burned in the college yard. The efforts of the Mathers, father and son, were to no avail. In 1701, Increase Mather was fired as President of Harvard College, and Samuel Willard, whose nephew had been executed in 1692, became the temporary President. The publication of Robert Calef's book destroyed, once and for all, the concept of the invisible world of the Devil and witches. The book put an end to the witch hunt. It disclosed that the old guard, consumed by avarice, envy, and pride, had no respect for the dignity and value of human life. Their sermons, court records, and publications were cunningly designed so as to hide the truth, and justify their actions to a gullible public and to posterity. To keep the witch hunt burning, they became masterful at spreading distrust and fear. At first, they easily deceived their new governor, Sir William Phips. When Phips arrived in New England as royal governor in May 1692, the old guard tricked him into delegating the responsibilities of the witch hunt to them. He trusted them because he felt compelled to turn his attention to a real danger; namely, the war with the French and the Indians. It was while he was away at the front during the summer, that the old guard carried out their greatest atrocities. Upon his return, he quickly realized that he had been mistaken in his trust, and he began to take steps to stop the witchcraft proceedings. Keen on retaining their usurped power, the old guard put up a stiff defense, but Phips finally prevailed. The whole tragic episode came to a conclusion in May 1693.

In 1697, four years after the end of the witch hunt, one of the judges, Samuel Sewall, handed a note to the Rev. Samuel Willard, minister of the Third Church (the old South Church) in Boston during a public fast. Sewall stood in church while the note was read aloud. "Samuel Sewall, sensible that, as to the guilt contracted upon the opening of the late Commission of Oyer and Terminer, he is more concerned than any he knows of, desires to take the blame and shame of it, asking pardon of men." William Stoughton, informed of Sewall's act, offered this arrogant rejoinder: "When he [Stoughton] sat in judgment he had the fear of God before his eyes, and gave his opinion according to the best of his understanding. Although it may appear afterwards that he had been in an error, yet he saw no necessity of a public acknowledgment of it."

The ordinary citizens commanded the wisdom and moral integrity which their leaders so sadly lacked. Except for Samuel Sewall, none of the members of the old guard ever acknowledged remorse or shame for the events that they had sponsored. Not only did they escape immediate judgment for their crimes, but they succeeded in clinging to the position and authority that they had won. Despite the revulsion of the general populace against what had happened, these men held on to their superstitions, insisting that they had done right. They repressed any motion, even the slightest, towards redress and restitution. Their chief, William Stoughton, retained power until his death in 1701. Even afterwards, the old guard conspired to frustrate and discourage every effort made on behalf of those imprisoned in 1692 and their families. Finally, when the rising tide of retribution became too great for them to resist, compensation was arranged through channels skillfully contrived to deny their responsibility in engineering the witch hunt. Those thought to stand closest to God had proved false. Thomas Putnam and Rev. Samuel Parris never made an apology. Cotton Mather, fond of preaching about damnation and hellfire, had made himself, by his own inflammatory acts, a prime candidate for both. Other ministers involved in the witch hunt either kept a convenient silence or tried to deflect their responsibility by appealing to abstruse theological arguments. It was left to the common people to step forward. And this they did. In a highly unusual act, twelve members of the witchcraft juries were moved to sign and circulate a declaration of regret.[5]

> We do signify to all in general, and to the surviving sufferers in special, our deep sense of, and sorrow for, our errors in acting on such evidence to the condemning of any person; and do declare, that we justly fear that we were sadly deluded and mistaken; for which we are much disquieted and distressed in our minds. We do heartily ask forgiveness of you all, whom we have justly offended; and do declare, according to our present minds, we would none of us do such things again, on such grounds, for the whole world.

[5] Robert Calef, *More Wonders of the Invisible World*, 339-341. It was signed by Thomas Fisk, Foreman, William Fisk, John Bacheler, Thomas Fisk, Jr., John Dane, Joseph Evelith, Thomas Pearly, Sr., John Peabody, Thomas Perkins, Samuel Sayer, Andrew Elliot, and Henry Herrick, Sr.

Chapter 2. Accident or arson?

Firestorms

Arson is the crime of willfully and maliciously setting fire to or charring property. Though the act typically involves buildings, the term arson can also refer to the intentional burning of other things, such as motor vehicles, watercraft, or forests. The crime is typically classified as a felony, with instances involving a greater degree of risk to human life or property carrying a stricter penalty. One of the main challenges to arson prosecutions is to distinguish between arson fires and accidental fires. Arson fires are fires set with intent to destroy or damage property. The legal definition of arson fires involves fires where the person setting the fire had the intent to commit harm by setting the fire, as well as setting the fire or being interrupted while in the process of setting the fire. Accidental fires are all other kinds of fires.

Accidental fires are usually not prosecuted as arson. If however, an accidental fire occurs because of demonstrably gross negligence or a casual disregard for the consequences of setting the fire, these fires can cease to be judged as accidental and may instead be seen as arson fires. An accidental fire is often set by a juvenile. In such situations, these juveniles may simply be manifesting an innate human interest in fire. More than half of the people arrested for setting fires of both types were under the age of 18 in 2003. Children under the age of seven are generally not setting arson fires. Accidental fires set by these children are almost exclusively the result of curiosity. A type of accidental fire that is not in dispute, however, involves campfires. Campfires at which every reasonable effort is made to control the fire and contain its blaze, but still spreads due to the spread of properly managed embers, can only be included in the category of accidental fires no matter how large the blaze which results.

Accidental fires in the home can have several causes. The forensic scientists employed to investigate fires are trained to examine whether a fire shares more similarities in burn patterns with accidental fires or arson fires. Common sources of accidental fires include cooking accidents, electrical appliances that have overheated, been left on for too long, or short-circuited, sparks from fireplaces or welding tools, cigarettes, or lightning strikes. A fire investigation is an unenviable task. The devastation, charred debris, collapsed structures, water soaked ashes, together with the smoke and stench, makes the task uninviting and seemingly impossible. In the past many investigators appear to have come to the task with inherent biases; fire brigade members have decided that all unexplained fires were due to electrical faults, whilst police and insurance investigators leaned towards "arson, by person or persons unknown.

Great fires of history

The **Great Fire of Rome** of 64 AD started on July 18. There was widespread devastation in the city. It took six days before the fire was brought under control. The various accounts either blame Emperor Nero for initiating the fire or else credit him with organizing measures to contain it and provide relief for refugees. According to Tacitus and later Christians, Nero blamed the devastation on the Christian community in the city, initiating the empire's first persecution against the Christians

No primary accounts of the fire survive. Varying secondary accounts are part of Roman history. There are at least five separate accounts written in ancient times by Roman authors. They are:

> ARSON. Motivated by a desire to destroy the city, Nero secretly sent out men pretending to be drunk to set fire to the city. Nero watched from his palace on the Palatine Hill singing and playing the lyre.
>
> ACCIDENT. The fire accidently occurred. According to Tacitus and later Christians, Nero blamed the devastation on the Christian community in the city, initiating the empire's first persecution against the Christians.

The **Great Fire of London** of 1666 started at the bakery of Thomas Farriner on Pudding Lane shortly after midnight September 2, 1666. The wind fanned the bakery fire into a raging firestorm. The fire spread rapidly across the City of London. However, it did not reach the district of Westminster or Whitehall (the Palace of the restored king Charles II). Finally, the strong east winds died down, and the Tower of London garrison used gunpowder to create effective firebreaks to halt further spread eastward. The fire consumed 13,200 houses, 87 parish churches, and St Paul's Cathedral. At the time London had a population of 80,000. The fire destroyed the homes of 70,000 of these inhabitants. The death toll is unknown. The social and economic problems created by the disaster were overwhelming.

> ARSON. Rumors arose that suspicious foreigners set the fire. The fears focused on the French and Dutch, England's enemies in the ongoing Second Anglo-Dutch War.
>
> ACCIDENT. The bakery accidently caught fire.

The **Great Fire of Chicago** of 1871 began on the night of October 8, in a barn located on the property of Patrick and Catherine O'Leary. The fire quickly grew out of control and moved rapidly north and east toward the city center. Legend says that the fire started when a cow knocked over a lighted lantern. However, Catherine O'Leary denied the charge, and the true cause of the fire has never been determined. The fire burned wildly finally coming under control on October 10 in a rainstorm. An estimated 300 people were dead and 100,000 homeless with 17,000 structures destroyed. At the time of the fire, Chicago's population was approximately 300,000. By 1890, the city had a population of more than one million people, second in America to New York City. In 1893 Chicago hosted the World's Columbian Exposition, an attraction visited by nearly 28 million people.

> ARSON. Rumors arose that the cause of the fire was suspicious
>
> ACCIDENT. A cow knocked over a lighted lantern.

Today, the Chicago Fire Department training academy is located on the site of the O'Leary property where the Great Chicago Fire started. In

1997, the Chicago City Council passed a resolution exonerating the cow. The fire was officially an accident.

Equal justice under law

The Salem witch trials may be described as a firestorm of the fiercest sort. Instead of houses, the reputations and lives of people were destroyed. In each previous New England witchcraft episode, the fire had burned itself out after affecting only one or two families. In the case of the Salem tragedy, scores of families were left in despair and some in utter ruin. The fire was sparked by a unique and fatal convergence of religious, social, political, and economic forces. But why, once ignited, why did it rage so wildly, gaining intensity as it claimed more lives? And what served to extinguish the flames? Like great firestorms in history, whether Rome, London, or Chicago, was the Salem catastrophe an accident, or was it arson? In other words, was the Salem calamity caused by a sequence of accidental events, or was it caused by a sequence of willful and malicious actions.

As we will see, there were strict laws against witchcraft in both Europe and America. All of the witchcraft trials followed the law. In the course of history, many ignominious and reprehensible laws have been enacted. The witchcraft laws in question were enacted in the Renaissance period in Europe and America. However, most were either repealed or ignored as the Renaissance came to an end. The Salem witch trials of 1692 have many defining characteristics. Among them are

1. Many thousands of witch trials occurred in the Renaissance. Salem is the only one for which an excellent paper trail is extant.
2. The Salem witch trials represent the last major firestorm.

In 1660, the Puritan government established in England by Oliver Cromwell fell, and the English monarchy was restored. Charles II, son of the beheaded king, was placed on the throne; this event is called the *Restoration*. At this point, some of the most repressive English Puritans who had served under Cromwell fled to New England, the last bastion of Puritan safety. Also some Puritan New Englanders, who had lived in

England during Puritan rule, went back to New England. Among them were Rev. Increase Mather and Rev. William Stoughton.

Note that the word “court” is used in two different senses. For example, the Massachusetts Superior Court is a trial court (i.e., a judiciary body in which defendant is found either guilty or not guilty). On the other hand, the Massachusetts General Court is the state legislature of the Commonwealth of Massachusetts. The name "General Court" is a hold-over from the earliest days of the Massachusetts Bay Colony, when the colonial assembly, in addition to making laws, sat as a judicial court of appeals. Before the adoption of the state constitution in 1780, it was called the Great and General Court.

In 431 BC, the Athenian leader Pericles encouraged belief in what we now call “equal justice under law.” Pericles stated that in Greek democracy "the law secures equal justice to all alike in their private disputes," However, in the history of the world, “equal justice under law” is the most widely violated legal principle. The trial court system in Puritan Massachusetts might well be regarded as an unfair and unjust system. However the same could be said of any court system existing in the seventeenth century.

Puritan's valued their religion zealously and it became part of everyday life in the colony of Massachusetts. The Puritan church was mixed with the Puritan state. Laws were a combination of state and religion. Any distinction between church and state was not clear. This situation was in contrast to the ideals of the Puritan founders, who originally wanted church and state to be separate, but able to work together. The church had so much power in the state, that it ultimately organized the civil government in Massachusetts. If a person criticized or defied the Puritan rule, it would be considered a sin against God.

In the medieval feudal system in Europe, there were two significant classes: (1) the upper class (kings, queens, dukes, knights, clergymen and such) and (2) the lower class (serfs, servants, men at arms and such). In the Renaissance a middle class emerged (merchants, weavers, carpenters, shoemakers, etc.) who had financial independence. The upper class did not mingle with the lower class. They were quite separate. The Puritans overwhelmingly were in the middle class. When they came to Massachusetts, they set up as a new kind of government. It did not have a king. However it soon developed an upper class and a lower class. The upper class was made up of church members; the lower class was not. However, all attended church services together and they freely mingled and intermarried.

The upper class has political power to force the lower class to do its bidding. Often a moral weakness develops in the person who exercises that power. It may take time for this weakness to become visible. The rulers in question begin as honest men. Their motives for wanting to direct the actions of others may be purely religious, patriotic and altruistic. Indeed, they may wish only "to do good for the people." But, apparently, the only way they can think of to do this "good" is to enforce restrictive laws. If these rulers stay in power long enough, they eventually conclude that power and wisdom represent the same thing. As they possess power, they must also possess wisdom.

There is a place for everything. In the Renaissance witchcraft laws had their place because they could force persons to conform to the official ideas of what was good. The more restrictions and compulsions the rulers impose on other persons, the greater the strain on the morality of the rulers. Their appetite for using force against people increases. If there is opposition, the rulers use some type of emergency, either declared or created, to justify their actions. Unfortunately, historians soon become accustomed to the seductive thesis that public office endows the official with both power and wisdom. At this point, the written history begins to lose his ability to distinguish between what was morally right and what was politically expedient. The proverbial saying 'power corrupts; absolute power corrupts absolutely' conveys the opinion that, as a person's power increases, their moral sense diminishes.

Kangaroo court

The term *kangaroo court* has various definitions. The Merriam-Webster Dictionary defines a kangaroo court as a "mock court in which the principles of law and justice are disregarded or perverted." According to one interpretation, a kangaroo court ignores recognized standards of law or justice, and often carries no official standing in the region in which it resides. In this sense, the Salem witchcraft court (known as the Court of Oyer and Terminer) was not a kangaroo court. According to another interpretation, a kangaroo court is a court held by a legitimate judicial authority, but one that intentionally disregards legal or ethical obligations. The defendants in such courts are denied access to legal representation and proper defense. In this sense, the Court of Oyer and Terminer was a kangaroo court. We will use this interpretation.

A show trial is a public trial in which the judicial authorities have already determined the guilt of the defendant. Show trials tend to be retributive rather than corrective. They are conducted for propagandistic purposes. The Salem witch trials with their kangaroo Court of Oyer and Terminer were show trials. The trials presented both the accusations and the guilty verdicts to the public to serve as both impressive examples and warnings to other would-be dissidents.

The show trial is merely a formality. The truth lies in pre-trial documents. For Salem, a plenitude of such documents survives intact. Preparatory papers such as depositions, indictments, confessions, petitions and even two death warrants are extant. The surviving records give the intimate facts in great detail. The words of the accused come to us exclusively from the writings of the accusers. The writings show that the transcribers were seldom impartial and far from giving thorough rendition. Often they transcribed not actual statements but their remembrance of what was said. In this way, they revealed their prejudices in a most striking manner. The result is indicative of their frightful intensions. The recorders mangle and strangle the voices of the accused. In so doing, they give credence as to the terror that was taking place. The accounts are conveniently inattentive to the role of accusers, usually not committing to paper the accusers' harsh proclamations. Some full transcripts of preliminary hearings were taken at the beginning of the Salem witch hunt. The transcripts testify to pandemonium in the courtroom.

As the witch hunt evolved into a firestorm, faithful transcribing was abandoned, and summaries were written instead. Sometimes highly revealing additions were added to the summaries. For example, it might be written that an accused witch had "a very wicked, spiteful manner." Another transcript might call the suspected witch a liar. In time the written accounts turned into sworn confessions. Such confessions are full of tall tales evidently induced by the leading questions of the examiners. An accused person would claim flight on a stick (broomstick) with the church deacon and others going to a satanic baptism. The minister's specter would be carried through the air with the accused witch, having earlier conferred in the orchard with a satanic cat. Such reports written down by various people were infuriatingly inconsistent. As would be expected, the writer would carefully avoid writing down the leading questions that elicited such imaginary tales. A child would be asked if her mother and father were with her on such an adventure. Naturally, the child would answer yes. This answer was later used as evidence that the child accused her mother and father of witchcraft. All such accusations were the result of the most blatant and heartless kind of trickery. This subterfuge will forever stain the character of perpetuators such as William Stoughton, John Hathorne and Rev. Cotton Mather. What terror went through the minds of the accused when they confessed to flying through the air or smothering a neighbor? How did those who withstood the vicious accusations and claiming innocence suffered death by hanging find the strength to do so?

Trial records

None of the official transcripts of the Court of Oyer and Terminer survive. Lack of court records is characteristic of show trials. The reason is that higher authorities want to deflect potential blame down to lower levels. However, in effect the transcripts of five of the most important trials do survive. Let us tell the story.

On Thursday September 22, 1692, eight condemned witches were hanged in Salem. In the evening, Justice William Stoughton, Justice John Hathorne, and Rev Cotton Mather met in Boston. These three were very important members of the Puritan old guard that ruled colonial Massachusetts. Their meeting place was Samuel Sewall's house in Boston. It was raining. Samuel Sewall as host was present at the meeting and so was his brother Stephen Sewall. Samuel Sewall recorded the meeting in his diary. Because he left the pages of his diary mostly empty throughout the witch hunt, any other private meetings of this small group can only be inferred. Stephen Sewall was the clerk of the court. The day before the meeting Stephen Sewall had received a letter from Cotton Mather requesting the trial records. Samuel Sewall brought with him the transcripts of the Court of Oyer and Terminer, dampened from the rain. He handed them over to Cotton Mather.

Cotton Mather wanted the records to use in his upcoming book on the trials of the witches. The book, *The Wonders of the Invisible World*, was rushed through press, the first (Boston) edition appearing in October 1692. It gives the transcripts of five of the trials at Salem[6]. Did Cotton Mather ever return the trial records to the Essex County Courthouse? Charles W. Upham, who in 1831 published his "Lectures on Witchcraft," wrote: "The journal of the Special Court of Oyer and Terminer is nowhere to be found. It cannot be supposed to be lost by fire or other accident, because the records of the regular court, up to the very time when the Special Court came into operation, and from the time when it expired, are preserved in order. A portion of the papers connected with the trials have come down in a miscellaneous, scattered, and dilapidated state." All the extant legal records are in *The Salem Witchcraft Papers* s available online (University of Virginia). What happened at the sessions of the Court of Oyer and Terminer must be determined from these records and from Cotton Mather's book. Concerning the preservation of other documents, Upham wrote:

---

[6] The trials included were those of George Burroughs ("one who had the promise of being a king in Satan's Kingdom"), Bridget Bishop, Susannah Martin, Elizabeth Howe, and Martha Carrier (who "the Devil promised should be queen of Hell).

> "The effect produced on the public mind, when it became convinced that the proceedings had been wrong, and innocent blood shed, was a universal disposition to bury the recollection of the whole transaction in silence, and, if possible, in oblivion. This led to a suppression and destruction of the ordinary materials of history. Papers were abstracted from the files, documents in private hands were committed to the flames, and a chasm left in the records of churches and public bodies. The records of the parish of Salem Village, although exceedingly well kept before and after 1692 by Thomas Putnam, are in another hand for that year, very brief, and make no reference whatever to the witchcraft transactions. This general desire to obliterate the memory of the calamity has nearly extinguished tradition. While writing the 'Lectures on Witchcraft,' I was occupying a part of the estate of Bridget Bishop, if not actually living in her house. Little, however did I suspect, while delivering these lectures in the Lyceum Hall, that we were assembled in her orchard, the scene of the preternatural and diabolical feats charged upon her by the testimony of Louder and others. Her estate was one of the most valuable in the old town. It is truly remarkable that the locality of the residence of a person of her position should have become wholly obliterated from memory in a community of such intelligence. Tradition was stifled by horror and shame. The only recourse was in oblivion; and all, sufferers and actors alike, found shelter under it."[7]

Hysteria

Of the Salem witchcraft affair, Nathaniel Hawthorne wrote, "If any one part of their proceedings can be said to deserve less blame than another, it was the singular indiscrimination with which they persecuted not merely the poor and aged, as in former judicial massacres, but people of all ranks; their own equals, brethren, and wives."[8] About fifty

---

[7] Charles W. Upham, *Salem Wit*chcraft 2:462-464.

[8] Nathaniel Hawthorne, *The House of the Seven Gables*, Chapter 1.

Andover residents were imprisoned for witchcraft in 1692, a number greater than Salem and Salem Village combined. Nowhere but in Andover do Hawthorne's words, "persecuted their own equals, brethren, and wives," take on such terrible meaning.

Contention, bickering, and altercations were present in abundance among the Puritans. In this atmosphere, accusations by one person against another were commonplace. Powerless to explain the reason for a sickness or catastrophe, the Puritan clergy turned to the Bible, and discovered witchcraft as the cause. "Witches are the doers of strange things. They do really torment, they do really afflict those that their spite shall extend unto," wrote Cotton Mather.[9] The policy of the church to blame witches as the cause of unexplained evils inevitably led to witchcraft accusations.

In modern psychology and psychiatry, hysteria is a feature of hysterical disorders in which a patient experiences physical symptoms that have a psychological cause, instead of an organic, cause; and histrionic personality disorder characterized by excessive emotions, dramatics, and attention-seeking behavior. Certainly the afflicted children exhibited such tendencies. However, often the term hysteria is extended to the entire disreputable episode as evidenced by its being called the Salem Witchcraft Hysteria of 1692. The following paragraph gives such an account.

> The Salem witch trials refer to a period of **mass hysteria and panic** that overtook colonial Massachusetts between 1692 and 1693. It is often regarded as one of the most fascinating episodes of American history. The story is so dramatic and so strange that it almost reads like fiction. Young girls underwent strange behaviors and had mysterious screaming fits. They were diagnosed as having been bewitched. Soon a hunt begins for the witches. The girls were urged to identify the persons who had bewitched them. Their initial accusations gave way to trials,

---

[9] Cotton Mather, *A Discourse on Witchcraft.*

> hysteria, and a frenzy that resulted in further accusations. The outcome was disastrous. Twenty people were executed for being "witches", and many more were accused and imprisoned. There were factors that made one more susceptible to accusations than others. With little opportunity to prove her innocence a woman could easily be convicted and hanged for witchcraft.

The above paragraph may be summed up by the statement (describing the case an accident):

> Mass hysteria and panic caused the Salem witch trials.

However, a more accurate representation would be the statement (describing the case for arson):

> The Salem witch trials caused mass hysteria and panic.

What then caused the Salem witch trials? In England the Puritan government came to an end and the king was restored in 1660. In New England in early 1692 the Puritan government was coming to an end and the king's appointed governor would replace the elected governor. Desperate, the Puritan old guard orchestrated the Salem witch trials as a last proclamation of their power against the devil. The old guard wanted to affirm that they were in power in Massachusetts and that they would stay in power one way or another, despite the king of England.

Puritans were noted for a spirit of moral and religious earnestness that informed their whole way of life. Their efforts contributed to the founding of colonies in New England as working models of the Puritan way of life. Puritans believed that it was necessary to be in a covenant relationship with God in order to be redeemed from one's sinful condition. Calvinist theology and polity proved to be major influences in the formation of Puritan teachings. This naturally led to the rejection of much that was characteristic of Anglican Church at the time. In its place the Puritans emphasized preaching that drew on images from scripture and from everyday experience. Still, because of the importance of preaching, the Puritans placed a premium on a learned ministry. The moral and religious earnestness that was characteristic of Puritans was combined with the doctrine of predestination inherited from Calvinism to produce a "covenant theology," a sense of themselves as the elect chosen by God to live godly lives both as individuals and as a community.

Puritans by their very nature were self-disciplined and courageous. There was nothing hysterical about them. An examination of the records gives no evidence of mass hysteria and panic in Massachusetts. All of the preliminary examinations were under the strict control of the authorities. None of the defendants became hysterical. The afflicted girls demonstrated their disorders in a controlled manner at the direction of the court. The same group of girls gave the same performance time and again in the preliminary examinations and in the Court of Oyer and Terminer in 1692 as well as in the Superior Court in 1693. All was well coordinated and by no means hysterical.

For example, the Court of Oyer and Terminer convened at Salem on June 30, 1692 for its second meeting. Five women were brought to trial: Sarah Good and Rebecca Nurse, of Salem Village; Susannah Martin of Amesbury; Elizabeth Howe of Ipswich; and Sarah Wildes of Topsfield. All were found guilty and sentenced to death. The five were executed on July 19, 1692; just nineteen days after the trial had started. The Court acted with impunity with meticulous self-discipline. There were no outbursts of hysteria in this trail, as in any other trial. The afflicted girls gave their usual performances according to cue.

Rebeca Nurse was highly respected, the epitome of an exemplary woman. When Rebecca Nurse came to trial, many testimonials about her Christian behavior, her care in educating her children, and her exemplary conduct were entered in court. The jury brought in the verdict not guilty. The afflicted girls, surprised and unhappy at this unexpected outcome, immediately put up a hideous outcry. In response, one of the judges expressed dissatisfaction; another judge said that Rebecca should be indicted again. The chief judge, William Stoughton, saying that he did not want to impose upon the jury, immediately brought up a technicality which was later shown to be false. He asked the jury to go out again and reconsider the verdict. This time the jury found her guilty.

Rebecca Nurse was a long standing member of the church in Salem Town. Rev. Nicholas Noyes, the younger of the two ministers of the church, claimed that her witchcraft represented an insidious attack by the Devil against the congregation. On Sunday July 3, 1693, he had Rebecca Nurse taken from her prison cell and brought to the meetinghouse. There, at the afternoon church service, he excommunicated her in front of the entire congregation.

Meanwhile, influential friends of Rebecca Nurse appealed to the governor, Sir William Phips, who reprieved her from the death sentence. The reprieve was not a pardon; it was only a temporary postponement of her execution. She remained in prison. When the afflicted girls learned of the reprieve, they renewed their outcries. A Salem gentleman prevailed upon the governor's council, and the reprieve was recalled. On July 19, 1692, Rebecca Nurse, age seventy, was executed with the other four.

Hysteria is exaggerated or uncontrollable emotion or excitement, especially among a group of people. Hysteria is a psychological disorder (not now regarded as a single definite condition) whose symptoms include conversion of psychological stress into physical symptoms (somatization), selective amnesia, shallow volatile emotions, and overdramatic or attention-seeking behavior. The term has a controversial history as it was formerly regarded as a disease specific to women. Hysteria may be a defense mechanism to avoid painful emotions by unconsciously transferring this distress to the body. People with histrionic personality have several of the following symptoms:

1. A need to be the center of attention
2. Inappropriate or provocative behavior while interacting with others
3. Rapidly changing emotions and superficial expression of emotions

4. Vague and impressionistic speech (gives opinions without any supporting details)
5. Easily influenced by others
6. A belief that relationships are more intimate than they are.

No one wants to hear how a group of envious men masterminded the Salem witchcraft trials. A much better story is obtained by describing how Salem Village found itself at the center of a notorious case of mass hysteria. A hysterical group of young women accused their neighbors of witchcraft.

The story revolves around the question: What caused the mass hysteria. This question has been answered by means of a variety of economic and physiological theories. Economic theories attribute the Salem trials to an economic downturn caused by the so-called "little ice age." The year 1692 had opened as a particularly troubling one in New England. The winter was cruel, taxes were intolerable; pirates were attacking commerce; smallpox was rife. The French were actively supporting the Indians on a bloody warpath. In fact, the year 1692, at the center point of the "little ice age," was one of the coldest years in the history of civilization. The cold caused worsening economics. Resulting food shortages led to anti-witch fervor in communities in both the United States and Europe. The economic hardships could have caused widespread scapegoating which, during this period, manifested itself as persecution of so-called witches. Such behavior was due to the widely accepted belief that witches were capable of causing physical harm to others and could control natural forces.

Socioeconomic problems were manifest in Salem Village. It was an agrarian and much poorer than neighboring Salem Town, a center of trade. Salem Village was torn apart by two opposing groups. As tensions between the two groups unfolded, they were influenced by anxieties and by differing levels of engagement with political and commercial opportunities unfolding in Salem Town. The result was increasing hostility; one group accused the other group of witchcraft.

Physiological theories for the mass hysteria include both fungus poisoning. Ergot is a type of fungus found in rye and other grains. It produces hallucinatory effects. It can also cause the affected to suffer from crawling sensations on the skin, vertigo, headaches, hallucinations, and seizure-like muscle contractions. Wet climate conditions and long storage times could have led to an ergot infestation of the grains grown in Salem Village. In 1692, some of the accusers exhibited such symptoms. A doctor had been called in to treat the girls but he could not find any underlying physical cause. Unfortunately, he stated that they suffered from possession by witchcraft, a common diagnosis at the time.

The hysteria is like a spark. It the spark lands on bare dirt or rock, it will go out. If the spark lands on tinder, it will start a fire. The authorities can extinguish the fire. The fire would be accidental. Otherwise, the authorities can fan the fire and cause a firestorm. In the Salem episode the authorities did not choose to extinguish the fire. Instead they fanned the fire into a firestorm. The firestorm would be arson. The Salem firestorm took the lives of innocent people and caused irrevocable harem to many families.

Arson is the crime of willfully and maliciously setting fire to property. The crime is typically classified as a felony, with instances involving a greater degree of risk to human life or property carrying a stricter penalty. As an analogy, we may think of the Salem witch trials as an extreme case of arson. What is most troubling is that the arson was carried out by the political authorities (such as William Stoughton and John Hathorne) and church authorities (such as Cotton Mather). The common motive appears to be envy and pride.

Witch trials other American colonies

Many reasons have been put forth for the igniting and spreading of the Salem firestorm. Some of the most popular factors are long-standing grudges; regional hostilities; teenage hysteria; delusion; confiscation of property; economic, ecclesiastical, and class tensions; food poisoning, long-incubated resentments; and distasteful aversions. A witchcraft accusation represents a spark. The governing authorities, whether secular or ecclesiastical, then choose either to let the spark ignite a witch hunt or to extinguish the spark. In effect the governing authorities make the choice to have a witch hunt or not. Once the fire is burning, governing authorities then make the choice either to pour fuel on the fire or to let the fire burn out. In the American colonies, it was only in Salem in 1692 where the authorities did not let the fire burn out so that only few witches condemned. Instead the authorities poured fuel on the fire, thereby creating the Salem witchcraft firestorm with many witches condemned. The evidence indicates that the Salem witch trials represented a government-manufactured crisis. Its ill-founded purpose was to preserve the power of the Puritan old guard in the transition of Massachusetts from a self-governing colony to a province of the English crown.

Let look what happened in other American colonies. Connecticut was founded by Puritans who held to the same hard lines as in Massachusetts. In fact, Connecticut was stricter. The idea of the devil taking an active role in everyday life was a genuine fear in **Colonial Connecticut**. Connecticut at the time was divided into two colonies: Connecticut and New Haven. Witchcraft officially became a crime in Connecticut in 1642: "If any man or woman be a witch—that is, hath or consulteth with a familiar spirit—they shall be put to death." New Haven enacted its witchcraft law in 1655: "If any person be a witch, he or she shall be put to death." Connecticut and New Haven had 43 witchcraft cases between 1648 and 1668, with 16 ending in execution.

There were only two witchcraft trials in **Plymouth Colony**, both decades before the Salem witchcraft trials of 1692. Both of the trials ended in not guilty verdicts. The accusers were fined by the court for having made false accusations. Clearly the governing officials had no tolerance for witchcraft. **Rhode Island** became an English colony in 1636. In the following years, many persecuted groups settled in the colony. The Rhode Island colony passed laws abolishing witchcraft trials, imprisonment for debt, and most kinds of capital punishment.

In **New Amsterdam,** the Reformed Dutch Church (Calvinistic in theology) was the predominant church. Superstition was general in the population. People believed in omens, signs, prognostications, and in such antidotes as charms and amulets. Comets and eclipses of both sun and moon filled everyone with fear. Thunderclaps were regarded as displays of God's wrath. In almost every house were such things as the Wheel of Adventure or the Spiritual Truth Sayer. There were also fortune-tellers. People believed in ghosts, in haunted places, in changelings, and in witches. However, no witches were ever persecuted in New Amsterdam. The Dutch and French churches of New Amsterdam asserted that "the apparition of a person afflicting another is very insufficient proof of a witch, and that a good name, obtained by a good life, should not be lost by mere spectral accusation."

In July 1683, **Pennsylvania** had its first and only witchcraft trial. The accused were two Swedish women, Margaret Mattson and Gethro Hendrickson. The accused and their husbands were immigrants from Sweden. As early immigrants they had their pick of the land and their choice was rich, fertile river land by the Delaware River. It is very possible that envy was behind the rumors that were spread following failures with the livestock of their English neighbors. The accused women spoke only Swedish. They appeared before Governor William Penn and a petit jury. Another Swede served as interpreter between the prisoners and the governor. There are no extant records for Gethro Hendrickson, but there are extant records for Margaret Mattson. Testimony was given that Margaret Mattson was a witch and that she had bewitched several cows 20 years previously. There was an appearance of a bright light and of the visage of an old woman standing at the foot of the bed holding a knife. When the heart of a calf that died by witchcraft was boiled, the witch Margaret Mattson appeared and advised that it would be better to boil the bones. In her defense, Margaret Mattson denied the testimony calling it hearsay. At the trial's conclusion, Governor Penn gave the jury their charge. The members found Mattson guilty of having "the common fame" of a witch, but not guilty in "matter and form as she stands indicted." A recognizance of 100 pounds for good behavior was demanded of Margaret Mattson; 50

pounds demanded of Gethro Hendrickson. Governor Penn never felt this was a ground-breaking case; in fact, he never wrote about it in later years.

Two of the earliest witchcraft cases in the **Maryland** State Archives involve executions aboard ships bound for Maryland from England. One was the case of the ship *The Charity of London*. It set sail from England for Maryland in 1654. Mary Lee was one of a small group of passengers. The ship came upon rough seas and violent winds. "The ship grew daily more leaky almost to desperation and the chief seamen often declared their resolution of leaving the ship if an opportunity offered itself." Rumor took hold that a witch had conjured the storms. The sailors believed that the foul weather "was not on account of the violence of the ship or atmosphere, but the malevolence of witches." The sailors decided that Mary Lee was the witch and petitioned the captain to put the woman on trial. Two seamen decided to take matters into their own hands. They seized Lee and searched her body for the Devil's markings. They found a damning mark. She was hanged and dumped overboard.

In **Maryland**, about 12 people were brought to trial for witchcraft over a period of a hundred years but only one was executed. In 1674, John Cowman was convicted for bewitching the body of Elizabeth Goodale. As he stood at the gallows, he received a pardon from the Governor. Rebecca Fowler was the one person executed for witchcraft in Maryland. In 1685 she was found guilty of bewitching several people in Calvert County. Her victims claimed that her evil incantations had left them, "very much the worse, consumed, pined & lamed." In 1715, Virtue Violl stood trial in Annapolis after a quarrel with Elinor Moore. Elinor Moore accused Violl of cursing her tongue, which rendered her unable to speak. The jury acquitted Virtue Violl of all charges.

In witchcraft cases, **Virginia** courts adhered to England's 1604 witchcraft law, a statute passed under King James I. The earliest witchcraft allegation in Virginia was made in 1626. The accused, Joan Wright, was a married woman and a midwife. Neighbors testified against her, alleging that, through witchcraft, she had caused the death of a newborn, killed crops and livestock, and accurately predicted the deaths of other colonists. Wright was acquitted despite her own admission that she did in fact have knowledge of witchcraft practices. In 1698 Grace Sherwood was accused by her neighbors of having bewitched their pigs to death. Another neighbor claimed that "Grace came to her one night and rode her and went out of the key hole or crack of the door like a black cat." Grace Sherwood brought defamation suits against the two accusers, but did not win either case. The rumors and accusations continued until 1706, when Sherwood stood trial before the General Court. The court justices decided to use the water test to determine her guilt or innocence. The test was so controversial that it was no longer used on the European continent at the time of Sherwood's trial. The authorities bound the hands and feet of Grace and threw her into water. If Grace were to sink, she would be innocent, because the water—a pure element—had accepted her. However, Grace floated and was presumed guilty. She was convicted and imprisoned, but by 1714, she had been released. Grace's case demonstrates the reluctance of the Virginia authorities to execute convicted witches. No person accused of the crime of witchcraft in colonial Virginia was ever executed.

No one was executed for witchcraft in **North Carolina**. In 1679 North Carolina law directed local officers to investigate felonies, witchcraft, enchantments, sorceries, and magic arts, among other crimes. The next year, a woman was jailed on a charge of witchcraft. Court records describe such women as "concerned with familiar Spirits under ye Notion of a Witch." In 1706 Walter Tanner accused Mary Rookes of being a witch. The court found her not guilty and fined Walter Tanner five shillings. Mary Rookes faced a similar charge brought by Thomas Collins, who claimed she had bewitched his wife. The court again found Mary Rookes innocent and fined Thomas Collins one shilling and costs.

Nathaniel Hawthorne

Nathaniel Hawthorne could not escape the oppression of Puritan society, not only from his childhood in devout Puritan family but also from his study of his own family history. Nathaniel Hawthorne's great

great grandfather, John Hathorne, was the chief witch hunter in the Salem witchcraft delusion of 1692. Because of the "persecuting spirit" of his Puritan forebears, Nathaniel Hawthorne changed his name from Hathorne to Hawthorne. He wrote, "I, as their representative, hereby take shame upon myself for their sakes, and pray that any curse incurred by them may now and henceforth be removed."

In his story *The Custom House*, Nathaniel describes the first of his ancestors, William Hathorne, as arriving with the Massachusetts Bay Colony in 1630 "with his Bible and his sword." A further connection can also be seen in his more notable ancestor **John Hathorne**, who exemplified the level of zealousness in Puritanism with his role as persecutor in the Salem witch trials. Nathaniel Hawthorne in his story *Main Street* writes

> "For listen to wise **Cotton Mather**, who as he sits there on his horse speaks comfortably to the perplexed multitude, and tells them that all has been religiously and justly done. ... Do you see that group of children, and half-grown girls, and among them, an old, hag-like Indian woman, Tituba by name? Those are the **Afflicted Ones**. Behold, at this very instant, a proof of Satan's power and malice! Betty Paris, the minister's daughter, has been smitten by a flash of Martha Carrier's eye, and falls down in the street, writhing with horrible spasms and foaming at the mouth, like the possessed ones spoken of in Scripture. Hurry on the accused witches to the gallows, ere they do more mischief. ... Among the multitude, meanwhile, there is horror, fear and distrust; and friend looks askance at friend, and the husband at his wife, and the wife at him, and even the mother at her little child; as if, in every creature that God has made, they suspected a witch, or dreaded an accuser. Never, never again, whether in this or any other shape, may **Universal Madness** riot in the Main Street."

Here Nathaniel Hawthorne highlights the four traditional scapegoats for the Salem witchcraft delusion:

1. John Hathorne (an agent of arson)
2. Cotton Mather (an agent of arson)
3. Afflicted ones (agents of accident)
4. Universal madness (agent of accident)

As noted, the first two of Nathaniel Hawthorne's scapegoats indicate that arson was the cause of the Salem witchcraft firestorm and the last two indicate that accident was the cause.

Theories to explain Salem

Between 1520 and 1650, the Reformation had a huge impact on European countries. By intensifying the awareness of evil, the Reformation produced anxiety and the fear of Satan. John Calvin stated,

> ...for after Satan has possessed us once and stopped our eyes, and God has withdrawn his light from us, so that we are destitute of his holy spirit and devoid of all reason, then there follow infinite abuses without end or measure. And many sorceries come from this condition.

The people were taught that the dangers of Satan in regard to a person were both physical and spiritual. Everyone, even the holiest individual, could be deceived and ensnared by the cunning treachery of Satan. These beliefs brought about a heightened awareness of the diabolical acts of witchcraft. European governments took up the cause and put accused witches on trial. They wanted to purify the land by getting rid of evil, even if it meant putting accused citizens to death

The Salem witchcraft episode in 1692 represents a decisive turning point in history. It laid the seeds of the American Revolutionary War. The witchcraft episode is made up of two parts. The first part occurred between February and June 1692. It is called Salem Village witchcraft. The second part occurred between July and October 1692. It is called Andover witchcraft. Historians have never thought Andover witchcraft important. They write about Salem Village witchcraft, at most with a footnote on Andover.

There was a great and decisive difference between Salem Village and Andover. In the Salem Village witch hunt essentially all of the accused refused to confess. In the Andover witch hunt essentially all of the accused did confess. Cotton Mather wrote a long letter on May 31, 1692, summarizing his views and offering firm advice on the impending trials. It said, "Do not lay more stress upon pure specter testimony than it will bear. I am far from urging the un-English method of torture, but whatever has a tendency to put the witches into confusion is likely to bring them into confession.

Because of his extensive writings in support of the doctrine, there can be no question that Cotton Mather believed in witchcraft. Nor is there any question that he believed in spectral evidence. In the summer of 1692, a question did arise. How much credence should be given to spectral evidence in prosecutions? From his writings it seems plain that, while Cotton Mather supported the admission of spectral evidence, he did not believe in convicting persons on that alone. Such spectral evidence was sufficient for conviction in the Salem Village witch hunt. However, as the trials proceeded, Cotton Mather and others felt that further corroboration was needed. It was well accepted that a personal confession was the best evidence of witchcraft.

The result was that in the succeeding Andover witch hunt essentially all the accused witches (about fifty) confessed to their guilt. Some of the clergy regarded such a confession as a valuable document that revealed the innermost secrets of nature. From the confessions, Cotton Mather hoped to lay bare the invisible world of the Devil. A major element of a confession was the admission that the accused wrote his or her name in the "Devil's book." Although witchcraft confessions are nothing more than intellectual fantasies, they do represent valuable historical documents. Not only do they tell us about witchcraft beliefs in 1692, but they also provide information about the personal lives of the people involved.

Of course, over the years many theories have been proposed to explain the Salem witch hunt. They are based on various ways to explain the incidents. As always, the question is "accident or arson?" The most popular theories nearly always favor accident.

Catastrophe theory (accident). In 1692, New England was at war with the French and Indians. When misfortunes of war struck, people blamed supernatural forces and found scapegoats in witches.

Hysteria theory (accident). In 1692, certain people in New England became clinically neurotic and even psychotic, resulting in group panic against alleged witches. In other cases, it was believed that fantasies and psychosomatic illnesses were responsible.

Poisoning theory (accident). Ergot poisoning is due to the ingestion of the alkaloids produced by a fungus that infects rye and other cereals. Ergot poisoning is also known as Saint Anthony's fire. It was held that poison of ergotism (caused by mold on rotten bread) affected people's behavior. However, it is hard to explain how so many people, even in one area, could become seriously ill or disturbed all at once. Also some believed that the effects of consuming bad mushrooms caused the mental instability.

Satanic Rebellion Theory (accident). Cotton Mather and others believed that Devil worship actually existed as a subversive attack on the ruling Christian order. Even today, historians of witchcraft take the confessions of witches (which were taken under threat and in some cases mild torture) as indicative of what the alleged witches actually believed. However, no credible evidence supports the existence of any actual satanic cults at the time. In Salem witchcraft, there seemed to be nothing beyond common superstition and simple folk traditions.

Misogyny Theory (arson). The witch hunt exemplified a social hostility toward women. Subordination of women, women's connection to folk-magic and healing, and women's views on social and economic conditions are regarded as important factors in the witch hunt. The majority of accused and executed witches were female, whether old or widowed or spinster or poor. However, many prominent women such as

Rebecca Nurse were also targeted. The Salem witch-hunt persecuted children of both sexes.

Conflict Theory (arson)**.** Reformation and its resultant fights between sects of Christianity led the Puritans to use witchcraft to attack Baptists or Quakers.

Exercise of power (arson). The Puritan old guard (who ruled Massachusetts) seized upon the opportunity presented by witchcraft allegations in Salem Village in early 1692. Instead of extinguishing the flame, the old guard fanned the flames and turned the conflagration into a firestorm. Their purpose was to affirm that they were in power in Massachusetts and that they would continue to be in power under the new royal charter. They exerted their power by fighting the devil and his attendant witches. The Puritan old guard maintained that a dangerous conspiracy of witches existed. The fear of witchcraft was exploited in order to centralize authority, increase bureaucratic jurisdiction, impose cultural uniformity, and dominate the Church.

Accident

The most favored type of theory claims that the Salem witchcraft affair was accidental. The spark that lit the fire was the unexplained sickness of little Betty Parris. The fire spread and became a firestorm despite the gallant efforts of the authorities to find and destroy the conspiracy of witches. No one was to blame. The girls' sicknesses excused them from culpability. All the others were just doing their jobs. A typical story of this sort is as follows.

In the winter of 1692 in Salem Village, little Betty Parris was sick, running about making strange shrieks and hiding under furniture. Her cousin Abigail Williams followed suit. Soon, other girls who had visited were having similar symptoms. Ann Putnam Jr., Mercy Lewis, Mary Walcott were affected. The contagion spread to other girls, including, Elizabeth Hubbard. To this day no one knows what really caused these hysterical outbursts. An untold number of reasons have been given. Diagnoses range from psychological and medical causes (such as asthma, epilepsy, or delusional psychosis) and extend all the way to the extreme of diabolical possession. Similar episodes have occurred worldwide. In Salem Village, the diagnosis was that these afflicted girls were bewitched. It was the beginning of the witch hunt to seek out the culprits. It was assumed that there was a deadly conspiracy of witches at play. It was the responsibility of the magistrates to use their authority and good judgment in order to ferret out this lethal intrigue of Satan's servants. The girls accused Tituba, Good and Osborn who were already under suspicion. The county magistrates Jonathan Corwin and John Hathorne issued arrest warrants for the three women accused. The three were examined. The magistrates watched the girls twist their arms and backs and contort their faces. The girls were bitten and pinched by invisible agents. Most of those present were filled with compassion, fully convinced that the girls were afflicted. The accused were sent to Salem Prison. The contagion spread. The afflicted girls soon named other others, including Rebecca Nurse. The girls' targets were not just older women. Four-year-old Dorothy (aka Dorcas) Good was arrested. The afflicted girls testified that Dorothy's specter would bite and pinch them. On March 26, Magistrate Hathorne, Corwin, and John Higginson interrogated Dorothy, and sent her to prison awaiting trial. Throughout the spring of 1692, the same afflicted girls went on accusing many other people. The flood of accusations overwhelmed the criminal justice system of Massachusetts. It simply was not suited to the task thrust upon them by the teenage girls. Unable to sway the girls' testimony, suspects began to confess to crimes they had not committed. The magistrates believed in the existence of a widespread conspiracy of witches. Cotton Mather gave his approval. As a result, evidence consistent with this belief was accepted. Evidence that did not fit this belief was rejected.

Arson

The central claim of the Puritan authorities in power was well stated in the confession of William Barker Sr., previously given in Chapter 1. Barker states that: "Satan's design was to set up his own worship, abolish all the churches in the land, to fall next upon Salem and so go through the country." In his confession, William Barker Sr. speaks of Mr. George Burroughs to be such a person as to set up the kingdom of the devil. The undercurrent was that Rev. Burroughs had Baptist tendencies, an anathema to the Puritan church. Was Rev. Burroughs an agent to set up his own worship?

In 1683, Burroughs, with his new wife, Sarah, left the ministry in Salem Village, and returned to his former ministry in Casco, Maine. Since no else had been willing to accept the rigors and dangers of such a remote frontier outpost, the position had remained unfilled during his absence. The first record of his return is in June 1683, when he relinquished 170 of the 200 acres which had been granted to him prior to the war. The town offered to give him 100 acres "farther off," in compensation. The town records contain Burroughs' reply, "As for the land taken away, he freely gave it to us, not desiring any land anywhere else, nor anything else in consideration." Compare the generosity of Rev. Burroughs with the greed of Rev. Samuel Parris in Salem Village!

Burroughs' fine gesture paints his character in a thoroughly selfless and virtuous light. Nothing has been found during the whole course of his ministry or personal life to suggest differently. The substantial coastal acreage that he gave to the town was situated on the Neck, the prime location in the fast-growing settlement. Meanwhile speculators like Bartholomew Gedney (of the Puritan old guard), an inhabitant of Salem, were making fortunes on Casco real estate.[10] (The old guard is the conservative and especially older members of an organization, such as a political party).

Sarah, the wife of George Burroughs, always had dreaded the Indians. Now, in the bitter winter of 1689–1690, she was frightened to stay in Casco, the furthest outpost in Maine, which was anticipating an Indian attack in the coming spring. Her husband, now attending to the spiritual needs of the settlers spread along the coastline from Casco south to Wells, decided to remove his family to Wells, considered secure. But

---

[10] Bartholomew Gedney was never himself an inhabitant of Casco or any other place in Maine. He owned a shipyard in Salem Town, and became a Salem magistrate as well as a major in the militia. He was one of the witchcraft judges who sentenced Rev. Burroughs to death in 1692.

before her husband could give her this promised security, Sarah died. Her body was placed on a ship for a final journey down the coast of Maine into her home port of Salem.

Burroughs, with his seven children, moved permanently to Wells in the early spring of 1690. He filled the vacant position as the town's new minister. Undaunted, he continued his ministry along the whole of the desolate coast. To the pioneering settlers of Maine, Burroughs had become the man of the hour. His vitality, courage, and leadership fitted him for any emergency. He was perceived by his parishioners as fearless, and he instilled a degree of his own hope and courage into them, enabling them to live through their dark time. Accounts reveal that their respect for him reached close to veneration. It was in Wells that Burroughs married his third wife, Mary.[11]

On May 20, 1690, the terror-stricken inhabitants of Wells sent by express the following letter to Major Charles Frost, the commander-in-chief of the army in Maine. "The Indians and French have taken Casco fort and, to be feared, all the people are killed and taken. We are in a very shattered condition, some are for removing and some are for staying. We must have more assistance." Two days later, the inhabitants of Wells dispatched a letter to the Council in Boston with this earnest appeal for help. "Our sad condition puts us on your charity. The enemy is very near us. Saco is this day on fire. If we have not immediate help, we are a lost people."

The few who escaped the slaughter at Casco fled south. All the garrisons from Casco south to Wells withdrew in a panic to Wells, where they were ordered to make a stand. This abandonment of the fortifications left the Indians free to overrun the New Hampshire border. Inhabitants of Fox Point in Newington were slaughtered. Captain John Floyd and his men pursued the Indians, forcing them to leave behind some of their captives and booty. Newmarket and Exeter were assaulted. The companies of Captain Wiswall and Captain Floyd

---

[11] Because of the destruction of records during the French and Indian wars, the maiden name of Burroughs' third wife is unknown.

fought bitterly with the Indians at Wheelwright's Pond in Lee. Captain Wiswall, his lieutenant, sergeant, and twelve of his men were killed. Captain Floyd kept up the fight, before being driven off the field. The victorious Indians moved westward leaving bloody tracks of destruction behind them. This was June 1690. (Captain Floyd was arrested for witchcraft on May 28, 1692.)

These were dark days for Wells. The citizens understood all too well that at any time they could be the victims of captivity or the most terrible murders. But led by the unwavering resolve and faith of their minister, they would not lose heart. Raids by small parties of Indians on northern New England farmhouses continued during the rest of 1690 and into 1691. In June 1691 a large force of Indians, over two hundred, attacked Wells, expecting an easy conquest. The assault, however, was bravely repulsed and the Indians withdrew, swearing revenge. Foiled in this attempt, the enraged Indians fell upon the little fishing hamlet at Cape Neddick, five miles south along the coast. There they killed nine men loading a vessel, set the buildings on fire killing the women and children, and disappeared as suddenly as they had come.

On July 21, 1691, George Burroughs sent the following dispatch from Wells to Boston. "We being at the front, remotely situated, for strength weak, and the enemy beating upon us, we are fair for ruin, and humbly conceive your honors are sensible of it. The enemy killed and drove away upward of one hundred head of cattle, besides sheep and horses; some of our corn is already lost, and more in great hazard. We therefore, distressed, make our humble address to your honors for men, with provisions and ammunition." The requested supplies never came; the cowardly and uncaring, safe and snug in Boston, felt no compunction to assist the settlers in their struggle for survival.

Once again, on September 28, 1691, with the embattled garrisons surrounded by Indians, Burroughs appealed to the Council in Boston. A young man, venturing forth less than a hundred feet outside the garrison to fetch some firewood, had been captured by the stealthy Indians. Burroughs writes, "Whereas it has pleased God, to let loose the heathen upon us, keeping us in close garrison, and daily lying in wait to take any that go forth, whereby we are brought very low, not all the corn is judged enough to keep the inhabitants themselves one half year. We therefore humbly request your honors to continue soldiers among us to remain with us for winter. We had a youth, seventeen years of age, last Saturday carried away, who went (not above gunshot) from Lieut. Storer's garrison to fetch a little wood in his arms. We have desired our loving friends, Captain John Littlefield and Ensign John Hill, to present this to your honors." The remarkable tenacity and bravery of Burroughs in this real war stands in stark contrast to Cotton Mather's sorry behavior in his imagined war against the witches!

Roving scalping parties continued to kill settlers in nearby New Hampshire towns during the remainder of the year 1691. At the same time the Indians were preparing for a more aggressive campaign against the remaining garrisons in Maine. In January 1692 the town of York, just south of Wells, was laid waste. Those who reached the garrisons were saved; those who did not met a horrible death, or a more cruel captivity. The minister in York, Rev. Shubuel Drummer, was killed at his own door, while trying to mount his horse. His clothes were stripped from his body. His wife and son, the only survivors in his large family, were carried into captivity, where she soon died. Cotton Mather, from eye-witness accounts, wrote that one of the "bloody tygers" was seen strutting about among the captives wearing the clothing of the murdered minister.

Wells, still with its minister and encouraged by his fighting spirit, staunchly persevered, despite being "destitute of clothing" for the winter's cold. Because of Burroughs' foresight in keeping the inhabitants away from their farms and within the garrisons, the town had been spared up to this point. But spring was approaching and the people knew that a large force might attack the garrisons momentarily.

The government in Boston utterly failed in its responsibility to assist the lonely outposts of Maine in this crisis. The appalling apathy of the Massachusetts authorities towards the fate of the great number of people pent up in the garrison houses was a betrayal, and one which verged on the criminal. On May 2, 1692, for a brief moment, the people of Wells thought that the aid they had so long hoped and prayed for finally had arrived. On that day Field Marshal John Partridge rode into Storer's garrison with a few men. But instead of carrying good news of reinforcements, Partridge carried an arrest warrant. Thomas Putnam and Jonathan Walcott had signed the complaint. It charged that Burroughs with high suspicion of sundry acts of witchcraft done upon the bodies of Mary Walcott, Marcy Lewis, Abigail Williams, Ann Putnam Jr., Elizabeth Hubbard and Susan Sheldon. To the astonishment of his parishioners and comrades, Rev. George Burroughs, the garrison's bastion of strength, a true minister of God, was arrested for witchcraft; the afflicted girls of Salem Village were claiming that "he was above a witch, for he was a conjurer." At the precise point when he was most needed, Burroughs was taken captive and carried from Wells to Salem prison to stand trial for his life.

Only four weeks later, in June 1692, the inevitable Indian attack did come. And when it came, the settlers stood ready. Fortified by the spirit, perseverance, and skills learned from their minister, they were able to survive the onslaught. Two months later, on August 10, 1692, Rev. George Burroughs, aged forty-one, was hanged in Salem. Like his fellow minister at York, his clothes were stripped from his dead body. Lots were cast for the expensive clothes of a minister. Rev. Cotton Mather watched on horseback, silent witness to this inhumanity.

The province of Maine had lost its last minister. George Burroughs had fought gallantly beside the soldiers, when all but one other minister in Maine had deserted their parishioners for the safety of Boston. Despite constant danger, Burroughs had ridden to the remnants of the coastal villages to minister to the people. He had offered courage to the dispirited and frightened soldiers, carrying supplies and fighting alongside them. In the stricken towns, he had comforted the wounded and buried the dead. Time and again, he had risked his life for all in need. Yet he died neither in battle nor in service to his people. On August 19, 1692 at Gallows Hill in Salem, George Burroughs was killed at the whim of a covert group of envious men who had the audacity to claim that they did God's will. Cotton Mather wrote:

> "Faltering, faulty, unconstant, and contrary answers are counted as some unlucky symptoms of guilt, in all crimes, especially in witchcrafts. Now there was never a prisoner more eminent for them, than G. B. [George Burroughs]. His tergiversations, contradictions, and falsehoods were very sensible. He now goes to evince it, *That there neither are nor ever were witches*. The jury brought him in guilty, but when he came to die, he utterly denied the fact, whereof he had been thus convicted."

My grandmother Anna Louise Wardwell (1846-1909) married my grandfather John Edward Robinson on October 19, 1870.

Chapter 3. Witchcraft

Witchcraft craze in Europe

Historically witchcraft represents various types of nature religion emphasizing the healing arts by magical means. Witchcraft also includes various kinds of magic or sorcery practiced in Asia, Africa, and Latin America. Witchcraft has played a role in European history, but what has been handed down comes from sources hostile to its practice. The traditional European viewpoint is that witchcraft was a type of harmful sorcery associated with the worship of the Devil. This diabolical interpretation of witchcraft was formulated in the late Middle Ages. Many of the beliefs about witches were based on delusion but some are said to be based on reality. The punishment of supposed witches by the death penalty first became common in the fifteenth century.

The doctrine of witches and familiar spirits was current from ancient times. Scripture depicts the witch's character, warns of its blighting influence, and enacted heavy penalties against employing its agency. The biblical authority was *Exodus* xxii, 18: "Thou shall not suffer a witch to live." Leviticus, xx. 27, states, "A man also or a woman that hath a familiar spirit, or that is a wizard, shall surely be put to death; their blood shall be upon them."

Deuteronomy, xviii. 9-12, says, "When thou art come into the land which the Lord thy God giveth thee, thou shalt not learn to do after the abominations of those nations. There shall not be found among you any one that maketh his son or his daughter to pass through fire, or that useth divination, or any observer of times, or any enchanter, or a witch, or a charmer, or a consulter with familiar spirits, or a wizard, or a necromancer; for all that do these things are an abomination unto the Lord."

Witchcraft as a living force in European life had its chief manifestations in the fifteenth, sixteenth and seventeenth centuries. During prior centuries, when faith was universal and doubt almost unknown, the Devil was regarded with something akin to contempt. Usually depicted as an insignificant imp, the Devil could have his malignity rendered harmless by the repetition of a prayer or by making the sign of the cross. With the onset of skepticism and heresy, the church began to picture the Devil as more terrible and to concern itself with his direct relations with human beings. It was in the thirteenth century that theologians worked out their theory of witchcraft, and in the fourteenth century the church drew all witchcraft cases into its own jurisdiction.

The first important book on the subject, the *Malleus Maleficarum* (Hammer of Sorceresses), appeared in Germany in 1486. Witch trials raged throughout Western Europe. Geographically, the center of witch persecutions lay in Germany, Austria, and Switzerland, but few areas were left untouched. The total number of victims is unknown. In southwestern Germany alone, however, it is said that more than 3,000 witches were executed between 1560 and 1680.

Henri Boguet was one of the judges involved in the trials, torture, and burning of many alleged witches in Burgundy at the end of the sixteenth century. His book *Examen of Witches* was based on his experiences. He introduces the book with these words:

> "It is surprising that there should still be found today people who do not believe that there are witches. For my part I suspect that the truth is that such people really believe it in their hearts, but will not admit it. They are refuted by Canon and Civil Laws; Holy Scripture gives them the lie; and repeated confessions of witches prove them wrong."

The period of the Northern European Renaissance spanned a period of about 200 years, roughly from 1500 to 1700. The Renaissance was a two-edged sword. On one side of the sword were art, music and literature. On the other side were heresy and witchcraft. For these two hundred years, a witchcraft craze terrorized certain parts of Europe. Of course, there were witch beliefs in every culture from the beginning of recorded time, even as there are today. Many of the medieval fables were little more than vestiges of old pagan beliefs about hobgoblins and fairies. Let us make clear that when we use the term "witch," we always mean "witch" in the sense used in the Renaissance. Such witches were considered malevolent and were prosecuted. Except for the period of the Renaissance, witches generally were ignored and left alone. The same is true as to the good witches in Wicca today.

Heresy is any belief or theory that is strongly at variance with the accepted beliefs of a religion. A heretic is a proponent of such beliefs. The Catholic Church considers obstinate and willful manifest heresy spiritually cuts one off from the Church, even before excommunication is incurred. Justinian I (c. 482-565) was an Eastern Roman (Byzantine) emperor in Constantinople. Justinian was a prolific builder. Most conspicuously, he had the Hagia Sophia, originally a basilica-style church that had burned down, splendidly rebuilt according to a completely different ground plan. At the completion of this edifice Justinian said, "Solomon, I have outdone thee" (in reference to the first Jewish temple). The Hagia Sophia, with its magnificent dome filled with mosaics, remained the center of the Eastern Church until the fall of Constantinople in 1453.

The Code of Justinian was the first of four parts of the Body of Civil Law, a collection of fundamental works in jurisprudence that was issued from 529 to 534 AD by order of Justinian I, Eastern Roman Emperor. Justinian achieved lasting influence for his judicial reforms by means of the summation of all Roman law. The Code of Justinian served to secure the status of Orthodox Christianity as the state religion of the empire by uniting Church and state, and making anyone who was not connected to the Christian church a non-citizen. There were provisions primarily aimed against heresies. A heretic was anyone not devoted to the holy Faith.

A more everyday supernatural danger for the medieval man or woman was the Devil's human servant, the witch. Witchcraft trials of both men and women became increasingly common in the fifteenth century. The chronicles report that Theson, King of the Franks, died in the year 583 as a result of witchcraft. From the 7th century to the 10th century, the penalty for witchcraft was very light. The punishment for someone using spells to become animals was three years penance for being devilish. The Church would act against strands of Christianity that it considered heretical, but before the 11th century these tended to center on individual preachers or small localized sects. However, in the 11th and 12th centuries organized heresies began to occur in Western Europe. Heresy became a major justification for the Inquisition and for the European wars of religion associated with the Protestant Reformation. It was believed that a witch drew powers not from a love of God, but by a pact with Satan. In 1305 Jeanne of Navarre, Queen of France, was reportedly killed by sorcery.

During the Middle Ages the teachings of the church made it clear that evil people would die in a state of sin and, therefore, go to Hell. Medieval creativity was at its most gruesome when describing the tortures of the damned. *Inferno,* which comprises one third of the book the *Divine Comedy*, by Dante Alighieri (1265-1321), epitomizes the medieval idea of Hell. In the book, the hero is given a tour through the nine circles of Hell by the Classical poet Virgil. They spiral lower and lower, until they reach the bottom, which is covered in ice. There, a winged Lucifer is in the process of devouring the three greatest sinners: Judas, flanked by Brutus and Cassius. Religious literature of the time also describes Hell in some detail.

Gutenberg in 1439 was the first to use movable type. It is not clear when Gutenberg conceived the Bible project, but for this he borrowed more money, and work commenced in 1452. The Pope appointed two Dominican Inquisitors to write a complete guide for the discovery, examination, and execution of witches. The resulting book was titled the *Malleus Maleficarum* (aka *The Hammer of* Witches), printed in 1490. It maintained that witches were in collusion with the devil. Because the book was printed, it enjoyed wide distribution. In order to identify witches and the practice of witchcraft, the book contained many items collected from the witch lore of Europe. It was designed to aid in the identification, prosecution, and dispatching of witches. It set forth all of the misconceptions and fears concerning witches and the supposed influence of witchcraft. Its false statements about witches came to be widely regarded as irrefutable truth.

When the *Malleus Maleficarum* was written, there were many scholars and theologians who voiced doubt about the existence of witches and largely regarded such beliefs as mere superstition. The *Malleus Maleficarum* vehemently attacked such doubters. It stated, “Whether the belief that there are such beings as witches is so essential a part of the Catholic faith that obstinacy to maintain the opposite opinion manifestly savors of heresy.” The *Malleus Maleficarum* essentially silenced those voices. It made very real the threat of one being branded a heretic, simply by virtue of one's questioning of the existence of witches and, thus, the validity of the Inquisition. It set into the general Christian consciousness, a belief in the existence of witches as a real and valid threat to the Christian world. The *Malleus Maleficarum* came not the beginning of witch persecutions, but it came at a peak point in European witchcraft accusations and executions. It was a foundation for treating witchcraft not as a superstition, but as a dangerous and heretical practice of person associating with the Devil, and thus becoming a great danger to society and to the church. It was used by witch hunters all over Europe.

Throughout history torture has been used for the purpose of obtaining information in interrogation. One early writer on the ineffectiveness of torture was Friedrich Spee (1591-1635), a German Jesuit priest, professor, and poet. Spee was a courageous opponent of witchcraft trials. Spee was the first person in his time to present strong written and spoken arguments against torture, especially with regards to its unreliability in obtaining "truth" from someone undergoing painful questioning. It was found that subjects would make up stories if it meant the torture would cease. Specifically, an accused witch under torture would affirmatively answer leading condemning questions in order to terminate excruciating pain. In fact, mild torture or even the threat of torture could often achieve the desired confession. It may be said that some authorities viewed torture as, essentially, an exorcism. They often proceeded from gentle to harsh torture. If the accused witch confessed under torture, they usually could get a confession not under torture, because the willpower of the accused person had been broken.

Galileo held the view that the Earth is not at the center of the universe but moves around the sun. In 1633, Galileo Galilei was brought before the Inquisition for heresy, but abjured his views and was sentenced to house arrest, under which he spent the rest of his life.

Pact with the devil

In the Northern European Renaissance (a period of about 200 years, roughly from 1500 to 1700), witchcraft was a crime of diabolism. It was involved with having a pact with the devil, whereby one exchanged one's eternal soul for monstrous powers. This characterization originated in a medieval campaign against magic and heresy, especially against heretics who challenged both doctrine and jurisdiction. By the late fourteenth century, however, canon lawyers, prominent inquisitors, learned academics, and several popes came to agree that by means of a contract with the devil, whether explicit or only implicit, a magician might work genuine harm in this world. These theorists also gradually worked out a composite view of all the different sorts of crimes and activities their heresy involved. It was increasingly believed that witch-heretics flew off to a Sabbath where they renounced their Christian faith and baptism, worshipped the devil, danced together, and enjoyed a cannibalistic feast, devouring children whom they had killed while using their fat or other body parts to make loathsome potions. They were also thought to receive instruction in working harmful magic by which they might destroy crops, interfere with the productivity of farm animals, and threaten the livelihood of people. Most vividly, witches were beholden to the devil or to lesser demons. During the fifteenth century large numbers of heretical "witches" or sorcerers began to be discovered, and increasingly the accused witches were women. Witchcraft was a supposed talent to summon evil spirits and demons to do harm to others. It was linked to religion and to government, as each had powers to punish those who dabbled in magic and sorcery.

Priests were able to exorcise those who had become possessed by malign spirits. The book *Highroad to the Stake, A Tale of Witchcraft* by Michael Kunze is history written as a novel. It follows the footsteps of an accused family along the path that led them to the stake. The episode takes place in the year 1600 in a small Bavarian village in Germany. The accused were simple, illiterate people. The authorities subjected them to extensive interrogation, often under torture. Their statements, recorded in Bavarian archives, make up the principal source of this account. The accused protested their innocence of witchcraft, yet the power of torture soon forced them to confess. They were just what the authorities had been looking for—criminals in league with the Devil. The fiction enters when Michael Kunze allows these convicted men and women to speak for themselves; how they lived, suffered and dreamed. The reality enters when Michael Kunze tells of those who operated the levers of power, the officials who sat in judgment: the governing class of clerics and doctors of law and of their subordinates, the sheriffs and jailors. The Duke who ordered the witchcraft trials was a ruler of the bureaucratic type: innocent yet guilty. European historians hold that the authorities that implemented and presided over the judicial proceeding bear the ultimate responsibility for the terrible events.

Zealous clerics in the Renaissance were increasingly fearful of nonconformity in a society of growing complexity. These clerics exaggerated the popular witchcraft credulities. Having systemized the kingdom of God, they logically constructed a kingdom of the devil. The medieval church constructed an organized systematic demonology with specific beliefs about the devil and witchcraft. With fevered imagination the clergy invested their demonological panoply with elaborate sophistication and projected these ideas into the minds of the populace. Government officials and clergy accepted the reality of witchcraft. They held no doubts about its diabolical nature. Biblical texts on the subject of witches and demons, with the express command "thou shalt not suffer a witch to live", supplied the principles. In their demented universe, witches committed blasphemous sacrilege in hideous conspiracies with the Devil. The witches were spirits given over to evil. They flew through the air on broomsticks to clandestine covens to worship the devil. The clergy preached that the Lords of Light and Darkness were face to face in a desperate war. The clergy with the sanction of the ruling powers brought to the citizenry a high level of paranoia. The people were led to believe that Satan was everywhere, and that day-to-day life was an individual duel with the devil.

To carry on a fight against an invasion of witches, the resources of church and state were mobilized. Fighting against the enemies of the faith, the witch hunters divided the world into the realms of light and darkness. They claimed that the accused witches were in league with the devil. To discover the secrets of this underworld, they sought out the confessions of these witches. However such confessions were seldom, if ever, freely given.

Despite the contemporary books and other witch-hunting propaganda, the most important materials are the court records of the trials of witches. In the last forty years, the study of European Witchcraft has turned to the systematic studies of the court records of the witch trials, such as trial verdicts, lists of confiscated goods, questions asked during interrogations, and the answers witches gave. These documents reveal the harsh treatment given to the accused witches. There are distressing original manuscript depositions taken from the victims in the torture chamber. The historical task is huge because the witch trials in Europe are scattered amongst literally millions of other trials.

From the eleventh to the fourteenth centuries when the Church was at the height of its power, very few witches died. Persecutions did not reach epidemic levels until after the Reformation, when the Church had lost its position as Europe's indisputable moral authority. The height of the persecution occurred during the Reformation, when the formerly unified Church shattered into Catholic and Protestant sects. The trials were concentrated in central Europe, namely in Germany, Switzerland, and eastern France. The further distance from that area, the lower the persecution generally got. In countries like Italy and Spain, where the

Catholic Church and its Inquisition[12] reigned virtually unquestioned, witch hunting was uncommon. The worst panics took place in areas like Switzerland and Germany, where rival Christian sects fought to impose their religious views on each other. For other countries the witch panics clustered around borders. France's major crazes occurred on its Spanish and eastern fronts. Italy's worst persecution was in the northern regions. Spain had a witchcraft craze which was centered on the Basque lands straddling the French/Spanish border.

Although it has become commonplace to think of the outbreaks of witch hunting as malevolent acts imposed by overpowerful elites, in reality the worst horrors occurred where central authority had broken down. Germany and Switzerland were patchwork quilts, loose confederacies stitched together from dozens of independent political units. England, which had a strong government, had little witch hunting. The country's one and only craze took place during the English Civil War, when the government's power collapsed. A strong, unified national church (as in Spain and Italy) also tended to keep deaths to a minimum. The worst panics definitely occurred where both Church and State were weak.

European church courts tried many witches but they usually imposed non-lethal penalties. A witch might be excommunicated, given penance, or imprisoned, but was rarely executed. The Inquisition almost invariably pardoned any witch who confessed and repented. The vast majority of witches were condemned by secular courts. Ironically, the worst courts were local courts. They condemned about ninety percent of all accused witches. National courts condemned only about thirty percent of the accused.

There are certain factors that increased a person's odds of being accused. Most witches were women, comprising approximately eighty percent of the accused. Many were poor or elderly; many were

---

[12] Many records say that a witch was tried *by inquisition*. It should not automatically be assumed that this meant *the Inquisition*, for *an inquisition* was the name of a type of trial used by almost all courts in Europe at the time.

unmarried or widowed. Often they were alienated from their neighbors, or seen as different or disliked. The majority of those accused were from the lower economic classes, although in some cases high-ranking individuals were accused as well. It has been asserted that the typical witch was the wife or widow, and she was well known for a quarrelsome and aggressive nature.

The most dramatic change in the historical view of European witchcraft is the death toll. Back before trial surveys were available, estimates of the death toll were essentially speculation. Historical accounts talked about crazes in which there thousands of executions. The witch hunters of the time wrote to convince people that witchcraft was a grievous threat, *so they often exaggerated the number of deaths and spread wild estimates about how many witches existed.* Estimates of the total number of executions for witchcraft for the period 1450 to 1750 are roughly between 40,000 and 50,000. However some estimates are 200,000 to 500,000 executed for witchcraft, and still others are 1,000,000 or more.

Today, historians are beginning to count the executions listed in an area's court records. Guess work is still involved, but the estimates are improving as further areas are studied. The studies based on trial records show that that historical numbers were inaccurate; they were much too high. Witch crazes were not everyday occurrences, as the historical literature suggested. To date, less than 15,000 definite executions have been discovered in all of Europe. Even though many records are missing, it is clear that total death toll could not be higher than 100,000. Briggs[13] concludes that there were about 100,000 European witchcraft trials with something between 40,000 and 50,000 executions, of which 20 to 25 per cent were men. Other studies give roughly the same numbers.

The concept of *spectral evidence* originally arose during the witch trials in Europe. It was held that the devil and his minions were powerful

---

[13] *Witches & Neighbours*, p. 8

enough to send spirits, or specters, to people in order to lead them astray. Spectral evidence is testimony in which the afflicted person claims that the accused witch's spirit (i.e. *specter*) causes the afflictions; no one other than the afflicted persons can verify such evidence. By admitting spectral evidence, the court allows the witness to give evidence as though there was no real difference between a person and a specter. Only the afflicted person can see the specter. No on else in court had the necessary spectral vision. In New England, many of the clergy argued against the use of spectral evidence, by saying that the specter might not be the person, but the devil himself. In such a case, spectral evidence would actually be the devil's evidence.

The countries involved in European witchcraft removed the legal limits on the application of torture to obtain confessions. The rise and decline of the witch craze coincides with the rise and decline of the use of torture. The use of legal torture coincided with the Northern European Renaissance, that is, from about 1500 to 1700. In other words, when legal torture started to be used, witchcraft confessions were forthcoming. The accused witch would either die under torture, or would confess and then be burned alive. When legal torture was finally banished, witchcraft confessions ended. The witchcraft craze ended too. The witchcraft confessions always were in line with the standard form of demonology propagated by the clergy. Improper leading questions in conjunction with excruciating pain explain the remarkable identity of the witchcraft confessions over this two hundred year period. England never used the conventional instruments of torture, but instead resorted to dire threats, the anguish of artificial sleeplessness, dipping tests, and other methods of persuasion. In many cases in England, but not all, the required confession would be forthcoming. When a confession was not obtained the authorities tried to convict the accused witch on the grounds of spectral evidence.

At this point we can differentiate three types of witch hunts, namely European, English, and Andover. European witchcraft refers to the northern European countries except England. English witchcraft refers to England and Salem Village. Andover witchcraft refers to Andover alone.

Confessions

Confessions were central to the process of investigating suspected witches. An accused witch could be questioned and even tortured with the aim of getting a confession. The overriding desire for the authorities to get a confession is explained by the fact that an accused witch could only be executed if the accused witch confessed.

Why did the accused confess to being witches? In Europe the reason was that most accused people confessed that they were witches because they were tortured into admitting it. When a person was suspected of witchcraft, they were arrested by the authorities (either secular or religious). They were tortured for days until a "confession" was made. While admitting guilt and repenting stopped the torture, it rarely stopped a death sentence. Torture was not limited to adults; children, the sick, elderly, were all tortured without mercy. One will admit to anything after enough torture. In some case the reason may have been threat of torture, or the promise of lighter punishment. Let us give an example. In the 1630s in Paderborn, a city in eastern North Rhine Westphalia, Germany, one tortured woman told her minister that she confessed falsely. He pleaded with her to recant the false confession so that the innocents she named could be freed. It is recorded that she replied: "But look, Father, look at my legs! They are like fire—ready to burn up—so excruciating is the pain. I could not stand it to have so much as a fly touch them, to say nothing of submitting again to the torture. I would a hundred times rather die than endure such frightful agony again. I cannot describe to any human being how terrific the pain actually is." (The Encyclopedia of Witchcraft and Demonology by Rossell Hope Robbins, Crown Publishers, Inc. New York 1959).

Let us summarize. In northern European witchcraft, a confession was used for conviction in a secular court. The confession would usually be obtained by physical torture, violent and sadistic. . In English witchcraft, heavy physical torture was not used. A confession would often be obtained either by milder forms of physical torture or by heavy forms of psychological torture. If the confession could not be obtained in such a way, then spectral testimony would be used for conviction. Witch trials were government-sponsored secular show trails used to inflict fear in the general populace. Witch trials often occurred in times of transition from one form of government to another. For example, large scale witch trials in England occurred during the English civil war.

In Massachusetts, the methods of English witchcraft were used, as would be expected in an English colony. Torture, except for a few mild cases was not used, so only a few confessions were obtained in the Salem Village phase. At the beginning of the Andover phase, a few mild cases of torture were used. However, that method was soon abandoned. Instead confessions were elicited on religious grounds (such as original sin and the Ten Commandments). The accused witches were talked into confessing. This approach was initiated by Thomas Barnard, the junior minister of Andover. Barnard took seriously the teaching of John Calvin. *A Prayer of Confession* by John Calvin is:

> Lord God, eternal and almighty Father: We acknowledge before your holy majesty that we are poor sinners, conceived and born in guilt and in corruption, prone to do evil, unable of our own power to do good. Because of our sin, we endlessly violate your holy commandments. But, O Lord, with heartfelt sorrow we repent and turn away from all our offenses. We condemn ourselves and our evil ways, with true sorrow asking that your grace will relieve our distress.

Because of Rev. Barnard, Christian charity and forgiveness came into play. The accused witches expected that forgiveness would follow confession. The secular rulers did not accept this interpretation, and wanted to proceed with the convictions of those who confessed. On September 17, the fifth (and last meeting) of the Court was held. The two Andover ministers (John Dane and Thomas Barnard) together with concerned Andover citizens did dignified and persistent work to end the witch trials. Forgiveness ultimately prevailed. Three of the accused were convicted in the Superior Court of Judicature in January 1693. However Governor Sir William Phips reprieved every convicted person. Sir William Phips issued a general jail release in May 1693.

Salem witchcraft followed the formula as used in England. Salem Village was the center of accusations in Salem witchcraft in from February to July 1692. Andover became the center from July to September 1692. But then Andover townspeople turned all the rules upside down. Under the leadership of its two ministers Francis Dane and Thomas Barnard and with the support of its elected officials, Andover interjected a strong dose of Christian forgiveness into the witchcraft proceedings. Andover was instrumental in the release of many of the witchcraft prisoners in the fall of 1692.

England and Scotland

In northern continental Europe, the mechanics of witchcraft accusations and convictions followed the same program during the entire Renaissance period. England was somewhat different. It was the one country that did not authorize the brutal European type of torture. However it did authorize the milder English type of torture. The English type included such things as deprivation of sleep and ordeal by water (i.e., an accused witch who sank was considered innocent, while floating indicated witchcraft.) Also England hanged convicted witches, and never burned them as was done on the continent and in Scotland.

The idea of black and white witches existed from time immemorial. However in the Renaissance, a new theory developed in Europe. It was that a witch would make a pact with the devil. Also it was held that witch did not act alone. If one witch existed at someplace, then there had to be more. This led to a shift in the persecution of witches. The difference between white and black witchcraft effectively ended. The use of torture on suspected witches inevitably revealed the names of other suspected witches. As a result many arrests for witchcraft would occur, in effect fanning the flames of a witch hunt turning it into a firestorm. Essentially no accurate records are extant for the arrest and punishment of witches in Europe.

James Charles Stuart (1566-1625) was the son of Mary, Queen of Scots, and a great-great-grandson of Henry VII, King of England. In 1567 James Stuart became King James VI of Scotland. Upon the death of Queen Elizabeth in 1603, the English and Scottish crowns were united, and James Stuart became King James I of England. He held the kingship until his death in 1625.

One of the most active centers of witch-hunting was Scotland, where it is reported that up to 4,000 people were burned for witchcraft. This was large number for such a small country and certainly it must be exaggerated. This atrocity is often attributed to King James VI of Scotland, later King James I of England. James's obsession with witchcraft is traced back to his childhood. The violent death of his mother, Mary, Queen of Scots, seems to have inspired a dark fascination with magic.

Mary had been convicted in 1586 and sentenced to death. On February 1, 1587, Queen Elizabeth had signed the death warrant. The scaffold was erected in the Great Hall. It was draped in black cloth. Mary was blindfolded, knelt down and positioned her head. Her last words were: "Into thy hands, O Lord, I commend my spirit." The first blow missed her neck and struck the back of her head. The second blow severed the neck, except for a small bit of sinew, which the executioner cut through using the axe. Afterwards, he held her head aloft and declared, "God save the Queen." It was reported that: "Her lips stirred up and down a quarter of an hour after her head was cut off." All of her clothing, the block, and everything touched by her blood were burned in the fireplace of the Great Hall to obstruct relic-hunters.

Prior to 1590 witchcraft was seen as a minor issue in Scotland. The year 1590 saw the start of a series of trials for treason. Three hundred witches were accused of gathering to plot the murder of King James VI. He had a morbid fear of violent death. During these trials King James VI suddenly developed a great interest in demonology and witchcraft.

Witches were accused of attempting to drown James by calling up a storm while he was at sea with his new wife. Other charges include the melting a wax effigy of James VI. There were perverted rituals in a church in Berwick. It is claimed about one hundred witches were actually put on trial, from which a large number were executed.

The violent death of his mother, Mary, Queen of Scots, seems to have inspired the king with a dark fascination with magic. It was reported that James knew of his mother's death before it did really happen, being, as he said, "spoken of in secret by those whose power of sight presented a bloody head dancing in the air." Two years after Mary's execution, another dramatic event deepened James's growing obsession with magic and witchcraft. In 1589 his betrothed Anne of Denmark embarked on a voyage to Scotland to meet her new husband. She turned back when ship almost sank in in a violent storm in the North Sea. James then set sail access to Denmark and get her in person. On the return voyage more storms battered the royal fleet and one ship was lost.

James blamed witchcraft, claiming that witches cast evil spells upon his fleet. Once in Scotland James ordered a witch-hunt on a grand scale. It was a firestorm and James was the arsonist. At least 70 suspects were arrested in the coastal Scottish town of North Berwick. Under torture, most of the accused witches confessed. According to the confessions, the accused witches described a lot of bizarre and gruesome spells and rituals that they made to whip up the storm. Satan himself, it was said, appeared to the witches and "promised to raise a mist." The accused witches bound the limbs of a dead man to the legs of a cat and then tossed it into the sea, and "there did arise such a tempest in the sea, as a greater hath not been seen." The accused witches were swiftly convicted and put to death.

As soon as the North Berwick trials had ended, James commissioned the publication of *News from Scotland*. It was a pamphlet that gave the whole North Sea saga in order to intensify the fear of witches. James wanted to warn his subjects of the evil that lay in their midst.

In 1597 James became the only monarch in history to publish a treatise on witchcraft. It was *Daemonologie* (aka the science of demons). The book has three sections on magic, sorcery and witchcraft and one on spirits and ghosts. It encouraged the persecution of witches with vigor and determination. James described witchcraft as "high treason against God," which meant torture was justified in obtaining confessions from the accused. Witches were arrested and of those arrested, about half were executed.

The persecution did not end. By the time he left for England in 1603, witches were still being arrested and of those arrested, half were executed. Between 1603 and 1625, there were about twenty witchcraft trials a year in Scotland – nearly 450 witches in total. As before, about half of the accused were found guilty and executed. *Demonology* is an essential source text on seventeenth-century witchcraft and the Scottish witch trials. It is a verification of King James' obsession with witches and their alleged attempts on his life. It gives many details about beliefs of magic and witchcraft in the Jacobean period.

Upon the death of Elizabeth I in March 1603 with no direct heirs, her throne passed to James Stuart. He left Scotland to become King James I of England. By the end of Elizabeth's reign, the number of witchcraft trials and executions in England had declined significantly. There was also a growing skepticism about the existence of witches. During the first year of the reign of King James I, *Daemonologie* was reprinted twice. Similar pamphlets stimulated the popular fear of witches. According to the Elizabethan law against witchcraft, convicted witches were severely punished only if they had committed murder or other injuries through their devilish arts. Barely a year after his accession, King James I ordered that the law be replaced by a much harsher version. James's determination to stamp out witchcraft in all forms was brutally apparent. He wanted the practice of any form of magic severely punished, regardless of whether it had caused harm to others. The resulting Witchcraft Act of 1604 made hanging mandatory for a first offence of witchcraft, even if the accused had not committed murder. In fact, the sentence of death was given even if the body of accused witch had a devil's mark on it. The act read: "If any person or persons... shall use practice or exercise any invocation or conjuration of any evil or wicked spirit, or shall consult, covenant with, entertain, employ, feed, or reward any evil and wicked spirit to or for any intent or purpose... [they] shall suffer pains of death."

The playwright Ben Jonson, friend of William Shakespeare, devised a number of masques for the entertainment of King James I and his court. The 'antimasque' to Jonson's *Masque of Queens* had a group of witches who represented "the opposites to good fame". In the instructions for the staging of the antimasque, there were 11 witches "some with rats on their head; some on their shoulders; others with ointment pots at their girdles; all making a confused noise, with strange gestures."

James Stuart (James VI of Scotland, later James I of England) was one of the most learned monarchs to ever sit on any throne. During his reign reading and learning flourished. The King himself wrote well and he wrote extensively. King James I became the patron to Shakespeare's troop of actors, which was renamed "The King's Men." The most famous of all the literary works inspired by witchcraft, was Shakespeare's *Macbeth*. The occasion of its inaugural performance was a visit by Queen Anne's brother, the king of Denmark, in 1606. We recall that it was James's voyage to his wife Anne's native land that had prompted his obsession with witchcraft.

Macbeth dramatizes the damaging physical and psychological effects of political ambition on those who seek power for its own sake. The character Banquo in the play was an ancestor of the Stewart kings of Scotland, adding in a prophecy that the descendants of Banquo would be the rightful kings of Scotland while the Weird Sisters served to give a picture of King Macbeth as gaining the throne via dark supernatural forces.

In Greek mythology, the Fates are three weaving goddesses who assign individual destinies to mortals at birth. Their names were: Clotho (meaning "The Spinner"), Lachesis (or "The Alloter") and Atropos (literally "The Unturning" or, more freely, "The Inflexible"). They had enormous power and even Zeus was unable to recall their decisions. Each of the three Fates had a different task, revealed by her very name: Clotho spun the thread of life, Lachesis measured its allotted length, and Atropos cut it off with her shears. In some renditions, each of the Fates was assigned to a specific period of time: Atropos – the past, Clotho – the present, and Lachesis – the future. In the visual arts, the three Fates are usually depicted as handsome women, but in literature, they are often imagined as old and ugly. In any case, they are almost always pictured as weaving or binding thread.

The Weird Sisters, also known as the Three Witches, appear in Shakespeare's play *Macbeth* (c. 1603–1607). They hold a striking resemblance to the three Fates of classical mythology. It appears that Shakespeare introduced them as a version of white-robed incarnations of destiny. Shakespeare's witches are prophets who hail Macbeth and predict his ascent to kingship. The filthy trappings of the witches and their supernatural activities set the tone for the play. Upon killing the king and gaining the throne of Scotland, Macbeth hears the witches ambiguously predict his eventual downfall.

Shakespeare's imagination was stimulated by various factors, including British folklore and the pamphlet titled *News from Scotland* that detailed the infamous Berwick witch trials of 1590. The witches involved confessed to attempt the use of witchcraft to raise a tempest and sabotage the very boat King James and Anne of Denmark were on board on their return trip from Denmark. The *News from Scotland*, states:

> Moreover she [the accused witch] confessed that at the time when his Majesty was in Denmark, she being accompanied with the parties before specially named, took a Cat and christened it, and afterward bound to each part of that Cat, the chiefest parts of a dead man, and several joints of his body, and that in the night following the said Cat was conveyed into the midst of the sea by all these witches sailing in their riddles or Cues as aforesaid, and so left the said Cat right before the Town of Leith in Scotland: this done, there did arise such a tempest in the Sea,

> as a greater has not been seen: which tempest was the cause of the perishing of a Boat or vessel coming over from the town of Brunt Island to the town of Leith, of which was many Jewels and rich gifts, which should have been presented to the current Queen of Scotland, at her Majesty's coming to Leith. Again it is confessed, that the said christened Cat was the cause that the King Majesty's Ship at his coming forth of Denmark, had a contrary wind to the rest of his Ships, then being in his company, which thing was most strange and true, as the King's Majesty acknowledges.

Evidenced of the attempt to raise a tempest is given in the following passage of the First Witch in *Macbeth*, I.iii.15–27

> I myself have all the other,
> And the very ports they blow,
> All the quarters that they know
> I' the shipman's card.
> I will drain him dry as hay:
> Sleep shall neither night nor day
> Hang upon his pent-house lid;
> He shall live a man forbid:
> Weary se'nnights nine times nine
> Shall he dwindle, peak and pine:
> Though his bark cannot be lost,
> Yet it shall be tempest-tost.
> Look what I have.

In England, King James I found a different situation. There the issue of demonic behavior had never been accepted. James toned down his rhetoric, because any association with the topic of witchcraft could become a potential embarrassment. Prosecutions for witchcraft did occur in England while James was king – such as in Lancashire in 1612. The 1604 Witchcraft Act went beyond the law introduced under Elizabeth I. However, only one clause in the 1604 Act was more harsh and severe. It was an execution for the first offence of raising evil spirits.

However, it was never used in the reign of James I and seems to have been only used once in 1645.

For King James, witches indicated a less than sophisticated society. England, he believed, was in a country in which he could demonstrate his intellectual —but the topics did not include witchcraft or demonology. King James was a religious scholar who had re-translated some of the psalms. He sought to unite the various groups in the Church of England through one universally accepted text of the Bible. Under the sponsorship of King James I, a new English translation of the Bible began in 1604 and was completed in 1611. It is known as the King James Version or as the King James Bible. Its majesty of style was a driving force in the shaping of the English-language. James gave the translators instructions intended to ensure that the new version would conform to the ecclesiology of the Church of England and its belief in an ordained clergy.

The Puritans

It is not easy for present-day Americans to visualize life in England in 1630. England at that time was in the process of emerging from the medieval system. In such a system, people generally were divided into two classes. The great majority was in the lower class, and they were expected to do the manual work that kept the society going. A small aristocracy represented the upper class. The oldest aristocratic son would inherit the father's estate and would become the new lord of the manor. The younger sons of the aristocracy would usually enter the church, the military, or universities, and under their guidance the system would be perpetuated.

Under the medieval system, the sons of the workers would generally have to follow in the footsteps of their fathers, and there was little, if any, opportunity for advancement or change for most of them. However, by the 1600's, a new group was springing up, and they were at the forefront of a technological revolution. This new group had technical skills which enabled them to earn money on their own and not be the dependents of the landed aristocracy. This was the beginning of the middle class.

This middle class formed the backbone of the Calvinistic movement. In England, Calvinists generally went under the name Puritans. Their churches were organized under the congregational principle. The Puritans stood in opposition to the religious establishment of England, which was under the control of the aristocracy. The established Church of England was an authoritarian church, organized in the shape of a pyramid from the peak of earthly authority (the King of England) downward through archbishops, bishops, and priests to the lowly communicant at the bottom.

The Puritans, or at least the extremists, criticized the existing form of the English churches, declaring their rituals false and counterfeit. As a means of purification, Puritan leaders went about establishing separatist congregations, voluntarily covenanting together to live as a people of God under ministers of their own choosing (rather than ministers set over them by a bishop). Moreover, the congregations were free to discipline their own membership and to admit only those who, so far as men in charity could judge, were sanctified and entitled to the promises of salvation and eternal life. Of course, an extreme position put forth publicly could subject a Puritan minister to persecution. Normally, the dissenting ministers would assume a low profile and remain within the national church as nonconformists, but all the time hoping for an ultimate reformation. However, the new world beckoned.

In 1630, John Winthrop, manor lord of Groton in Suffolk, England, led a small group of Puritans to New England. On the way across the Atlantic on the flagship *Arbella*, Winthrop delivered a sermon which he summed up with the sentence "We shall be as a City upon a Hill." There would be a community as the center and the seat of the church. Beyond would be fields which the people would cultivate and on which they could graze their cattle. In a larger sense, it would be a city of God, a society where ideas of Christian brotherhood and right conduct would be expounded from every pulpit. The new American city was founded at a place called Shawmut by the Indians. Soon the name of this new town was changed to Boston, after the Boston in Lincolnshire, England, from which the Lady Arbella Johnson and her husband had come, and in whose church John Cotton was still preaching.

But why should these events, which took place many centuries ago and involved only a handful of people, be of interest to us today? The usual answer is, "We Americans are still living out our historical 'city on the hill' vision of the world. In this originally Puritan concept, America was to stand to the world as a beacon of hope and purity. The American Puritans were disciplinarians. The congregations were supposedly voluntary associations of the brethren, but actually they gave rise to a collectivist discipline marked by a tense mutual watchfulness. Despite what is said about "Puritan individualism," there was never any respect for privacy. The Puritans believed that they were living in a world of chaos and crime, and directed their efforts to be constantly on guard against sin. Their admonitions were continuous and insistent, and they enforced their concept of moral discipline to what might be considered as an unreasonable degree. Puritans believed is strict adherence to the law. Offenses that merited criminal punishment in New England included: (1) Crimes against the church (disturbing the congregation, contempt of the ministry, absence from service). (2) Contempt of authority (criticism of the government, berating public officials, seditious speeches). (3) Disturbing the peace (disorderly conduct, drunkenness, card playing, dancing and other vanities). (4) Crimes against persons (assault, slander, defamation). (5) Crimes against property (theft, borrowing and not returning, sloth in business, wagering)

In each congregation there was a type of minor intimidation, which was maintained by the "godly" elders to enforce this discipline. The eminent British Puritan Richard Baxter said that the enforcement of the new moral order was made possible "by the zeal and diligence of the godly people who thirsted after the salvation of their neighbors."[14] In each town there were informers who spied on their neighbors and reported any suspicious behavior to the clergy and the magistrates.

Any deviant behavior was criminal. The Puritans did not take into account any subtle shading between various forms of misbehavior; everything not white was black. No distinction was made between persons who flatly violated the law and those who merely infringed somewhat on the prescribed customs. The Court took notice of any persons who drank too much, who dressed in inappropriate clothes or indulged some other form of scandalous behavior, who let their hair grow too long, who talked too much or engaged in frivolous games. The word of God governed everything, and had to be protected with all the state's machinery. The Court's responsibility extended to every form of behavior that might offend in the eyes of God. The punishments were severe: the stocks, banishment, whippings, and executions.

The Court ordered that "no person shall spend his time idly or unprofitably, under pain of such punishment as the Court shall think meet to inflict; and for this end it is ordered that the constable of every place shall use special care and diligence to take knowledge of offenders of this kind."[15] The community as a whole was expected to bring any deviancies to the Court's attention. Puritan discipline was a matter of community vigilance. Each citizen was expected to guard the public morals as carefully as those of his own household. In protecting the morality of the townspeople he had the license to spy on his neighbors, to inquire as to their doings, and disrupt their privacy. Nathaniel Hawthorne described New England as a place "where iniquity was dragged out into the sunshine."

The obligation of a citizen to do moral housecleaning included the stern duty of reporting any members of his own family who deviated from the strict Puritanical code. Governor John Winthrop, in his explanation of

---

[14]*Reliquiae Baxterianae*, M. Sylvester, ed., London, 1696, 87.

[15] Essex Court Records, 1:109.

this responsibility, wrote, "A godly minister, upon conscience of his oath and care of the commonwealth, reported to the magistrates some seditious speeches of his own son, delivered in private to himself." In the tightly disciplined Puritan community, people were sensible to each other's affairs and ready to interfere when any hint of sin or scandal threatened. The towns were small and compact, the people watchful, and every person was ready to report the movements of his neighbors to the magistrates. A woman who had lost her temper when the cow kicked over the milk pail would be brought trembling into court. Secure in the belief that they were doing their duty to both her and to the Lord, her accusers would cite her delinquencies into the public record so she could be punished as a criminal. In 1692, she would be hanged as a witch.

Many scholars seem to connect the spiritual roots of the Puritans with a sense of guilt. Always, these scholars seem to arrive at the conclusion that a single controlling idea, particularly as symbolized in the satanic character of the Faustus story, could explain more clearly than any other conception the essential nature of the New England mind. In the writings of the New England divines Increase Mather and Cotton Mather, there is a reliable transcription of the dark ideas that tortured the Puritan conscience. From their works can be derived an insight into the principles of good and evil which molded the convictions of the Mathers and the other clergy and which was passed down to their congregations in their sermons.

It is perceived that these Puritan ministers subscribed to a moral code of exquisite simplicity. The forces of good, all stemming from God, were pitted against the evil hosts of Satan. Though both God and the Devil were hidden powers, each pursued his own ends in antagonism to the other, and each used his own instruments. Moreover, each had the same territorial design: the conquest of man's spiritual kingdom. John Milton's great epoch poem *Paradise Lost* represents the classic expression of Puritan thought.

In the spiritual war that continually raged, the Devil relied upon temptation. Because man was irretrievably tainted by original sin, his soul was in constant jeopardy. Consciously or unconsciously, he could establish a fatal pact with the Devil. Therefore, the Puritan clergymen had to exercise constant vigilance in order to attack evil wherever it appeared. In this prodigious struggle, both of the Mathers observed that the most shocking example of moral depravity was a person who sold his soul to the Devil. This person would gain the transitory pleasures of temporal existence, but would lose eternal salvation.

So far as Increase Mather was concerned, Dr. Faustus was the most notorious perpetrator of this type of apostasy. As a consequence, Increase Mather assigned himself the task of compiling a list of the sins of this infamous magician. He owned the principal works of the sixteenth and seventeenth-century commentators on this arch-necromancer, and he wove this material into his *Remarkable Providences* (1684) and *Cases of Conscience Concerning Evil Spirits* (1692). In his scholarly investigations of magic under the Christian tradition, Increase Mather had often encountered the names of Simon Magus, Cyprian of Antioch, Theophilus of Adana, Gerbert, and Zyto. However, Increase Mather saw that these potent wizards, even though they trafficked with the powers of hell, had never suffered the doom of Dr. Faustus, who alone had sold his soul to the Devil.

According to the invoices of a number of Boston booksellers at that time, only the Bible, hymnals, and a few school texts were in greater demand than *The History of the Damnable Life and Deserved Death of Dr. John Faustus*. This English translation of the of the famous *Historia von D. Fausten* was a popular and much read book in New England. Being acquainted with its wide circulation among his parishioners, Increase Mather was granted countless opportunities to use this material from his pulpit in Boston. The damnation of Faustus was in accord with the clergyman's conscience. In terms of Puritan dogma, Faustus committed the sin most abhorrent to the New England mind. Faustus had sold his soul to the Devil. In so doing, he had denied God and lost forever the hope of redemption through salvation.

Increase Mather's absorption with Faustus is understandable in view of his Puritan conscience. The sincerity of his belief in the possibility of personal communion and pact with the Devil was unequivocal. His opinions on the subject were typical for clergymen in those times. But the feature of Faustus' apostasy that weighed most heavily on Increase Mather's mind was the arrogant rejection of salvation. By implication, an epidemic of similar conduct among the inhabitants of New England would seriously menace the security of Christendom. Nor did he forget that the forests surrounding the settlements were peopled by Indians who were part of the satanic legions.

Because salvation through the love of God was the central doctrine of their religion, it followed that subordination of present pleasures to future good was a primary tenet in the conduct of social and religious life. Increase Mather realized that the sorcerer Faustus had been seduced by his very preference for the illusive pleasures of earthly existence. To add to this ignominy, Faustus had resorted to magic in an attempt to circumvent the inscrutable workings of the divine mind.

The real import of the Faustus story is bound up in the theme of temptation. The Devil's emissary Mephistophiles conspires to give satisfaction to every desire the magician Faustus might have, blinding him to the pre-eminent good represented in divine grace. Mephistophiles exposed the magician to temptations that were anathema to the Puritan ethic. The demonic agent supplied him with further magical means to obtain gratuitously any immediate necessity. These easily acquired materialistic gains drove Faustus beyond the pale of society. The most insidious temptation which Mephistophiles devised was embodied by proscription in the Puritan moral code, namely, the sensuous appeal to the beautiful. The evil of beauty in the Puritan ethic lay in its ability to obscure the idea of God. The truth of this conception was supposedly proved in the religious art of the Catholics, not only in rich vestments and beguiling liturgical music, but also in the paintings and statues which fostered a Devilish iconolatry. When, with the aid of Mephistophiles, Faustus evoked Helen of Troy, he ensnared himself in the atheistic cult of Greek paganism in which beauty was its own excuse for being. Increase Mather could only see that beauty seduced the hearts of men away from God.

Further adding to the horror of these lapses of morality was the conjurer's unquenchable intellectual curiosity when he conspired with the Devil to trespass the portals of forbidden knowledge. Faustus longed for an insight into the mysteries of the universe that went beyond the revelations of scripture, and to fulfill this desire he considered the loss of his soul but a trivial affair. The Puritans construed any attempt to attain self-sufficient knowledge without the benefit of heavenly dispensation as a mortal sin.

The final outcome in which the notorious heretic Faustus suffered a violent death at the hands of the Devil's cohorts was justified in the eyes of Increase Mather. Obviously, Increase Mather could find no better example of moral irresponsibility so as to give his sermons the quickening leaven of fire and brimstone.

To most Americans, witchcraft suggests a specific isolated historical event, the Salem witchcraft delusion of 1692. However the Salem witch hunt can be considered in conjunction with the many witchcraft crazes that swept over Europe in the sixteenth and seventeenth centuries. From this viewpoint Salem was not a unique event. What is unique about Salem is that it came after the great European witchcraft epidemics had ceased. By 1692 most learned people knew, or should have known, better. There was no major witch hunt after Salem, although isolated events occurred for nearly another one hundred years.

In Western countries a witch became to be regarded as an agent of Satan and an enemy of God. By the sixteenth century, the educated Europeans had connected malfeasance with Devil worship, resulting in the concept of an invisible world run by the Devil. In this unseen world, a witch would attend black Sabbats, worship Satan, and reject Christianity. The result was the witch crazes which swept Europe and America until its culmination at Salem. It was an age when Satan had become a vivid reality. It was believed that the Devil was constantly using his ingenuity to defeat the divine will, and employing his hellish agents to plague and tempt the select of God. The foremost literary work on this domain of Satan is Cotton Mather's book *The Wonders of the Invisible World* (1692), one of the great best-sellers of all time.

It seems a contradiction that witch hunting developed simultaneously with the great cultural movements of the sixteenth centuries. The renaissance in art and literature, the Reformation and the Counter Reformation, overseas explorations, and the rise of modern science seem like a strange background for witchcraft atrocities. A closer look, however, shows that witch hunting was a means for the educated elite to impose its values and standards of behavior on lower social levels. The elite groups, such as lawyers, judges, theologians, physicians, large landowners, and political rulers, were the ones who vigorously asserted the reality of cults devoted to the Devil. By transmitting these fears to the uneducated majority, they were able to divide and rule. Rival religious were labeled heretic and satanic in origin, and so-called undesirable people could be driven out by calling them Devil worshipers and witches. The witch hunts were the inevitable consequence of the elites' hunger for power together with the popular superstitions and fears which they induced and promoted.

Because educated people today are the ones who associate witchcraft with irrationality, we might expect their counterparts in the past to have spoken out against the witch trials. Eventually this action did happen at the end of the witch craze. In Salem, the merchant class as exemplified by Thomas Brattle and Robert Calef did eventually bring rationality to the scene. However the college-educated clergy were at the forefront of the witch hunts. It was educated men like these who gave the Western concept of witchcraft its most disturbing characteristic. In non-Western cultures, a so-called witch was one who performed magic, which could be evil. But the educated Europeans created a demonic image of the witch by associating harmful magic with religious dissent. Educated people connected sorcery with heresy.

Witchcraft, considered a crime against the church, was dealt with in the Puritan court system, showing the close connection between politics and religion. Puritans feared anyone or anything that was different from them, and then accused them of being witches. "The Crucible", by Arthur Miller, is a characterization of the Puritan community of Salem as a theocracy. Hard work and church consume the majority of the people of Salem. The government of Salem, and of Massachusetts as a whole, is a theocracy. Salem witch trials of 1692 ended when the colonial governor transferred the trials to the Superior Court in 1693, which did not accept spectral evidence.

The Puritan Theocracy consisted of a government ran by religious authorities. Religious men ran their government. The Puritans considered all government actions to be necessarily good or sanctioned by Heaven. Which meant that any attempt by anyone to question, corrupt, or resist any of the government's actions was considered by the government and other Puritans to be an attempt to overthrow God. The government was to be governed by their religion.

The minister of the church was selected by the congregation and the town government paid his salary. The minister was also a government official who exerted an enormous political influence in the community. Only someone who the minister certified as "godly" could be elected to office. Non-Christians could not hold political office. Only church members could vote in political elections. Any rebel against the civil government was a traitor to God, and any criticism or rebellion against Puritan rule was also a sin against God.

Puritans believed that man existed for the glory of God. Man's first priority in life is to do the will of God in order to receive future happiness. They believed in demonic forces. They believed in some accusations of witchcraft. Puritans believe that marriage represents one of the most significant human relationships established in conception, love, and salvation. Husbands were the spiritual head of the household while women were to demonstrate religious obedience under male authority. Marriage represented not only the relationship between husband and wife but also the relationship between spouses and God. The Puritan belief held that the Puritans were a chosen people that the devil would do anything to destroy. They didn't believe in celebrations, dancing, or anything of that sort. Puritan goal was to purify themselves and their communities from any appearance of evil. In our government & court system today we believe in the separation of church and state, but the Puritans believed in combining the two to use to their best advantage. The court system was based off of the bible. The Puritan church did not save or exempt anyone from being dealt with by civil authority. If someone were accused of breaking God's law they were presented before the town elders. They mostly used public humiliation as a form of punishment. Stocks were two heavy wooden planks with holes cut out to hold the ankles and wrists. The pillory held the criminal while standing, and had holes for the head and hands. The community would yell insults and chunk leftovers at the criminal. Letters were sometimes sewn onto a criminal's clothing or branded on the flesh. The letters would represent specific crimes. The dunking stool was a plank of wood balanced at its center, like a see-saw, a stool was strapped to the end of the plank where the woman would be tied, and placed over water. A judge would assign a number of dunks based on the level of offense, and the criminal would face the judicial system wet and humiliated. Jail, whippings, brutal punishment, hanging, beating, & execution were also used. Puritans were mainly agricultural people. They lived in villages and owned private fields. The typical village was made up of houses grouped around the meetinghouse, where the pastor, the most important figure in the community, held long religious services. Puritan society required that its members follow strict guidelines of social order. Those who think or act independently are seen as a threat to the community & they must be eliminated. The Puritan community in Massachusetts was a collection of godly communities tied together by an agreement with God in order to ensure the public welfare. Puritans placed family at the center of their societies as an organization to facilitate their devotion to God.

Puritan old guard

Puritan New England was founded idealistically as a haven of religious liberty, yet it would in turn persecute religious dissenters. The Puritans fled to New England not to permit unfettered religious liberty but to acquire the "gospel liberty" to erect a godly society—a "New Israel"—in accordance with their specific beliefs. The Puritans considered themselves as a righteous group surrounded by enemies. Their religious and political psychology was reflexively defensive. Puritan believed that God blessing on their society was grounded on order and obedience. The New England Puritans has an obsession with conspiracy theories. The Native Americans were in a conspiracy against them. The Quakers were in a conspiracy against them. The Baptists were too. In 1692 so were covens of witches. This conviction helps clarify the motivations of Puritans and the rationale for some of the acts of intolerance that still give them a bad reputation.

Except for the brief tenure of Sir Edmond Andros as governor, Puritan New England was self-governed until 1692. A staunch group of Puritan leaders held rule. Among these were those that held strictly to old tradition. They were the Puritan Old Guard. The included key members of the legislative body (board of assistants or council). Accustomed to ruling with an iron hand, and fearing the general franchise granted by the new charter, they sought to keep the population under their control at all costs.

John Winthrop in 1630 established Massachusetts as a Puritan state. The Puritan settlers wanted to create a very different world from the one they had left behind. However they took with them a curious heritage, a strong belief in the power of witchcraft and magic. They transplanted the old legends to their new homes. A large number of the pioneers of New England came from the eastern part of old England where the fear of witchcraft had been the strongest. In fact many of them had emigrated in the first place because they had believed that the authorities were too tolerant of witchcraft. The witchcraft mania broke out in Essex County, Massachusetts in 1692. The same pattern of witch persecution in old England was recreated there.

The legal structure of Massachusetts had no time to grow and mature gracefully. Designed for immediate use, it combined elements which did not mesh together. It was a dogma which drew largely from the militancy of the Old Testament but also upon English law with its traditional safeguards. The early history of New England was marked by a continuing controversy about the place of civil laws in a religious community. The Puritan settlers believed that their colony represented the nation described in I *Peter* 2:9,10, "But ye are a chosen generation, a royal priesthood, a holy nation, a peculiar people; that ye should show forth the praises of him who hath called you out of darkness into his marvelous light."

The leaders of New England were bent on establishing the Kingdom of God in the new world. The ruling class set themselves up as "visible saints," and required everyone to live as they believed God intended people to live. Drawing their authority from Holy Scripture, the Puritan leaders regulated their society accordingly. Soon a rigorous control of personal behavior was imposed on everybody in New England, Puritans and non-Puritans alike. Swearing, drunkenness, and any other kinds of licentious behavior were severely penalized. The law and government were in effect derived from the hell-and-brimstone sermons delivered from the pulpits. The Puritans were no more believers in the political rights of individuals, or in democracy, than in religious toleration, and the leaders of Massachusetts denounced both with equal vehemence.

The intolerance of the old guard in imposing despotism upon those under their control is inherent in Puritan thinking. The Puritan elite were the "elect," God's representatives on Earth. They believed that the Puritan community of New England resulted from a plan of God to plant his kingdom on new soil. To them, the Indians were as savages who to the devout Puritan appeared like devils from hell itself. They believed that the Native Americans practiced diabolic rituals. The Indian shamans and medicine men were regarded as witch doctors, which openly practiced the magic that the Puritans most feared.

Although the intention was to build a heaven on earth, the fate of New England was otherwise. The Puritan leaders had created such a hell that after the first great wave of immigration during the 1630s many new settlers shunned New England like a plague. It became common knowledge that the Quakers had suffered terribly under the despotism of the Puritans. The stocks, whipping posts, and gallows were in constant use in New England for the preservation of God's kingdom. Anyone who offended against the scruples of Puritan morality had a great price to pay. It was an offense in Massachusetts to walk the streets on a Sunday other than to church. A young couple in Connecticut was arrested for sitting under an apple tree on a beautiful Sunday afternoon. Not only were all people required to attend both morning and afternoon services on Sundays, but also services called lectures on Thursday afternoons.

Charles Francis Adams, the eminent scholar and a descendant of American presidents, in his book *Massachusetts, Its Historians and Its History*, writes: "The witchcraft mania of 1692 in Massachusetts was no isolated or inexplicable manifestation; on the contrary, it was the most noticeable instance of the operation of law: given John Winthrop's journal in 1630-1640, Salem witchcraft at a somewhat later period might with safety be predicted. The community was predisposed to the epidemic." However, Adams goes on to say that the Puritan leaders in waging their vigorous struggle for self-government and a church free from English control unwittingly indoctrinated New Englanders with the seed of democratic ideas far different from professed beliefs.

Because Puritan New England was a theocracy, the church had a significant hand in the government, so the clergy as well as the politicians formed the elite ruling class. The clergy also made sure that they were paid quite well, so they also represented a moneyed class. The Cotton family and Mather family provide the most eminent representatives of the clergy in Puritan New England. The activities of these families are intertwined in the unfolding of the Puritan experience in New England.

Witchcraft in Massachusetts

Here we present a discussion on perceptions and illusions, and how they influence thinking. Perception includes not only how the world is experienced through the five senses, but also how the signals from the senses interact with our intelligence. Although all organized knowledge starts from perception, science seems to work better when instruments or instructions replace the human observers. Sensation, or the awareness of shape, color, sound, touch, and smell is often deeply mysterious. However, the mystery deepens even more though the aspects of artificial intelligence afforded by computers. These machines seem to make possible some kind of perception by processing information without awareness.

Illusions are discrepancies from the truth. All perceptions are subject to errors, but illusions have errors of perception built into their mechanism. Unless an illusion has a striking inconsistency, it will often pass unnoticed. Illusions of the senses present a fundamental embarrassment to the concept that knowledge is securely based on perception. Typical kinds of cognitive illusions are illusions resulting from such things as ambiguity, distortion, paradox, or fiction. There are many questions still unanswered. However, when answers are found they often shut off possibilities of new understanding.

There is one event in Puritan Massachusetts which took place in 1692 for which no fully satisfactory explanation has ever been given, and indeed it appears that no complete solution can ever be found. It is a grim story and one which plunged those families involved in ignominy, and it might be better forgotten. It certainly has no place in this day and age, and in fact it is nearly impossible for the modern reader to conceive of such a situation, let alone understand it. There is good reason to omit this unpleasant drama altogether and instead concentrate on the many positive aspects that have taken place over the intervening years. On the other hand, it may be time to make as full a disclosure of the story as we can by bringing together the various documents.

Stories are not immortal. Most are forgotten, and soon buried in the deep grave of eternity. There are many stories of injustices, crimes, and misery. Sometimes a story is about a hero; sometimes, a victim. A story may be lost many years in oblivion and then is finally found and retold. People grow wiser, and shun reminders of the past. But sometimes the past will not be forgotten, and it is necessary to recall our own history with its adventures and trials. In these cases we need stories, and what we can learn from them.

This story revolves around the question of witchcraft in Salem in 1692. The answer to this question can never be ascertained with certainty. Various accounts come from family traditions. The great bulk of accounts are based on historical fact. The most important source is *The Salem Witchcraft Papers*, availed online by the University of Virginia. It contains verbatim transcripts of all the extant legal documents of the Salem witch trials. Yet legal documents alone seldom reveal the innermost thoughts and aspirations of people. Throughout history, witch hunts or their counterparts have occurred. All are impostures driven by deceitfulness and sanctioned by the governing authorities. They feed upon underlying fears of the people. The underlying cause of the witch hunt is always envy in one or more of its many forms.

Not all witch trials ended in conviction and death. In England, where many forms of torture were prohibited, only about twenty percent of the accused witches were executed (by hanging); in Scotland, where torture was used, nearly half of all those put on trial were burned at the stake, and almost three times as many witches (1,350) were killed as in England. Some places had fewer trials than others. In the Dutch republic, no witches were executed after about 1600, and none were tried after 1610. Accusations of witchcraft in Spain and Italy were handled by the Inquisition, and although torture was legal, only a dozen witches were burned out of 5,000 put on trial. Ireland apparently escaped witch trials altogether. Many witch trials were provoked, not by hysterical authorities or fanatical clergy, but by village quarrels among neighbors.

About three-quarters of all accused witches were women. Traditional theology assumed that women were weaker than men and more likely to succumb to the Devil. Woman, having been formed from a bent rib, was supposedly an imperfect being, and always considered as a deceiver. It may in fact be true that having few legal rights, they were more inclined to settle quarrels by resorting to magic rather than law. However blatant misogyny was always evident.

All these aspects of witchcraft crossed over to the Americas with European colonists. In the Spanish and French territories cases of witchcraft were under the jurisdiction of church courts, and no one suffered death on this charge. It is reported that the Indians in New England were puzzled by the concern of the settlers, and thought them more sinful than the French colonists to the north, for among the French "the Great Spirit sent no witches." In the English colonies about 40 people were executed for witchcraft between 1650 and 1692, half of them in the famous Salem witch trials of 1692. Witch trials declined in most parts of Europe after 1680; in England the death penalty for witchcraft was abolished in 1736. In the late seventeenth and eighteenth centuries one last wave of witch persecution afflicted areas of Eastern Europe, but ended by about 1740. The last legal execution of a witch occurred in Switzerland in 1782.

Some historians argue that the Salem witch trials were the result of governance in keeping with the Puritan world view. The church and the state made up one entity. God and the devil were active in man's experience of life. Other historians argue that the Salem witch trials were the result of apprehension and varied social forces under a flawed court system adjudicating the interplay of good and evil. It is often claimed that no one was responsible. If anyone were to blame, it was Cotton Mather, or else William Stoughton, or else the circle of afflicted teenage and pre-teenage girls, or a combination of all. The belief that Christianity was the true religion was the motivation for this need to control the population.

Cotton Mather

John Cotton (1584–1652) was a renowned English minister who in 1633 immigrated to America. His congregation in England followed him to New England, and he became minister of the First Church in Boston. Richard Mather (1596–1669) came to Massachusetts in 1635. He settled in Dorchester (just south of Boston then, and now part of Boston) and preached for nearly thirty-four years. Two of John Cotton's sons, and four of Richard Mather's, graduated from Harvard College and entered the ministry. Both John Cotton and Richard Mather were Moses-like figures, leaders and lawgivers to the American Puritans.

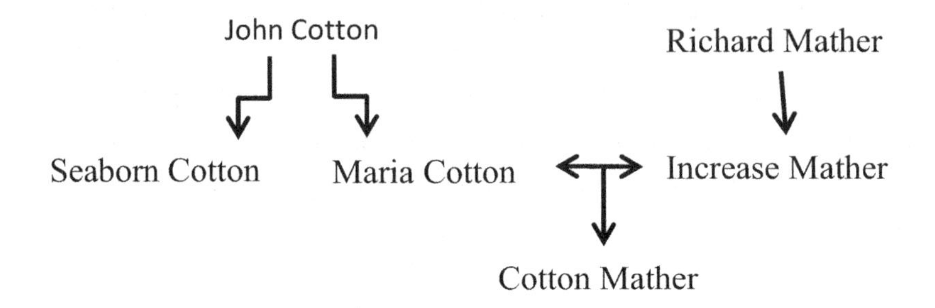

The two sons who play a role in this story are John Cotton's son Seaborn Cotton, and Richard Mather's son Increase Mather. The critical link between the two families comes by way of John Cotton's daughter, Maria Cotton, who married Increase Mather. Their offspring, Cotton Mather, was named so as to perpetuate this bond between the two families.

Increase Mather became the minister of the North Church in Boston. He married Maria Cotton in 1662 and on the February 12, 1663, the couple's first child, Cotton Mather, was born. Increase Mather was to become the president of Harvard College. By 1674 his son Cotton Mather had mastered the entrance requirements for Harvard College and was admitted. The college laws required for admission a working knowledge of Latin and Greek. Cotton Mather entered at the age of eleven and a half, the youngest student admitted to the college in its history. At the time of his admission, physical and administrative problems had put the college in the sorriest state in its history. The College Hall, a two-story wood building enclosing most of the college facilities, was collapsing. When Cotton Mather attended, the total enrollment at Harvard was never more than 20 students all together; in his own class there were only four. Because Harvard was the training ground for the New England ministry, its sinking condition was a matter of deep public concern.

The students' ages ranged from about 15 to 18. As an eleven year old boy with a stutter, Cotton Mather was discouraged after some of the students had threatened him. Following only a month at college he returned home and stayed there for the rest of the freshman year, studying with his father and on his own.

His experiences that first month at Harvard are worth recounting. He found himself one of a group of thirteen boys, including his own first cousin, John Cotton Jr. Cotton Mather's immediate classmates were three: cousin John Cotton Jr., who became a preacher; Urian Oakes, the consumptive son of the college president, and Grindall Rawson, who was the son of the secretary of Massachusetts Colony, and who later would become the strictest of clergymen. The normal time spent for the undergraduate degree was three years, so there were two classes above the freshman class of Cotton Mather. In the class right above (the junior class), there were six boys, three of whom were sons of ministers, one the son of a captain, one the son of a weaver, and one the son of a strict schoolmaster. Four of the six boys in this class became ministers. In the top class (the senior class), there were three boys, two of which would become ministers. One of these two boys was the son of Reverend Thomas Shepard whose terrible depictions of hell fed his parishioners with appetite for horror. The other of the two future ministers was the son of a wheelwright; this young man was older than the others in the college, being 21 when Cotton Mather entered.

The third member of the senior class was Thomas Brattle who in his lifetime made use of his calm judicial mind to see beyond the prejudice and hysteria of Cotton Mather and his father Increase Mather, and thereby become a veritable thorn in their flesh. If Cotton Mather represents everything bad about Puritanism, then Thomas Brattle represents everything that is good. If history were fair he should be the most famous American Puritan, not Cotton Mather.

The demoralized atmosphere at the college during Cotton Mather's second year was deepened by a violent event that his father had predicted. Early in 1674 his father, Increase Mather, had foreseen that God would strike New England by sword. The summer of 1675 fulfilled the prophecy: King Philip's War erupted, a war of annihilation by the Indians. The fighting came within 20 miles of Cambridge. Cotton Mather heard his father's many prayers to God for victory, and believed them efficacious. Increase set, by a stroke of providence. In less than a week the thing was accomplished. Philip was shot and quartered, and his remains sent to Boston and Plymouth.

Now newly 14, Cotton Mather saw the accomplishment of another of his father's prophecies, that Boston would be punished by a judgment of fire. In the morning of November 27, his family's house burned down along with 45 other houses and the North Church. At this time he became acquainted with a fellow student, Thomas Barnard of Hadley. Cotton Mather easily went through the required junior and senior curriculum at Harvard. Cotton Mather graduated in 1678; Thomas Barnard graduated one year later, in 1679. Thomas Barnard became the assistant minister in Andover. After Cotton Mather graduated from Harvard, he spent a brief time studying medicine, but then turned his attention to the ministry. He became the assistant minister in his father's church, the North Church.

In a world peopled by evil spirits, the Puritan elect found it easy to accept statements by their clergy that the plan of the Devil was to overthrow the kingdom of God that they were creating. Their survival was at stake, and from dispatches from the old country there was ample evidence that the Devil was at work in assaulting the righteous through his instruments, the witches. The New England colonies started introducing laws against witchcraft as early as 1641. The Puritan old guard persecuted, prosecuted, and punished people accused as witches.

There was always a steady trickle of accusations, yet at no time did it reach the level of persecution in England until 1692. It is a matter of speculation why the witch fever never arose until that year. Something was needed to transform the latent witch fear into open persecution. History has laid the blame on Rev. Cotton Mather.

The cry against the witches was built up by Cotton Mather. In 1690 he told a youth group that

> "the Devil from the mouth of a possessed person, within the hearing of several standers-by, threatened me with much disgrace for what I was doing."

In preaching about the current war against the French and Indians in 1690 he said:

> "The Devils are stark mad that the house of the Lord our God has come to these remote corners of the world; and they fume; they fret prodigiously."

In 1691 he preached:

> "How many doleful wretches have been decoyed into witchcraft itself, by the opportunities which their discontent has given to the Devil to visit them and seduce them?"

These few citations are from a mass of Cotton Mather's published and unpublished writings on this subject in the years 1690 to 1692. His paranoia was transmitted to the civil authorities who then took action against these imagined enemies of the state in the witchcraft persecutions of 1692.

By 1692 the Puritan old guard of Massachusetts was under serious threats. The most serious one came from the people themselves, who in a quest for democracy were questioning the very basis of the theocratic government. Only the "elect," about four percent of the people, were allowed to vote and participate in government. These elect were the "visible saints" of the Puritan church, the only ones who had church membership. The rest of the people were denied this privilege. The Puritan beliefs were based on contrasts. As there was good, there had to be evil. As there was a God, there had to be a Devil. As there were "visible saints" chosen to do God's work on Earth, there had to be witches who were instruments of the Devil. From this logic it followed that if one denied the existence of witches, one did not believe in God, the ultimate heresy.

As the leading young clergyman, Cotton Mather undertook the task of establishing the existence of witches "to glorify the Lord Jesus Christ." In his sermon *Discourse on Witchcraft* in 1688, he wrote:

> "Witchcraft is a most monstrous and horrid evil. Witchcraft is a renouncing of God, and advancing a filthy Devil into the throne of the most high. Witchcraft is a renouncing of Christ, and preferring the communion of a loathsome lying Devil before all the salvation of the Lord redeemer. Witchcraft is a siding with Hell against Heaven and Earth; and therefore a witch is not to be endured in either of them. It is a capital crime."

Cotton Mather was a scholar and possessed considerable influence among the old guard Puritans. He undertook the task of convincing the people that the Devil had selected covens of witches to destroy New England. He was obsessed, under the spell of his own dogma. He was a purveyor of the philosophy of fear. He was a man of "overweening vanity," and an ardent mover of the search for witches, always haranguing the people for more strenuous actions. Through his popular writings Cotton Mather had direct influence on the general populace. His friends in high government circles listened to his advice..

The linking of Cotton Mather with the Salem witchcraft trials began in his own time and persists to the present. In 1688, four of the children of John Goodwin of Boston were generally believed to be bewitched, and for this crime "an ignorant and scandalous old woman," as Cotton Mather described a poor washerwoman named Glover, was condemned and executed. With this first-hand experience, Mather produced in 1689 his first book *Memorable Providences, Relating to Witchcraft and*

Possessions. He describes the "afflictions" of the four children as follows. "Sometimes they were deaf, sometimes dumb, sometimes blind, and often all this at once. Their tongues would be drawn down their throats, and then pulled out upon their chins to a prodigious length. Their mouths were forced open to such a wideness that their jaws went out of joint, and anon clap together again, with a force like that of a spring-lock, and the like would happen to their shoulder blades and their elbows, and hand wrists, and several of their joints. They would lie in a benumbed condition and be drawn together like those who are tied neck and heels, and presently be stretched out, yea, drawn backwards to such an extent that it was feared the very skin of their bellies would have cracked. They would make most piteous outcries that they were cut with knives, and struck with blows that they could not bear." All their afflictions were during the day; they slept comfortably at night.

By being the most active and forward of any minister in the Goodwin case, and by printing an account of it, Mather contributed much to the kindling of the witchcraft flames at Salem Village in February 1692, and as the months wore on, he continued to fan the fire even after the Salem witchcraft episode came to its ignominious end in 1693.

Salem witchcraft followed the formula as used in England. Salem Village was the center of accusations in Salem witchcraft in from February to July 1692. Andover became the center from July to September 1692. But then Andover townspeople turned all the rules upside down. Under the leadership of its two ministers Francis Dane and Thomas Barnard and with the support of its elected officials, Andover interjected a strong dose of Christian forgiveness into the witchcraft proceedings. Andover was instrumental in the release of many of the witchcraft prisoners in the fall of 1692.

A penny loaf was a small bread loaf which cost one old penny at the time when there were 240 pence to the pound. A penny loaf was a common size loaf of bread in England regulated by the Assize of Bread

Act of 1266. In late 1692, the whole edifice of Salem witchcraft, like London Bridge, came falling down.

London Bridge is falling down,
Falling down, falling down.
London Bridge is falling down,
My fair lady!

Build it up with penny loaves,
Penny loaves, penny loaves.
Build it up with penny loaves,
My fair lady!

Penny loaves will tumble down,
Tumble down, tumble down.
Penny loaves will tumble down,
My fair lady!

The Puritan old guard tried to build up the Salem witchcraft again with a new set of trials in early 1693, but to no avail. Witchcraft was declared a superstition. Witchcraft accusations effectively came to an end in New England. Except for a very few short outbreaks elsewhere in the world the persecution of witches was over. Of course, in some circles, belief in the existence of witches and witchcraft persisted, but the subject was no longer acceptable in public discourse.

Invisible spiritual world

In the seventeenth century the microscope opened up a new world of observation, and profoundly revised current thinking. For the first time, it was realized that there were huge numbers of living microscopic animals quite invisible to the naked eye. The interior of nature, once closed off to both sympathetic intuition and direct perception, was now accessible with the help of optical instruments. The discovery of the invisible world of microbes unlocked a source of problems. Scientists and philosophers were presented with the task of reconciling the ubiquity of life with human-centered theological systems.

In 1688 in England, Sir Isaac Newton wrote *Principia Matematica*, in which he gave the "System of the World." His book has governed the scientific understanding of the visible universe ever since. In the same year in New England, Cotton Mather wrote *Memorable Providences Relating to Witchcraft and Possessions.* This book, published the next year, was Cotton Mather's first attempt to give a scientific account of the invisible world of the Devil. The book is based on his first-hand observation; he uses as data the experiences of the Goodwin children in the summer and fall of 1688. Cotton Mather wrote,

> "Haec ipse miserrima vidi," or "these things these wretched eyes beheld."

The Latin words "Haec ipse miserrima vidi" come from Virgil's *Aeneid.* Actually Virgil wrote, "quaeque ipsa miserrima vidi, et quorum pars magna fui," with translation, "and those terrible things I saw, and in which I played a great part." With more honesty, Cotton Mather would have written, "those terrible things I saw, and in which I played a great part." Yes, Cotton Mather did play a great part in the travesty of the Salem witch trials.

Cotton Mather resolved 'never to use but just one grain of patience with any man that shall go to impose upon me, a Denial of Devils, or of Witches. ... I shall count him down-right Impudent if he asserts the Non-Existence of which we have so palpable Convictions of." The book *Memorable Providences* was not challenged. In fact, few learned persons of that time would express any doubt about the "facts" presented in the book, readily accepting the preternatural agency of witchcraft as the cause of the children's afflictions. Mr. Richard Baxter, an eminent English cleric, in a preface to an edition published in London in 1691, says, "The evidence is so convincing that he must be a very obdurate Sadducee who will not believe."[16]

---

[16]Cotton Mather (*Discourse*, 99) wrote, "Since there are Witches, we are to suppose that there are Devils too. It was the heresy of the ancient *Sadducees* in Act. 23:8. *The Sadducees do say, That there is neither Angel nor Spirit.* And

At the height of the Salem Witchcraft Trials in 1692, Cotton Mather wrote his book *Wonders of The Invisible World*. It presents his historical and theological observations upon the nature, the number, and the operations of the devils. It was published by the Special Command of His Excellency, the Governor of the Province of the Massachusetts-Bay in New-England. In this case the book was severely challenged. In fact, the book destroyed the reputation of Cotton Mather. Cotton Mather suffered shame and dishonor beginning in his own time and continuing to the present day.

Magic and Science

The seventeenth century marks a turning point in history because it represents the period in which ancient science is transformed into modern science. The traditions of civilization, which started in Mesopotamia and Egypt, reached a climax in the Hellenistic Age of Greece, and were extended by the Roman Empire. After the decline of Alexandria, Greek science lingered in Byzantium, and was spread by Islam from Baghdad to Spain. In the 12th century Christian Europe started picking up these ideas. Not only was there a revival of learning, but trade grew and technology and hygiene improved. Developments or redevelopments such as the clock and the magnetic compass changed the eternity of the religious man into the time of the secular man, and space as order into space as opportunity for expansion and independence. The 14th and 15th centuries saw the increasing breakup of the theoretical religious unity of the Middle Ages, as new trade routes beckoned for the acquisition of new-found wealth. The scientific tradition persevered by Islam started mankind on a new venture during the 15th century. This century gave birth to one of the most fundamental technical advances, the development of printing. Printing multiplied the means for both propaganda and enlightenment.

The Renaissance came into prominence in Italy, and spread throughout Europe. The thrusting spirit catapulted science over earlier obstacles,

---

there are multitudes of Sadducees yet in our day; fools that say, *Seeing is believing;* and will believe nothing but what they see."

but it did so in a manner that left many problems in a state demanding profound reconsideration in the centuries to come. Science started to crystallize from several different sources and in many different places. Artists like Leonardo da Vinci (1452-1519) were among the most enterprising workers in optics, mechanics, and anatomy. Leonardo's break with Aristotle in mechanics had been anticipated by Buridan (c1297-c1358), and had to be re-done, in the 17th century, by Galileo. The interplay between theoretical knowledge and practical knowledge always is basic in the process of interpreting the history of science. Theoretical maps devised by monks with the aid of travelers' tales gave way to the practical pilots' charts of the Mediterranean.

A drawback to the pre-science of the 16th century was the isolation of things capable of a fruitful union. Generally this isolation kept discoveries away from the vast fields of application which awaited them. A case in point is alchemy. Alchemy is characterized by mysticism in inappropriate places and a cult of secrecy. Medieval people craved order in science as well as life. When they were halted in finding true laws of nature, they made recourse to symbolism. Things with the same number were linked together following the number-mysticism of the ancient Greeks, in particular, Pythagoras.

Greek chemistry had four elements: fire, air, water, and earth, which in turn were compounded in pairs of hot, dry, cold, and wet. The four elements responsible for human health correspond to them: blood for a sanguine temper, black bile for a melancholic temper, phlegm for a phlegmatic temper, and yellow bile for a choleric temper. Before the dodecahedron was discovered there were only four regular polyhedra known: the tetrahedron, octahedron, the icosahedron, and cube. These corresponded to the four elements. When the fifth (and last) regular polyhedron (the dodecahedron) was discovered, a fifth element was postulated to represent the entire non-worldly universe. This fifth element was the quintessence (the fifth essence) thought to be the substance of the heavenly bodies and latent in all things.

The number seven, which is four plus three, took on special significance. Seven represents three-dimensional space made up of the horizontal directions, north, east, south, and west, and the vertical directions, up, center, and down. There are seven musical notes. There are seven planets of the ancients (including the Sun and Moon). The Sun stood for gold, the Moon for silver, Jupiter for tin, Saturn for lead, Mars for iron, Venus for copper, and Mercury for mercury.

One man can serve as an example of a sixteenth century scientist, or mystic, depending upon how one chooses to view him. He is Paracelsus, a German-Swiss alchemist and physician, born in 1493 and died in 1541. In the eyes of his contemporaries, Paracelsus was a sorcerer and a wonder healer. Tales of his miraculous cures went throughout Europe. Envious doctors would attribute these cures to magic arts, and even say that his powers came from the Devil. Even the great English poet John Donne (c1572-1631) wrote that Paracelsus carried out Lucifer's orders "by thy [the Devil's] minerals and fire." Paracelsus had prophesied that "natural magic" would make it possible to see beyond the mountains, to hear across the ocean, to divine the future, to cure all diseases, to make gold, to gain eternal life. Asserting that "nothing is so secret that it cannot be made apparent," he presumed knowledge of the occult and the hidden forces of nature. Yet, this necromancer, this practitioner in the occult science, praised reasoning and experiment as the true source of knowledge. This alchemist urged his fellow adapts to stop making gold; instead, find medicines. His challenge opened up the possibility of a science of biochemistry, and indeed was the forerunner of the revolution that was to take place in medicine and chemistry.

These writings of Paracelsus give instances of both of best of scientific thought and the worst of mysticism. How can we understand this puzzle? Was Paracelsus a medieval magnus or a modern scientist? Was he an impostor who put forth careless speculation and ill-conceived experiments, or was he a deep thinker whose genius saw the future direction of science? However, he was not alone. He has these two conflicting aspects of character in common with many great scientists who followed him, in particular Kepler and Newton.

It is well-known that Johannes Kepler (1571-1630) spent a good part of his time in astrology. Even his early models of the solar system are based on the five regular polyhedra. However it is not so well-known that Sir Isaac Newton (1642-1727) spent the major part of his productive lifetime working not in chemistry, but in alchemy, the same kind of alchemy as did Paracelsus, who was born a full century and a half before him.

Newton's scientific career was almost entirely contained in his years at Cambridge University from 1660 to 1696. During virtually this whole period he was in a state of intellectual isolation, isolation broken only in the final academic years after the publication of the *Principia* in 1688. The catastrophic decline of the University after the Restoration in 1660 left it an intellectual wasteland. Cambridge lacked any scientific community into which Newton might fit. His devotion to alchemy during this period shows that his isolation was in fact mitigated by the clandestine fraternity of alchemists. Newton's interest in this black art was neither a youthful adventure nor an aberration of intellectual burn-out. His devotion to alchemy fell in the middle of his scientific career, and it spans the time of most of his achievements in mathematics and physics upon which his fame rests. In fact, alchemy appears to have been his most enduring passion. Whereas mathematics and physics only riveted his attention during brief periods, alchemy held his interest without a major interruption for almost thirty years. In the 1660s, he was devoted to mathematics, and in the process invented calculus. Optics concerned him briefly in the late 1660s and early 1670s, but he never seriously returned to it again. He devoted himself to physics for two limited periods, once in the 1660s and again from 1686 to 1688 when he wrote the *Principia*. Meanwhile his devotion to the black arts went on unchecked. Even while writing the *Principia*, he would leave his desk to tend to his alchemical furnaces. In the five years after the completion of the *Principia*, he spent his entire time in a monumental study of alchemy. The little time he spent in mathematics, mechanics, and optics produced calculus, the laws of motion and universal gravitation, and the spectrum of light, but these short periods were just inconvenient interruptions in his primary labors in the mysticism of alchemy.

Let us now return to Paracelsus. The methodology of science rests on the freedom to push research into fields which before had been forbidden as improper. The medieval mind regarded the unseen or invisible aspects of nature as provinces surrendered to demons. Now these provinces would be opened to scientific exploration. Science expanded the concept of nature; it reduced the realm of the occult. However, such deductions frightened scholars of the 16th century. Uncovering the occult was not only dangerous, but it was impious. This crossing of the threshold into free scientific inquiry could also be interpreted as a form of heresy. These religious qualms were in a large measure responsible for the accelerating witch hunts in sixteenth-century Europe.

Paracelsus serves as the model of Dr. Faustus of legendary fame. Fascinated historians have sifted out records of people who actually had the name of Faustus. All lived in the first half of the sixteenth century, Paracelsus' time. However none of these show any of the true heroic Faustian features, as Paracelsus does. The legend of Dr. Faustus represents a myth, a myth that had a tremendous influence in the sixteenth and seventeenth centuries. In the pursuit of knowledge, modern scientists and their backers have spent their fortunes and risked their lives. But the legendary Dr. Faustus risked even more than life. He was willing to forego salvation and risk damnation in order to gain power over the mysteries of nature. All his travels and studies had been without satisfaction, so he turned to black magic and made a pact with the Devil to give him knowledge of space and matter. He was then able to travel through the air, draw wine out of dry wood, and call back Homer's heroes from Hades. But in the end Faustus paid the price. The Devil claimed his due.

One of the numerous Faustus books was that of Johann Spies of Frankfurt in 1587. Its description title reads: History of Dr. John. Faust, the notorious sorcerer and black artist: How he bound himself to the

Devil for a certain time: What singular adventures befell him therein: What he did and carried on until finally he received his well-deserved pay. Mostly from his own posthumous writings; for all presumptuous, rash and Godless men, as a terrible example, abominable instance, and well-meant warning, collected and put in print. "Submit yourselves therefore to God: resist the Devil and he will flee from you." (James 4:7). The book immediately sold out, and numerous editions followed.

Invisible subatomic world

Cotton Mather (1663-1728) had an overriding interest in the invisible world. Was Cotton Mather a unifier or a diversifier? That is an age old question. Unifiers are people whose driving passion is to find general principles which will explain everything. They leave the universe looking a little simpler than before. Diversifiers are people whose passion is to explore details. They leave the universe a little more complicated than before.

In 1674 Antoni van Leeuwenhoek (1632-1723) in Delft looked through the microscope that he had carefully constructed. The specimen was a small glass tube containing water from the Berkelse Meer, a lake a few kilometers away. Leeuwenhoek was shocked because he did not see pure clear water. Instead he saw another world, a world unknown to mankind. It was an aquarium filled with minuscule little animals swimming in all directions, each about one thousand times as small as a tiny cheese mite. Some were shaped like spiral serpents, some were globular, and some were elongated ovals. Leeuwenhoek has discovered the microscopic world inhabited by microorganisms. They are organisms (such as protozoa, bacteria, fungi, viruses) too small to be seen with naked eye but visible under a microscope. They are also called microbes. Through his skillful observations, insight and unmatched curiosity, he revolutionized biological science by exposing microscopic life to the world. Leeuwenhoek showed that the biological world was much more diversified than before. He had discovered an invisible word replete with life.

Emil Johann Wiechert (1861-1928) was a German physicist and geophysicist who made many contributions to both fields, including being among the first to discover the electron and presenting the first verifiable model of a layered structure of the Earth. Wiechert was one of the first to suggest the presence of a dense core in the earth. Composed primarily of liquid iron and nickel, the core controls Earth's magnetic field which protects us from the sun's solar winds. Wiechert contributed to other branches of geophysics, particularly atmospheric electricity. Under his direction various methods were developed for measuring potential gradients and conductivity in the atmosphere. Wiechert was a diversifier. In 1896 Wiechert delivered a lecture which contained this passage:

> "So far as modern science is concerned, we have to abandon completely the idea that by going into the realm of the small we shall reach the ultimate foundations of the universe. I believe we can abandon this idea without any regret. The universe is infinite in all directions, not only above us in the large but also below us in the small. If we start from our human scale of existence and explore the content of the universe further and further, we finally arrive, both in the large and in the small, at misty distances where first our senses and then even our concepts fail us."

In other words, Wiechert said that there is an invisible world in the large and also an invisible world in the small. We, as human beings, can never see what is inside the invisible world. In other words, we can grasp what magnetism does, but we are unable to fathom how. In this regard, Voltaire (1694-1778) referred to Job 38:11: *Usque huc venies et non procedes amplius; et hic confringes tumentes fluctus tuos*, which translated is: "This far you may come, but no farther, and here your proud waves must stop!" In other words, we can understand the universe and all of its workings only up to a point, and no further. The "proud waves must stop," but what are the waves?

Louis de Broglie (1892-1987) made groundbreaking contributions to quantum theory, an essential aspect of a unified field theory (UFT). In

1924, de Broglie maintained that just as light has wave and particle properties, all microscopic material particles (e.g., electrons, protons, atoms, molecules) also have dual character. They behave as a particle as well as wave. Such a wave is called a *matter wave*. It is also called a *de Broglie wave* and also a *probability wave.* (A probability wave is a wave whose amplitude at a given region and over a given time interval corresponds to the probability of observing a given particle within that region in that time.) The concept that matter behaves like a wave is also referred to as the de Broglie hypothesis. This means that an electron which has been regarded as a particle also behaves like a wave. Thus, according to de Broglie, all the material particles in motion possess wave characteristics. However, the dual nature is significant for only microscopic bodies. For large bodies, the wavelengths are too small to be measured. Probability waves play a central role only in the subatomic world of quantum mechanics.

The wave-particle duality refers to the exhibition of both wavelike and particle-like properties by a single entity. For example, electrons undergo diffraction and can interfere with each other as waves, but they also act as point-like masses and electric charges. The measurement of the wave function will randomly "collapse", or rather "de-cohere", the probability wave into a sharply peaked function at a well-defined position (subject to uncertainty), a property traditionally associated with particles. More precisely, a wave function collapse is said to occur when a wave function (initially in a superposition of several eigenstates) appears to reduce to a single eigenstate (by observation). Such a collapse is the essence of measurement in quantum mechanics and connects the probability-wave function with classical observables like position and momentum. In simple words, the measurement of a probability wave yields a particle. We can observe the interference of mechanical waves whenever we throw stones into a pond. We can never observe the interference of probability waves because the very act of observation collapses the waves into particles, which in turn are subject to the Heisenberg Uncertainty Principle.

Quantum mechanics solved problems of the stability of atoms and the nature of spectral lines. It also brought chemistry into the framework of physics. Quantum electrodynamics (i.e., the quantum field theory of photons, electrons, and positrons) gave rise to Standard Model. This model unifies physics, except for gravitation, dark matter, and many unexplained numerical quantities. The Standard Model is a set of equation that can fit onto a single sheet of paper. This sheet of paper arguably represents the greatest intellectual achievement of mankind up to the present. It is a major step toward the Holy Grail; namely, a unified field theory (UFT). It is a theory that allows all that is usually thought of as fundamental forces and elementary particles to be written in terms of a single field. There is currently no accepted unified field theory, and thus it remains an open line of research.

The resolution of microscope refers to the shortest distance between two points that a user can still see as separate images. The resolution of Leeuwenhoek's microscope (which used light) was sufficient to see microbes. An electron microscope is a microscope that uses a beam of accelerated electrons as a source of illumination. Because the wavelength of an electron can be up to 100,000 times shorter than that of visible light photons, the electron microscope has a higher resolving power than a light microscope and can reveal the structure of smaller objects. Can atoms be seen under an electron microscope? The answer is partially yes. In certain situations, the images can be interpreted as representations of atoms or even atomic nuclei. Has anyone ever seen electrons and protons under an electron microscope? Electrons and protons are subatomic particles that travel as waves. A subatomic particle is smaller than an atom. When we talk about waves at the atomic level, it is about matter waves (i.e., probability waves which are 3D graphs that describe the probability of finding an electron at a certain point around a nucleus). Electrons are much smaller than most atomic nuclei, so we are able to use them as a medium to view the features of atoms. Electrons are incredibly tiny and have extremely low mass. They move extremely fast, and due to the Heisenberg Uncertainty Principle, their exact position is practically unknowable. We can only approximate their position to within a certain uncertainty.

Without being able to acquire an exact position makes it impossible to view an electron. That aside, their mass is so low, that even the smallest interaction with them (involving another electron or photon) will send them flying off so that we cannot view them and in addition we have an even worse understanding of their exact location. Because there is no way to see electrons, we use the electron cloud model of the atom, which indicates where electrons are likely to be, and never where they actually are. The electron cloud is nothing but a probability field.

Columbus had a magnetic compass, but he had no way to estimate his longitude. If he had had some way to estimate longitude, he would not have concluded that he was in the East Indies when in fact he was in the Caribbean. Accurate navigation at sea also requires a sextant and a marine chronometer (an accurate clock that can withstand storms at sea). The sextant measures the inclination of a star or the sun, and helps to determine latitude. The chronometer gives longitude.

Magnetic surveys have been made by geophysicists for the past 100 years. But geophysical methods are crude in comparison to the high-resolution procedures used by a bird or turtle. Animal navigation is the ability of many animals to find their way accurately without maps or instruments. Birds such as the Arctic tern, insects such as the monarch butterfly, and fish such as the salmon regularly migrate thousands of miles to and from their breeding grounds, and many other species navigate effectively over shorter distances. An ant continuously determines its position relative to a known starting point (e.g., its nest) while travelling on a crooked path. At every point along its journey, the ant can always return directly in a straight line to its nest. Sahara desert ants forage for insects that have died of heat stress. These ants can sustain surface temperatures of up to 70 °C (178°F). The ant will venture out a distance as much as a half of a kilometer on a tortuous path that continually meanders and twists in all directions. The ant completes its journey when it finds a dead insect. The ant then goes directly back to its nest by the shortest route. This skill is necessary to its survival under the harsh desert conditions.

With respect to size, this ant travels farther from its nest than any other animal that lives on the Sahara. There are no landmarks on a desert. It is all sand. An ant does not know where or when it will find a dead insect. As a result, at each point along its path, the ant computes the distance and direction to its nest. How does the ant do this? Ants can do this in the dark, so they do not need the sunlight. At the same time the ant must correct for terrain. It takes more steps to traverse a fixed horizontal distance on a bumpy terrain than on a flat terrain. However, the ant gets the correct value in either case. It seems that ants have a "mental integrator" which allows them to accumulate changes in direction, and from there to keep track of their location. The same seems to apply to moles when they dig their underground tunnels. The "mental integrator" is a form of dead reckoning (as used by Columbus) which requires a magnetic compass to determine direction. It is generally accepted that many animals obtain their orientation or navigational behavior by magnetic field variations. They have internal compasses just as real as the compass that Columbus used. What kind of compass within an ant or a mole can sense and amplify something as weak as Earth's magnetic field?

Magnetoception is the ability of an animal to perceive Earth's magnetic field. The earth's magnetic field can have a decisive effect on living things. By magnetoception, animals can find food, return their nests, and meet each other. Bats and geese use magnetoception for navigational, altitude and location purposes. Magnetoception allows honeybees to possess the extraordinary ability to create a map of their surroundings. Invertebrates with magnetoception include fruit flies, lobsters, and certain bacteria. Vertebrates with magnetoception include many species of birds, turtles, sharks, and stingrays. The type of magnetoception present in sea creatures like sharks, stingrays and chimaeras is called inductive sensing. The mollusks (Tochuina tetraquetra) orient themselves between magnetic north and east before a full moon. The evidence is that magnetite in the beak of a pigeon accounts for its ability to navigate using magnetoception.

The use of magnetic fields to navigate is found in magnetotactic bacteria. They are crucial for understanding other forms of magnetoception in animals. Magnetotactic bacteria move according to the direction of the North Pole, and hence they are magnetosensitive bacteria. The sensitivity of magnetotactic bacterium to the Earth's magnetic field arises from the fact the bacterium precipitate chains of crystals of magnetic minerals within its interior. These crystals, and sometimes the chains of crystals, can be preserved in the geological record as magneto-fossils. Reports of magneto-fossils extend to 1.9 billion years in the past.

Magnetism is an effect of quantum mechanics. At the subatomic level an electron acts as a tiny magnet. It is a rotating electrically charged particle. Thus, to obtain a fine representation of the magnetic field one must go beyond geophysical prospecting, and descend down into the subatomic level, which is the realm of quantum mechanics. In that domain, traveling electrons and other subatomic entities are exist as matter waves (also known as probability waves), not as individual particles. Probability waves within the magnetotactic bacterium interfere and entangle in a state that is affected by the earth's magnetic field. The resulting probability wave can then influence a chemical reaction at the molecular level. Such chemical reactions provide the bacterium with the ability to navigate. The same type of behavior is present in all animals that use magnetic navigation.

Who is it? Is it diversifier Prof. Wiechert with his misty distances beyond which our senses and our concepts fail us? Or is it unifier Prof. de Broglie with his probability waves that bring us closer to a unified field theory (UFT)? We do know that animals have systems of intelligence that operate at the quantum level. At this level, it is impossible to directly observe the interference of probability waves. We have the mathematical theory of probability waves, but we cannot observe them in practice. At present it is impossible to conceive of any artificial (i.e., man-made) system whatsoever that could ever replicate, in the slightest way, the intelligence of a bacterium, much less than that of an ant. These forces of animal life are part of the invisible subatomic world.

Life utilizes macro forces, allowing plants and animals to manipulate their environment at the visible level. Life also utilizes micro forces allowing plants and animals to manipulate their environment at the invisible quantum level. Micro biology goes beyond simple chemistry and instead focuses on life's ability to actually control quantum forces. Plants monitor and react to the world around them. In some cases, they remember the stresses and stimuli of the past. They are aware of the community of plants around them. They monitor underground signals and react to the stresses that their neighbors experience. Aphid-infested plants are able to signal the other plants, connected through mycorrhizae, of an imminent attack. In this way the other plants have time to mount their own chemical defenses. Plants use underground fungal networks to warn neighboring plants of impending insect attack, uniquely illustrating the complex and highly designed interconnected cooperation found in nature. These forces of life are part of the invisible subatomic world. We cannot find out the composition of life because it exists at the quantum level which we can never reach.

In a certain sense, Cotton Mather was right in saying that there is a visible world and an invisible world. We as human beings live in the visible world. However, by subatomic probing we have discovered the existence of the invisible world of quantum mechanics. We can understand molecular chemistry because it is in the visible world. We can never understand the mystery of life because it is in the invisible world. The wave nature of a particle (such as an electron) is expressed by a probability wave. It represents the probability of an observer measuring a particle at a given place and time. Until the particle is measured, it is in every place it is allowed to be. Once it is measured, the probability wave of the particle collapses and forces the particle into a single specific place. The probability of a particle being observed in a specific place is given by its wave nature, and the world of particles is inherently probabilistic. We cannot visibly discern now or ever the intricate internal structures of the interaction of probability waves of subatomic particles. *Usque huc venies et non procedes amplius; et hic confringes tumentes fluctus tuos.*

Chapter 4. Salem Village witch hunt

Salem Village

Salem Village, the northwestern section of Salem Township, was made up of a group of scattered farms. The village center was five miles northwest of Salem Town. A meetinghouse, parsonage, and a tavern were at the center. The meeting house in Puritan New England served as the church building and town hall; the tavern served as the community center. Although not well known today, strong drink in moderation was not a sin for our Puritan forebears. Other things well accepted today, however, were most sinful, especially anything to do with witchcraft and sorcery. Samuel Parris was the minister of the church and Nathaniel Ingersoll owned the tavern.

Nathaniel Ingersoll was a man of industry and thrift. As a licensed innkeeper, he could even sell liquor by the quart on Sunday. He was a lieutenant of the Salem Village militia company and a deacon in the church. A close neighbor was his nephew, Jonathan Walcott, who was the captain of the company and also a deacon. A couple of miles away lived Thomas Putnam, the sergeant of the company and the parish clerk.

The witch hunt started in the parsonage of Rev. Samuel Parris. In the household were two servants whom Parris had brought from Barbados. They were John Indian and his wife, Tituba. Tituba knew about magic, fortune-telling, incantations, and necromancy (or spirit communication with the dead) from her native West Indies. In the winter of 1691-92 a small group of girls were in the habit of having Tituba to teach them about the black art. They included Parris' daughter Elizabeth Parris, aged 9, his niece Abigail Williams, aged 11, Others were Sergeant Thomas Putnam's daughter Ann Putnam Jr. aged 12, and his servant, Mercy Lewis, aged 17; Dr. William Griggs' maid, Elizabeth Hubbard, aged 17; and Captain Jonathan Walcott's daughter, Mary Walcott, aged 17.

The girls began to act in strange and unusual manners. They acted in the same way as Cotton Mather had described for bewitchment in his recent book on witchcraft. In their "fits" they would get into holes, and creep under chairs and stools. They would use various odd postures and antic gestures, uttering foolish, ridiculous speeches which made no sense. Dr. William Griggs, the local physician, was called in to examine the afflicted girls. He could not give any physical reason for their behavior. Instead he said that they were bewitched. These girls came to be known as the afflicted children. Rev. Parris summoned other clergy and held days of fasting and prayer. John Indian tried an experiment to find out the witches causing the afflictions. He made a cake of rye meal with the children's urine, and baked it in the ashes. When he gave it to a dog to eat, the afflicted children went into their fits and named some people who afflicted them. The first named was Tituba herself. The children said that she appeared to them as a specter, pinching, pricking and tormenting them. They fell into strange positions, and became convulsed and distorted.

The number of afflicted persons increased. The circle was joined by Elizabeth Booth and Susannah Sheldon, each 18, and Mary Warren and Sarah Churchill, each 20. Most of the newly afflicted were girls. But there were also a few wives and other women, as well as a boy or two. Notable was Mrs. Ann Putnam, the sergeant's wife, a well-educated woman of 30, but so high-strung that her fits were even more pronounced than those of the girls. She was deeply engaged in the village quarrels; and she played an important role in supporting her daughter, Ann Putnam Jr., and the other afflicted girls in their accusations.

In their fits, the afflicted cried out upon the witches who were tormenting them. In addition to Tituba, the afflicted cried out upon two other women: Sarah Good, aged 38, and Sarah Osborne, aged 50. Sarah Good was poor and homeless, and Sarah Osborne was a bed-ridden woman in poor health. Both were persons so ill thought of that the accusations were readily accepted. Each of these three accused persons satisfied the prevailing stereotype of a witch.

As in other cases of hysterical young girls, the whole episode could have ended at this point if no action were taken. However, Thomas Putnam, Edward Putnam, Joseph Hutchinson, and Thomas Preston filed a legal complaint against the three women. Such a complaint represented a red-hot spark. As in some other colonies, the authorities could dismiss the complaint, thus extinguishing the spark. Instead the Massachusetts authorities decided to let the spark ignite some tinder and burst into flames.

More particularly, on March 1, 1692, the Salem magistrates John Hathorne and Jonathan Corwin issued warrants for the arrest of the three women, Tituba, Sarah Osborne, and Sarah Good, accusing them of witchcraft. The two magistrates, in their impressive magisterial clothing and the insignia of official station, rode on horseback for the five-mile journey from Salem Town to Salem Village. The attending constables and marshals, bearing long staffs, wore the bright red coats that were the official dress of men charged with the enforcement of law. The entrance of this troop into the village was marked with all the grandeur and splendor which they had at their command. The examinations were to be held in Ingersoll's tavern, but the crowd was so great that they were held in the meetinghouse.

The chief accusations against Sarah Good were that she had spoken angrily to some neighbors and soon after some of their cattle sickened and died; that she threw the children into fits; and that she tried to persuade Ann Putnam Jr. to sign the Devil's book. According to lore, the Devil's servants, the witches, went about with that infernal book soliciting signatures; each signature was equivalent to a deed surrendering the signer's soul to the Devil. Similar accusations were made against the other two women. During each examination the afflicted girls raved and screamed. Ten could turn their hysteria on and off according to the need at hand. At the indignant denials by Sarah Good and Sarah Osborne, the tumult of these paroxysms became frightful. When Tituba was questioned, she claimed that she had been taught in her own country in the Caribbean about witchcraft. Soon she started to confess. She said that the Devil urged her to sign his book, and told her to work mischief on the children. When she said that she enchanted the girls, their symptoms vanished and perfect calm ensued.

Much later Tituba gave the account that Rev. Parris did beat her and abuse her in other ways to make her confess and accuse her "sister witches." She said that everything that she did by way of confessing or accusing others was because of such usage. Tituba was searched and they found the marks of the Devil upon her body. The three women were committed to prison and put in chains. Sarah Osborne was in jail only a little while, dying there on May 10, 1692. Sarah Good was destined to die on the gallows that summer. Tituba was allowed to become an accuser instead of a prosecuted witch. She stayed in prison for more than a year and then was sold in slavery to a new owner for payment of her prison fees.

Tituba vs. John Hathorne

In the Salem Village examinations on March 1 and 2, 1692, Magistrate John Hathorne questioned Rev. Parris' salve Tituba. Hathorne led off with leading and bullying questions in order to trick Tituba into incriminating herself along with as other innocent people. However, Tituba was able to turn the entire process around. She induced Hathorne to ask questions that were even more ridiculous than her outlandish answers. The net result was a story so fantastic that it would well serve the needs of the authorities. Tituba told about witches gathering in the Village. She described encountering the specters of four of them, led by a man dressed in black. Hathorne provoked her to tell what the man dressed in black said she must do. Tituba's eyewitness testimony about the witches' specters meeting inside Parris's house hit the courtroom like a bombshell. It meant that Satan's attack against the family of the minister was an organized assault led by outsiders, and it captivated the imagination of the Village and the Salem magistrates. Finally, Tituba revealed that there were nine witches' marks in the man's book, thereby doubling the number she had initially seen meeting in Parris's house.

Tituba knew how witchcraft was practiced on the Caribbean Islands. In European type witchcraft, a witch was an agent of the Devil, and an enemy of the state. In the Caribbean type of witchcraft, a witch was a magical entity, not an enemy of the state. There was no connection at all between Tituba's and Cotton Mather's understandings of witchcraft. Hathorne had little interest in Tituba. He only wanted to use Tituba to gain evidence against Sarah Good and Sarah Osborn. Through her testimony, Tituba provided the authorities with stories about the invisible world of witchcraft which they craved to hear—stories about strange monsters, yellow birds, hairy imps, two-legged creatures with wings, wolves, and the Devil in a serge coat, sometimes black, sometimes another color. Sarah Good and Sarah Osborn, in pleading their innocence and denying any part of this imaginary world, were to perish; Tituba was to survive and live.

Witch hunt sanctioned on April 11, 1692

The next women accused were Martha Corey and Rebecca Nurse, both church members. Because they were respected women of good character, the whole community was thunderstruck. Church members had elevated place in the Puritan society. At this point the authorities should have quit. They did not quit; they wanted a firestorm'

On March 21, 1692 Martha Corey was examined before the magistrates at the meeting house in Salem Village. A throng of spectators were present to see the novelty. Rev. Nicholas Noyes, the assistant minister at Salem, began with prayer. After the prayer the prisoner was called in to answer the allegations against her. She said that she desired that she might go to prayer. In answer, magistrate John Hathorne said that he did not come to hear her pray, but to examine her.

The afflicted children fell into their usual fits and performed their hysterical outbursts while the women were under examination. The afflicted accused Martha Corey of afflicting them by biting, pinching, and strangling. And they said that in their fits they saw her likeness coming to them and bringing a book for them to sign. Magistrate Hathorne asked Martha Corey, "Why do you afflict those children?" She said, "I do not afflict them." He asked her, "Who does then?" She said, "I do not know. How should I know? They are poor distracted creatures, and no heed to be given to what they say." Hathorne replied, "It is the judgment of all that are present that they are bewitched, and only you say they are distracted."

The afflicted girls said that they saw the Black Man whispering into Martha Corey's ear while the examination was taking place. They said that her familiar, a yellow bird, was sucking between her fingers. An order was given to look to see if there were any sign of a bird. The girls said, "It is too late now, for she has removed a pin, and put it on her head." Upon searching Martha Corey' head, the officials found a pin there sticking upright. When the accused made any motion of their bodies, hands or mouths, the afflicted would cry out. When Martha Corey bit her lip, they cried out of being bitten. If she grasped one hand with the other, they cried out of being pinched by her, and produced marks. For some other motion of her body, they complained of being pressed. When she leaned to the seat next to her, or if she stirred her feet, they stamped and cried out of pain. Despite everything, Martha Corey refused to confess. She was committed to prison.

On March 24, 1692 Rebecca Nurse was brought before magistrates Hathorne and Corwin in the Salem Village meetinghouse. She was one of three sisters, daughters of William Towne. Her two sisters, Sarah Cloyce and Mary Easty, were arrested soon after her. They and their husbands were all persons held in high esteem. However they were on the side of the town of Topsfield in a fierce land dispute with the town of Salem Village. The dispute had engendered hard feelings between them and the Putnam family of Salem Village. This feud had left a grudge, and in revenge the Putnams accused the sisters of witchcraft. Adding to the troubles, Rebecca Nurse and her husband had opposed Rev. Samuel Parris in church disputes.

Rev. John Hale, minister of Beverly, began the examination with prayer, after which Rebecca Nurse was accused of much the same crimes as Martha Corey. She made similar answers, asserting her own innocence with earnestness. The afflicted were the familiar circle of Salem Village girls. In addition, Sergeant Thomas Putnam's wife, Mrs. Ann Putnam, complaining bitterly that Rebecca Nurse was tormenting her, made a most terrible shrieking heard throughout the neighborhood. Rebecca Nurse was committed to prison.

Now comes one of the lowest points reached in Salem witchcraft. Dorothy (aka Dorcas) Good, Sarah Good's four-year-old child, was apprehended. The afflicted girls said this baby girl bit them, and showed marks like those from a small set of teeth upon their arms. Any of the afflicted that the child cast its eye upon would complain she was in torment. Dorothy Good was put into prison. Because the tiny wrists and ankles of this small girl slipped out of the chains, special manacles and fetters had to be made for her. After her mother, Sarah Good, was executed on July 19, 1692, little Dorothy still was kept in prison.

On April 3, 1692 Sarah Cloyce, sister of Rebecca Nurse, had been with difficulty prevailed upon to be present at the church service. Upon entering the building, she heard Rev. Parris name as his text: "Have not I chosen you Twelve, and one of you is a Devil." There is some doubt as to whether it was because of her sister's being committed, or whether it was the choice of that text, but she rose up and went out. The wind shut the door forcibly. This slamming of the door convinced some that she went out in anger, and so it gave them occasion to accuse her. On April 4, 1692 Sarah Cloyce was complained of and arrested.

Also arrested on the same day was Elizabeth Proctor, a midwife. Testimony against Elizabeth Proctor claimed that she was responsible for the death of a man because Dr. Griggs had not been summoned "to give him physic." [Physic is an old word for medicine. A physician is one who gives medicine.]

The firestorm now was going at full speed. It had turned into a firestorm. It was out of control. On April 11, 1692, an important turning point occurred. Sarah Cloyce and Elizabeth Proctor, were examined in the large meetinghouse in Salem Town. On this occasion, the Provincial government took formal charge of the witch hunt. Simon Bradstreet was now the governor. He had won thirteen annual elections by the ruling class (the freemen, the male church members, who made up about four percent of the population) to that office. He was 86 years old, the grand old man of his time. Aged and ill, Simon Bradstreet did not attend the examination.

Important magistrates of the Puritan old guard carried out the examination. They were Thomas Danforth (the deputy governor), Isaac Addington of Boston (the secretary of the province), Major Samuel Appleton of Ipswich, James Russell of Charlestown, Capt. Samuel Sewall of Boston, Jonathan Corwin, and, of course, John Hathorne. (Appleton, Russell, Corwin, and Hathorne were related by marriage. Corwin and Hathorne had conducted all the previous examinations at Salem Village.) The examinations were officially described as taking place "at a Council held at Salem." William Stoughton was the only member of the hard core of the old guard who was not present at this time. In addition to the magistrates, several ministers were present.

William Rayment, age 26, testifying for Elizabeth Proctor, said that when he was at Ingersoll's tavern on March 28, 1692 an afflicted girl cried out, "There is Goody Proctor. There is Goody Proctor. I'll see her hang!" When Goodwife Ingersoll sharply reproved the afflicted girls, Rayment said that "they seemed to make a joke of it." The accused, whenever possible, tried to present evidence showing the imposture of the afflicted girls, but it did no good. In court, the afflicted girls made hideous clamors and screeching for the benefit of the high dignitaries present. This examination firmly establishes the complicity of the ruling old guard in the actions of the witch hunt. The presence of these officials, their lines of questioning, and their verdicts made clear that the highest levels of government and church sanctioned the witch hunt. These Council members concurred in the methods used in the witch hunt, thereby stamping it with their seal of approval. In effect, John Hathorne was given full authority to continue his outrageous methods of finding and arresting suspected witches. Elizabeth Proctor's husband John Proctor came to attend and assist her as well as he might. The afflicted cried out against him also. They did it with so much earnestness that he was committed with his wife.

Why did the Salem magistrates believe the afflicted girls? That is a most important question. If the magistrates had refused to act on the girls' accusations, the legal process would have been nipped in the bud. The court's reliance on the girls' spectral evidence is perplexing. As the seventeenth century progressed, magistrates and juries grew increasingly reluctant to convict people of witchcraft. The zeal of the Salem magistrates in 1692 went against thirty years of judicial restraint in witchcraft cases in New England. Between 1665 and 1692, only one individual was executed. In Europe there was an overall reluctance to convict an alleged witch on the basis of spectral evidence alone. The courts wanted a confession, and unfortunately the confession was usually obtained by torture.

In the Salem Village with hunt, torture was generally not used, and according very few people confessed. Asa result, accused witches were convicted on the basis of spectral evidence alone. Leading ministers of Boston, who were familiar with European witchcraft, warned against using spectral evidence alone. They realized that confessions were needed in order to justify the cruel business. At the start of the Andover witch hunt the authorities decided to use mild forms of torture on a 72 years old widowed woman and on children. Their confessions were obtained. All of a sudden, the tide turned. The authorities then made arrest after arrest in Andover, and all of the accused witches made a confession, except for three. We have the improbable situation that in the Salem Village witch hunt, essentially none of the accused confessed, whereas in the Andover witch hunt essentially all of the accused confessed.

Governor Sir William Phips

Rev. Cotton Mather was the most prominent member of the strict Puritan clergy. He was the assistant minister at the North Church in Boston. Through his published sermons he exerted authority over many of the clergy. His father Increase Mather was the minister of North

Church, but he had been in England for the past four years. A new royal charter for New England had been signed by the King in England in October 1691. The crown chose Sir William Phips, aged 31, as the new governor. Phips was a ship captain born in Maine. He had given to the crown gold that he had recovered from a sunken Spanish ship. In this change of government, Increase Mather had been allowed to name the new Council members. Except for a few changes, the new Council members would be the Puritan old guard. Way. In mid-February the old guard received this good news together with a copy of the new charter. The also learned that the new governor would be soon on his way to Boston.

Instead of being happy, the old guard feared the worst. From the beginning, Puritan rule was absolute in Massachusetts. Only Puritans could vote and hold office in Massachusetts. Within a few months, the new charter would be in place, and then, as night follows the day, the new charter would "let slip the dogs of war"; namely Anglicans, Baptists and Quakers. These groups could now vote and in time they could overthrow the strict Puritan rule. In the past the Puritans had forcibly expelled dissenters like Roger Williams, Ann Hutchinson and her followers (including the Wardwell family), and the Quakers. It was time again to do something to keep the masses in check. In February a stroke of luck came; namely, witchcraft in Salem Village. The Hathorne family had extensive property in Salem Village, and knew the town well. An investigation of the witchcraft there could be revealing. In March, the magistrates John Hathorne and Corwin began arresting and examining the people accused of witchcraft. By May, many had been arrested. However, acting governor Simon Bradstreet did not permit indictments, thereby preventing the witchcraft cases to proceed to a grand jury. In so doing, Bradstreet deliberately blocked trials for those arrested for witchcraft. He left this responsibility to the new governor, Sir William Phips. Bradstreet had an aversion to witchcraft allegations, and he was doing whatever he could to stall things in the hope that Governor Phips would be able to mitigate the affair.

Many modern historians assert that Hathorne and Corwin were just trying to stop a witchcraft threat and maintain local government control until Governor Phips and the new charter arrived. In fact, Hathorne and

Corwin had intentionally started a witchcraft firestorm to which the rest of the old guard gave their consent on April 11, 1692. Franklin Delano Roosevelt, 32nd president of the United States, once said: "In politics, nothing happens by accident. If it happens, you can bet it was planned that way." The purpose of the firestorm was to impart fear in the general populace so that the old guard could keep governing under the new charter as they did under the colonial charter. Also in the process they could inflict damage on certain non-conformists whom they regarded as enemies. The firestorm was planned by the old guard to retain control. The plan worked, but only in the short run. Phips was recalled to London in 1694 and Stoughton served as acting governor until 1699. By then Stoughton was in poor health and he died in 1701.

On May 14, 1692 the frigate *Nonesuch* from England arrived in Boston. Sir William Phips, the new royal governor, was on the ship and was ready to take up his duties. He carried with him the royal charter with which to govern New England. Increase Mather returned from his four year sojourn in England on the same ship. William Stoughton became the new royal lieutenant governor.

Sir William Phips was told that the prisons in Essex and Suffolk counties in Massachusetts were crowded with accused witches and wizards. His new government did not interfere with the witchcraft prosecutions in progress. Examinations and imprisonments went on as before. The number of complaints increased every day. The afflicted girls continued to cry out against those in prison, saying that the prisoners' specters still tormented them. The girls said that irons on the prisoners' legs and arms would hold back their specters. The tumult was so great that Sir William Phips yielded himself to the views of the leading men in the Council, and in particular his lieutenant governor Stoughton. Sir William Phips, to his shame, gave the order to put irons on the imprisoned.

Consider the constant torture inflicted by ironsAt the same time consider how ridiculous it was to believe that physical irons could confine ethereal specters.

Stoughton recommended the establishment of a flagrantly illegal tribunal, by means of a special executive commission. Governor Phips followed Stoughton's advice, and on May 25, 1692 instituted a Court of Oyer and Terminer to try the suspected witches. (*Oyer* and *Terminer* are Norman French for "to hear" and "to determine) In one stroke, the legal machinery was by-passed, and its concomitant legal safeguards were avoided. In fact, the very existence of the court was illegal. Phips unwittingly had created a kangaroo court, a tool giving arbitrary power to the Puritan old guard; its use would not go wanting.

On May 27, 1692 the members of the court were appointed. As would be expected, William Stoughton (Harvard, 1650) was named chief justice. The eight justices were Nathaniel Saltonstall (Harvard, 1659), John Richards, Peter Sergeant, Wait Still Winthrop (Harvard class of 1662 but did not graduate), Samuel Sewall (Harvard, 1671), John Hathorne, Jonathan Corwin, and Bartholomew Gedney. The court could be made up of any five of the nine. These justices, all members of the board of assistants in the provisional government, were recently appointed members of the Council under the new charter. The French and Indians were making attacks upon the frontier towns of Maine. Phips turned his full attention to mobilizing an army, and from time to time, Phips left Boston to command the army in Maine.

First Trial, June 2, 1692

The Court of Oyer and Terminer set up in 1692 for the purpose of trying the accused witches was a kangaroo court. There was nothing unusual about this situation in those days. Prejudicial biases by the decision-maker or by political decree are among the most publicized causes of kangaroo courts. Their proceedings often give the appearance of a fair and just trial, even though the verdict was already decided before the trial actually began.

The authorities proceeding in the witch-hunt by the end of May had imprisoned about 100 persons. John Hathorne spent most of his time in the summer and early autumn of 1692 holding the preliminary hearings, as he had done since March 1. Between June 1, 1692 and October 15, 1692, more than one hundred accused persons appeared before John Hathorne; he committed them all to prison. For many of these, he was able to extract signed confessions.

The first meeting of the Court of Oyer and Terminer began in Salem on June 2, 1692. There were seven justices sitting for this session. They were the chief justice, Stoughton, and six associate justices, Nathaniel Saltonstall, John Richards, Bartholomew Gedney, Wait Still Winthrop, Samuel Sewall, and Peter Sergeant. Four were very close friends of Cotton Mather, namely Stoughton, Richards, Winthrop, and Sewall.

Only one of the imprisoned, Bridget Bishop, was brought to trial at this session. She had been first arrested on April 19, 1692. This first trial was a test case, and a large number of accusers and accusations were brought against her. She was charged with such things as the losses the neighbors met with in their cattle and poultry, or by overturning their carts. The testimony included spectral evidence given by John Louder of Salem, aged 32. He stated that upon awaking in the dead of night he "did clearly see Bridget Bishop, or her likeness, sitting on my stomach." Two workmen testified that they found puppets in her cellar. The puppets were made of hog bristles and rags, and were stuck with headless pins. Upon search a witch mark was found upon her body. The jury found Bridget Bishop guilty, and she was sentenced to die. To the end she did not make the least confession of anything relating to witchcraft. The court adjourned to June 30.

In Salem prison voices in low whispers passed the word that Bridget was going to hang. A terrible shudder went through all the inmates. The prison walls seemed to reel. With a noose about her neck, she was to die a death of shame. In each one's mind the terror was felt. The night before the execution, there was a silence in the prison. No one could sleep with the hangman so close at hand. At dawn on June 10, 1692, a day of dark disgrace, the dreadful figure of the Sheriff entered the prison and took away Bridget. She walked with a stumbling gait, for fettered legs were now lame.

John Hathorne, on horseback, was a prominent figure in the procession which followed her to the place of execution. She rode in an open horse-drawn cart, forced to stand so the hundreds of spectators could see her better. As she passed the church, she happened to cast her eyes in that direction. Rev. Cotton Mather claimed that a board on the inside of the building broke from the heavy nails which held it and flew to the opposite wall with a crash that could be heard throughout Salem.

Outside town the cart turned from the main street into a narrow road that led up to a rocky mound. This was Gallows Hill. With three fathoms of hempen rope, Bridget Bishop was hanged by the neck from a tree. Her body was thrown into a shallow, unmarked grave which had been dug among the rocks close by. Out of her grave, it was said, a wild red rose grew.

The insane proceedings of this Court were too much for justice Nathaniel Saltonstall of Haverhill. Not being able to prevail against the tide, Saltonstall resigned from the Court after this first meeting. When he returned to his home in Haverhill, Saltonstall spoke out so strongly against the witch hunt that the afflicted girls started to cry out against him. Some of them said that they had seen his specter at several witch meetings. The courageous man continued to oppose the proceedings, and his attitude encouraged others to take similar stands.

Bishop's execution also alarmed some ministers as to its injustice. Because of this negative reaction, Rev. Cotton Mather realized that it was possible that the witch trials might be brought to a halt. With the aid of some ministers in his camp, he drew up a statement entitled *The Return of Several Ministers* By design this document was equivocal, just as the three witches' advice to *Macbeth* in Shakespeare's play. Cotton Mather's document was worded "in a double sense." It gave more encouragement for the Court to proceed in their dark measures than cautions against them. Cotton Mather's concluding section is:

> "Nevertheless, we cannot but humbly recommend unto the government, the speedy and vigorous prosecution of such as have rendered themselves obnoxious, according to the direction given in the laws of God, and the wholesome statutes of the English nation, for the detection of witchcrafts.

This conclusion took away the force of any cautionary sections. This document appeared like it gave the Court instructions carefully to weigh the evidence, whereas in reality it encouraged the Court to do the opposite. It was presented to the Council on June 15, 1692, and the prosecutions went on with more vigor than before. This incident brings out the nature of the intertwined features of Cotton Mather's personality. Cotton Mather was intent on carrying out his witchcraft plan. But in order to succeed he had to give the appearance of respectability. In his deception, Cotton Mather was able "to keep the word of promise to our ear, but break it to our hope." Cotton Mather demonstrated here that he had full control of the Court.

By summer 1692, a certain degree of reaction appeared to be taking place, so Cotton Mather was called upon by the governor to employ his pen in justifying what had been done. The result was his *The Wonders of the Invisible World*, published in October, 1692, in which he gives an account of some of the trials and adds an elaborate dissertation on witchcraft in general. In his book, Cotton Mather proclaims:

> "There is little room for hope, that the great wrath of the Devil will not prove the present ruin of our poor New England."

As a rejoinder, we take this passage from the notebook of my great aunt Hanna Wardwell:

> Learn the folded hands are not always idle ones and there is a silence which is more triumphant that a shout.

Chapter 5. Andover witch hunt

Prelude to Andover Witchcraft

At first, the witchcraft delusion was confined to the environs of Salem Village, but soon the accusations began to spread to other towns. Let us trace how the contagion infected the town of Andover.

In 1644 the General Court in Boston granted the ownership of the entire Andover Township to a group of men under the leadership of Simon Bradstreet. These men, known as the first settlers or proprietors, numbered twenty-three. The first settlers were responsible for deciding how to divide the abundant land. From the beginning, there was a hierarchy of rank and wealth among Andover families rather than equality. The first families formed a small closely-knit group, most of whom were interrelated by marriage.

The exclusionary town policies practiced so long by the first proprietors created deep resentment and anger in some Andover residents. However at the beginning of 1692 the town of Andover seemed to be heading toward reconciliation and prosperity at long last. The bitter and prolonged feuding between the two ministers, Francis Dane and Thomas Barnard, had subsided; the grumblings against the old proprietary families' control of town affairs had quieted. But a foreboding of trouble came suddenly in May when Martha Carrier was arrested for witchcraft in the Salem witchcraft affair.

The Salem witchcraft affair may be conveniently divided into two major episodes, the Salem Village witch hunt and the Andover witch hunt. The arrest phase of the Salem Village witch hunt occurred during the four-month time period from March 1, 1692, to July 1, 1692. All the arrests associated with this episode were made in that interval. Only one Andover resident was arrested during that period: Martha Carrier, on May 31, 1692.

The arrest phase of the Andover witch hunt began after the arrest phase of the Salem Village witch hunt was over. All the arrests made in the Andover witch hunt occurred during the eight-week period from July 15, 1692, to September 7, 1692. Nearly fifty residents of Andover were arrested in that short period. The first arrest was that of Ann Foster of Andover on July 15. The final arrests of the Andover witch hunt represented a spectacular outburst: eighteen arrests made at the Andover touch test on September 7, 1692.

In stark contrast to the Salem Village witch hunt, nearly all those arrested during the Andover witch hunt quickly confessed. The nearest and dearest relations of the Andover accused pleaded with them to confess. Because of their husbands' urging, and their children's entreating upon their knees, the Andover accused said they were guilty. Only husbands and children from Andover urged their wives and mothers to confess; none from other towns did this.

Roger Toothaker, his wife Mary (Allen) Toothaker, and their children lived in Billerica, a neighboring town of Andover. His wife Mary was the daughter of first settler Andrew Allen of Andover. Roger was a physician and his wife was a midwife. Like many of the medical people of his day he believed that some of the ailments that could not be treated were due to witchcraft. In fact, Dr. Toothaker spread the story that his daughter had killed a witch named Button. The daughter was 23-year-old Martha (Toothaker) Emerson. Roger Toothaker said that his daughter had learned the method from him. The daughter had wanted to help a person who complained about being afflicted by a "witch" named Button Following her father's instructions, the daughter put an earthen pot containing the witch's urine into a hot oven and stopped up the oven. A suitable incantation was made:

> "Boil thou first in the charmed pot. Double, double, toil and trouble! Fire burn and cauldron bubble. Then the charm is firm and good."

The next morning the witch was dead, according testimony given later in the witch trials.

Dr. Toothaker's bragging about his witchcraft prowess seems to have led him into a trap. On May 18, 1692, three of the Salem Village afflicted girls, Elizabeth Hubbard, Ann Putnam Jr, and Mary Walcott, accused Dr. Toothaker of witchcraft. Elizabeth Hubbard was the servant of his Salem Village counterpart, his rival, Dr. William Griggs.

Ten days later, on May 28, 1692, Dr. Roger Toothaker's wife Mary (Allen) Toothaker, and their nine year old daughter Margaret Toothaker were arrested for witchcraft. As the wife of a doctor, Mary Toothaker would help nurse patients back to health. Also arrested on the same day was Mary's sister, Martha (Allen) Carrier. Martha Carrier lived in Andover, and this was the initial accusation in that town. Also arrested on May 28 was Elizabeth (Jackson) Howe. The two Allen sisters, namely Mary (Allen) Toothaker and Martha (Allen) Carrier, were related by marriage to Elizabeth (Jackson) Howe through an intermediary, Rev. Francis Dane of Andover. Thus two sisters, nurse Mary Toothaker and Martha Carrier, and their cousin-in-law, Elizabeth Howe, were arrested together.

After his arrest on May 18, 1692, Dr. Roger Toothaker's life was short. He died in Boston prison less than one month later, June 16. Because it was an unexpected death, the authorities took great pains to cover themselves. They summoned 24 able and sufficient men to view the body and attest that he came to his end by a natural death.

The nurse Mary Toothaker, now a widow, was examined before John Hathorne on July 30. She testified that in May she was under great discontentedness and troubled with fear about the Indians, and used often to dream of fighting with them. Her fear was so great that she imagined that the Devil appeared to her in the shape of a tawny man, and promised to keep her from the Indians, and that she should have happy days with her son. And the Devil promised if she would serve him she should be safe from the Indians. Her plight did not impress Hathorne, and the widow Toothaker and her 9 year old daughter Margaret were imprisoned as witches.

The widow Toothaker's fear of the Indians was well founded. On August 1, 1692, while the widow and her daughter were in jail, the Indians raided Billerica, and a number of persons were slain. They burned down the empty Toothaker farm. The widow Toothaker and her daughter were to languish a year in prison before being released in the general amnesty in May 1693 when they returned to Billerica. However, their joy was short lived. Two years later, on August 5, 1695, the widow Mary (Allen) Toothaker was killed by the Indians that she so feared, and her younger daughter Margaret Toothaker, by now 12 years old, was taken captive, never to be seen again.

The arrest of Martha (Allen) Carrier on May 28, 1692 was the beginning of real troubles in Andover. Her husband was Thomas Carrier. He was born in Wales. Thomas Carrier's tombstone, which was erected many years after his death, has an incorrect death-date. He did not die in 1739, but rather, on May 16, 1735, aged 109. In 1649, during the English civil war the victorious Puritans captured King Charles. They sentenced him to death. According to Charlotte Helen Abbott's unpublished history of the Allen family of Andover, Thomas Carrier "alias Morgan" is said to have been one of the bodyguards of Charles I of England. Abbott gives his birth year as 1626. According to Abbott's account, in 1649 on the day of the execution of the monarch, the regular executioner could not be found. Thomas was required to act as headsman in his place, and was the man who beheaded the King. Abbott says: "The tale probably followed him and he seems to have been unwelcome here [Andover], the settlers believing that he brought bad fortune." He and his wife, Martha, were later blamed for the epidemic of smallpox that broke out in Andover in 1690, causing many deaths including several members of Martha's own family (her parents, her two brothers, and a brother-in-law).

After the trial of Charles I in January 1649, 59 judges signed his death warrant. If rumors were fact, Thomas Morgan wielded the axe that sent the whole kingdom of England into misgiving and terror. Of course, at the time there was no disclosure of the name of the executioner, and it is certainly doubtful that it was Thomas Morgan.

After the dark years of Puritan rule, the people of England restored the monarchy in 1660, and crowned Charles II as the new king. The 59 judges, along with several key associates and numerous court officials, were the subject of punishment for regicide. Of those who had been involved in the trial and execution, 104 were specifically excluded from reprieve, although 24 had already died, including Cromwell, John Bradshaw (the judge who was president of the court), and Henry Ireton (a general in the Parliamentary army and Cromwell's son-in-law). These 24 dead men were given posthumous execution. Their remains were exhumed, and the dead bodies were hanged and beheaded. Their headless bodies were cast into a pit below the gallows. Their heads were placed on spikes at the end of Westminster Hall. Many other living men were hanged, drawn and quartered, while 19 were imprisoned for life. Twenty-one of those under threat fled England, mostly settling in the Netherlands or Switzerland, although three settled in New England. On the same tide were some returning New Englanders, who were living in England during Puritan rule. Among them were Rev. William Stoughton and Rev. Increase Mather. Clearly these two Puritans were wondering how long would it be before the crown performed similar revenge upon Massachusetts. (William Stoughton was the chief justice for the witchcraft trials in 1692.)

Thomas Morgan, the supposed regicide, also fled to New England. Martha Allen was the daughter of Andrew and Faith (Ingalls) Allen. Andrew Allen was one of the original 23 settlers of Andover. In 1674, Martha married Thomas Carrier (1630–1739). After the marriage, they relocated to neighboring Billerica, some ten miles southwest of Andover, and lived in the north part of town near her sister Mary. Martha had eight children, one of whom died in infancy. In 1685, Thomas Carrier moved his family to Andover. Finally tragedy was about to strike his family. They were stricken with small pox in late 1689. The small pox epidemic ravaged the Allen family. Martha (Allen) Carrier's sister died of small pox December 14, 1690, the sister's son having died the day before. One of Martha Carrier's brothers died October 14, 1690, of small pox, and then his son died November 26, 1690. Her other brother also died of small pox the same day, and his wife died one month later of small pox on Christmas day, 1690. Instead of feeling compassion for the troubles of Martha (Allen) Carrier, the townspeople, or at least some of them, had resented her presence in Andover. The selectmen of the town of Andover took note that Martha (Allen) Carrier and some of her children were "smitten with that contagious disease the small pox, and that they are to take care not to spread the distemper with wicked carelessness which we are afraid they have already done," dated October 14, 1690.

Martha (Allen) Carrier had many things going against her. Some people had heard malicious rumors about Thomas Carrier's part in the regicide and blamed him personally. Others were aroused by the suspicion that the small pox epidemic in Andover had been caused by Martha (Allen) Carrier. Most damaging was the sharp wit of Martha combined with her sharp tongue. Some of her choice expressions are preserved to this day.

Let us give an example. Land had been granted to Benjamin Abbot, aged 31, in the south part of Andover close to the Carrier farm. He saw no harm in indulging in a little encroachment on Martha's land, thinking that if he put up his stone walls soon enough there would be nothing the Carriers could do about it. However Martha was not one so easily fooled, and she went about putting an end to his mischief. She became very angry, and in a confrontation she said:

> "I will stick as close to you, Benjamin Abbot, as the bark sticks to a tree. You will repent of this before seven years comes to an end." She further said, "I will hold your nose as close to the grindstone as ever it was held since your name was Benjamin Abbot."

Benjamin Abbot was glad to use these outbursts as evidence against her in her forthcoming trial on August 3, 1692.

Elizabeth (Jackson) Howe was arrested on the same day as Martha (Allen) Carrier and Mary (Allen) Toothaker, May 28, 1692, under the same complaint for afflicting the Salem Village girls. Elizabeth (Jackson) Howe was married to James Howe Jr. They lived in the Ipswich Village close to the Topsfield border. Her husband James Howe Jr was blind, so he had to be led. The evidence used against Elizabeth (Jackson) Howe was meager. The Howe family had a falling out with the Pearly brothers and their wives. After this falling out, Samuel Pearly claimed that Elizabeth (Jackson) Howe afflicted his ten year old daughter. However, the two ministers of the town of Rowley, Samuel Phillips, aged 67, and Edward Payson, testified that they had gone to Samuel Pearly's house in Ipswich. They said that when they were in the house, the child had one of her fits, and when the fit was over, Elizabeth Howe went to the child, took her by the hand and asked her if she had ever done her any hurt. The child answered no, never. But later the ministers heard the brother of the afflicted girl tell his sister to say Goodwife Howe is a witch. The ministers rebuked the brother for his boldness in stirring up his sister to accuse Goodwife Howe. The ministers testified that there was no wonder that in her fits the child mentioned Goodwife Howe, when the child's nearest relations were so frequent in expressing their suspicions in the child's hearing that Goodwife Howe was an instrument of mischief. Moreover, Rev. Payson added that the afflicted daughter fell into one of her usual strange fits because of something that her mother spoke to her with tartness. During her fit she did not mention Elizabeth Howe. We see therefore that this poor child was used by her own family to settle a grievance with the Howe family.

The arrests of the Toothaker family members, Martha Carrier, and Elizabeth Howe make up the prelude to the Andover witch hunt, which started with the arrest of Ann Foster on July 15, 1692. Both Elizabeth Howe and Martha Carrier would be hanged. Two unmarried daughters of Elizabeth Howe, Mary and Abigail, lived out their lives in the homestead of their parents. The two women remained secluded and alone beneath the shadow of the cruel attainder of their mother. After Abigail's death, Mary stayed on by herself, with only the past memories of her mother to comfort her. When Mary died, the house, considered haunted, went to ruin and decay. Eventually only the bare foundation was left, known as Mary's cellar. By the nineteenth century, all appearance of a cellar was gone, and the location was thereafter called Mary's hole. Today there is not even the slightest vestige of a hole. The long-gone house of Elizabeth Howe and her blind husband is remembered only as part of one of the saddest chapters in Massachusetts history.

Samuel Wardwell foretells his death

Let us now go back to mid July 1692. Joseph Ballard was a citizen of Andover. His wife Elizabeth had come down with a high fever. Joseph Ballard had no idea of what caused her sickness. Joseph went to his his brother John Ballard and told him about the sickness. John Ballard also lived in Andover. John's wife Rebecca was the sister of Samuel Wardwell's wife Sarah. Rebecca Ballard was the Godmother of the new baby Rebecca Wardwell of Samuel and Sarah. The brothers-in-law Samuel Wardwell and John Ballard and their families used to get together. When they met in July, Samuel Wardwell said to John Ballard: "Your brother Joseph Ballard has reported that I have bewitched his wife." John Ballard was taken aback. He then went and told his brother Joseph Ballard: "Samuel said to me that you have reported that he [i.e., Samuel Wardwell] has bewitched your wife." Joseph Ballard answered John in these words: "I have no knowledge that my wife is afflicted by witchcraft." Immediately Joseph Ballard went to Samuel's farm and told Samuel Wardwell: "I doubt that you [i.e., Samuel Wardwell] are guilty of hurting my wife. For I have no such thoughts; nor have I spoken any such words of you or any other person. Therefore I do not know whether you [i.e., Samuel Wardwell] are guilty [of witchcraft]." Samuel answered: "I admit that I said that to your brother John." In effect he said he was guilty of witchcraft, even before witchcraft was suspected in Andover. Samuel Wardwell had foretold his death. Samuel Wardwell would be found guilty of witchcraft and be hanged for it.

Wardwell's neighbor, Ephraim Foster, living in the north part of Andover, believed in Wardwell's ability to prophesy. When Ephraim, aged 20, married Hannah Eames, aged 16, in 1677, Wardwell predicted that they would have five daughters before a son should be born to them. This had proven true. Their oldest child, daughter Rose Foster, was born in 1678. Their next two daughters died young, in Ephraim's mind possibly from witchcraft. Then daughters Hannah and Jemina were born. Their first boy, their sixth child, was born in 1688. In 1692 eldest daughter Rose was ill, believed to be afflicted by witchcraft.

Ephraim Foster had often seen Wardwell tell fortunes and observed that in so doing Wardwell always "looked first into the hand of the person, and then cast his eyes down on the ground before he told anything." To Ephraim this indicated that Wardwell was in league with Satan, master of the underworld.

In 1692 blacksmith Thomas Chandler, an original proprietor of Andover, said, "I have often heard Samuel Wardwell of Andover tell young persons their fortune. He was much addicted to that, and made sport of it." Abigail Martin Jr., aged sixteen, added, "I testify that some time last winter Samuel Wardwell was at my father's house with John Farnum. I heard John Farnum ask Wardwell his fortune, which he did. Wardwell told him that he was in love with a girl, but he would be crossed, and should go to the southward, which Farnum admitted to be his thought. Wardwell further told Bridges he had like to be shot with a gun, and should have a fall off from his horse. Farnum afterwards admitted that Wardwell told right. And further I heard him tell James Bridges his fortune. Wardwell said that Bridges loved a girl fourteen years old, which Bridges admitted to be the truth. But Bridges could not imagine how said Wardwell knew; for he never spoke of it. John Bridges, father of James Bridges, said he heard James say, 'I wonder how Wardwell could tell so true.'"

Andover historian Sarah Loring Bailey wrote in 1880, that, in Samuel Wardwell, "we see one of those odd geniuses, or wonder-loving characters, of whom every community has some always, who deal in the marvelous, tell great stories, dupe the credulous to the amusement of the crowd, and who, in an age of superstition, were apt to claim a knowledge of future events, and who, perhaps, believed in a measure in their own supernatural gifts."[17]

---

[17] Sarah Loring Bailey, *Historical Sketches of Andover*, 211.

Horse and man were dispatched to take two of the afflicted girls of Salem Village to Andover to seek out the witch. At the sight of Ann Foster, the afflicted girls fell into their usual fits, and a warrant was made out for her arrest for witchcraft. Ann Foster's arrest came on July 15. She was taken to Salem and thrown into prison.

Ann Foster, aged 65, was a widow with some status in the town of Andover. Her deceased husband Andrew Foster was a Scot, and an original proprietor of the town of Andover in 1643. They had five children born between 1640 and 1655. Her husband Andrew Foster died In 1685. His widow Ann continued living on their farm. Her daughter Hannah Foster had married Hugh Stone in 1667. After 22 years of married life, in the year 1689, a terrible thing happened. Hannah's husband in a fit of drunken rage murdered her. He was apprehended, and was hanged the same year.

Second Trial, June 30, 1692

By mid-July 1692, the trial of Rev. George Burroughs and Martha Carrier was coming up. It was scheduled for the first week in August. Chief justice William Stoughton wanted more evidence to use against these two accused witches. Martha Carrier came from Andover. In the *Wonders of the Invisible World*, Cotton Mather wrote elaborate accounts of five of the trials at a Court of Oyer and Terminer, held in Salem, 1692. They were the trials of (1) Rev. George Burroughs; (2) Bridget Bishop, alias Oliver; (3) Susanna Martin; (4) Elizabeth Howe, and (5) Martha Carrier. Cotton Mather begins his account of the five trials with George Burroughs:

> This G. B. was indicted for witchcraft, and in the prosecution of the charge against him, he was accused by five or six of the bewitched, as the author of their miseries; he was accused by eight of the confessing witches, as being an head actor at some of their hellish rendezvouses, and one who had the promise of being a King in Satan's Kingdom, now going to be erected.

Cotton Mather ends his account of the five trials with Martha Carrier.

> This rampant hag, Martha Carrier, was the person, of whom the confessions of the witches, and of her own children among the rest, agreed, that the Devil had promised her, she should be Queen of Hell.

The Second Trial, June 30, 1692, resulted in the conviction of Sarah Good, Rebecca Nurse, Susanna Martin, Elizabeth Howe, and Sarah Wildes. The execution of these five convicted witches occurred on July 19 on Gallows Hill. The elderly widow Ann Foster was arrested in Andover just four days before that disgrace on Gallows Hill. It was particular cruel for people in Andover because the executed Elizabeth (Jackson) Howe was a member of Rev. Francis Dane's extended family.

Ann Foster was a tough old Scot and not easily intimidated, but still she was no match for the trickery and rough tactics performed by the authority of magistrate John Hathorne. Ann Foster was examined on record on July 15, July 16, July 18, and July 21. She was not allowed to sleep but was kept awake between these official examinations by constant interrogation and forced walking in the prison. She was broken physically and mentally. In that way, the inquisitors were able to obtain their desired result. It was testimony against Martha Carrier and Rev. George Burroughs for use in their upcoming trial [i.e., The Third Trial, August 5, 1692]. Also obtained by the inquisitors was testimony against "two men besides the minister Mr. Burroughs, & one of them had gray hair." This man with gray hair is an obvious reference to Rev. Francis Dane, the elder minister of Andover. Rev. Francis Dane had faithfully served the spiritual needs of Ann Foster and her family over her lifetime.

In Andover, one of the two main objectives of the authorities was to destroy the reputation of Rev. Francis Dane. They dared not go at him directly, so instead they attacked members of his immediate family and also members of his extended family. The other main objective of the authorities was to destroy the families of the well-placed and prosperous leading citizens (i.e., the original proprietors) of Andover. This group included the famines of John Osgood, Richard Barker, and of course Andrew Foster. Ann Foster was the trial case and, when their action worked so well, the authorities went forward with a full-scale firestorm in Andover.

All the accusations against Andover's Martha Carrier came from residents outside of Andover. However Andover resident Joseph Ballard opened Pandora's Box when he accused Andover resident Ann Foster. Pandora's Box contained all the evils of the world. When opened all the evils flew out, leaving only "Hope" inside when the box was closed again. One of the evils was manifested by Joseph Ballard's attendance on Gallows Hill of the mass execution of the five unfortunate victims on July 19. In particular, he saw Elizabeth Howe hang. She was a member of Rev. Francis Dane's family.

Joseph Ballard was a neighbor of Ann Foster in Andover. Yet he had been responsible for putting her in the dungeon-like Salem prison. On July 19, his wife, Elizabeth was now even more ill; her burning fever was to bring her death a week later, on July 27. Yet on July 19, Joseph Ballard was not with his wife in Andover, but in Salem. Salem was a day's horseback ride from Andover. After witnessing the mass execution on Gallows Hill, Joseph Ballard went to the authorities in Salem Town and swore out a complaint for the arrest of the daughter [Mary Lacey] and granddaughter [Mary Lacey Jr.] of the ill-fated Ann Foster, then undergoing torture in the Salem jail. Cotton Mather wanted further testimony against Martha Carrier of Andover, and Ballard's new complaint was a step in the right direction. Joseph Ballard posted a bond of 100 pounds sterling,[18] a great deal of money then, "to prosecute this my complaint to the effect as the law directs." Joseph Ballard did not go to Justice Dudley Bradstreet in Andover for his complaint. Somehow he knew that Dudley Bradstreet would not be as accommodating as the authorities in Salem.

---

[18] The act of posting a bond with a complaint is an important historical fact. A bond was mandatory in all capital cases. The reason is that a bond establishes that the accusing men were willing to risk their money on their actions. However, in most cases, the magistrates disregarded legal precedent in that they failed to require accusing men to post a monetary bond with their complaints.

The accused daughter Mary (Foster) Lacey had married Lawrence Lacey in 1673, and they were respected citizens of Andover. The accused granddaughter Mary Lacey Jr., aged 15. Because of Joseph Ballard, complaint of July 19, mother and daughter were arrested and imprisoned, the mother on the very day July 19 and the daughter the next day, July 20.

The senior Mary Lacey sharply reproached her mother, Ann Foster, for pleading not guilty. "Oh, mother, how do you do? We have left Christ and the Devil hath got hold of us. How shall I get rid of this evil one? I desire God to break my rocky heart that I may get the victory this time."

Mary Lacey Jr. confessed glibly. She exclaimed "Where is my mother that made me a witch and I knew it not?" Mary Lacey Jr. then went on with more disordered thoughts. She had not always obeyed her parents, and had once run away for two days. To her the Devil had come in the shape of a horse. "A little more than a year ago, I was in bed and the Devil came to me." Asked if that was the first time, she answered, yes.

The young adolescent Mary Lacey Jr. was is such a state of terror that she played into John Hathorne's hands. When Hathorne asked a flagrant leading question, she fell right into his trap. For example when he asked, "Did you at any time use to ride upon a stick or pole?" she took the bait and subconsciously went along with what he said. She answered, "Yes, sometimes above the trees." Hathorne then asked another leading question, "Do not you anoint yourselves before you fly?" to which she answered, "No, but the Devil carried us up upon hand poles." Hathorne operated on the principle: "Ask a stupid question, and you will get a stupid answer."

The testimony of Mary Lacey Jr., taken by trickery and force, to implicated Martha Carrier's children. These children were arrested on July 21. The testimony of Mary Lacey Sr. also was forced to implicate Martha Carrier's children, as well as Martha Carrier, Elizabeth (Jackson) Howe, Rebecca (Towne) Nurse, Mary (Perkins) Bradbury (of Salisbury), and even her own mother, Ann Foster. However, except for the Carrier children, all those she implicated were already accused, so she gave no new names.

The successful arrest of Ann Foster, Mary Lacey, and Mary Lacey Jr., three generations of a family of a first settler of Andover, opened the door to further accusations. The circle of afflicted girls of Salem Village was joined by a circle of afflicted girls of Andover. When afflicted girls came into any place where there were ill people, the girls fell into their fits. When asked who it was that bewitched the person, they would name one who they said sat on the head, and another that sat on the lower parts of the bewitched. In the weeks following Ballard's action nearly fifty residents of Andover were complained of and arrested.

This period of madness took place in Andover over a period of about eight weeks from July 15 to September 10. The Andover circle of afflicted girls stayed the same throughout the Andover witch hunt. Others (such as Mary Lacey Jr.) were allowed into the circle on special occasions, but afterwards they were relegated to the witch-class and never became a regular member of the circle.

The treatment of the Carrier children represents one of the darkest incidents in the annals of American history. Cotton Mather and William Stoughton were determined to finish off the children's mother, Martha (Allen) Carrier and would stop at nothing. The magistrates were going to force her own children to testify against her. Her sons, Andrew Carrier, and Richard Carrier were imprisoned on July 21, whereas her son Thomas Carrier Jr. and her little daughter Sarah Carrier were arrested and imprisoned on August 10. On July 22, their cousin, Martha (Toothaker) Emerson of Haverhill, was arrested.

The Carrier boys were not ready to confess anything, so Hathorne authorized physical torture, which was a departure from his usual method of non-physical torture (the so-called English torture). Evidence of this is given in Hathorne's own words. "Richard and Andrew Carrier were carried out to another chamber and their feet and hands bound. A little while after Richard was brought in again." Hathorne said,

"Richard, though you have been very obstinate, yet tell us how long ago it is since you were taken in this snare [of witchcraft]?"

A more graphic description is given in the letter of the prisoner John Proctor, present in the same prison, which reads in part: "Two of the five are young men (Carrier's sons), who would not confess anything till they tied them neck and heels, till blood was ready to come out of their noses, and it is creditably believed and reported this was the occasion of making them confess what they never did by reason. They said one had been a witch a month, and another five weeks, and that their mother had made them so, who had been confined here this nine weeks."

The examination of little Sarah Carrier on August 11 demonstrates clearly the falseness and imposture in the flagrant leading questions of magistrate Hathorne.

> **Hathorne,** "How long has thou been a witch?"
> **Little Sarah**, "Ever since I was six years old. I am near eight years old. Brother Richard says I shall be eight years old in November next."
> **Hathorne**, "How do you go to those you afflict, in body or spirit?"
> **Little Sarah**, "In spirit. Mother carried me thither to afflict."
> **Hathorne**, "How did your mother carry you while she was in prison?"
> **Little Sarah**, "She came like a black cat."
> **Hathorne**, "How did you know that it was your mother?"
> **Little Sarah**, "The cat told me so."

Magistrate John Hathorne was willing to deceive this little seven-year-old child by giving credence to the idea that cats could talk. Not even little Sarah truly believed this fantasy, as she was making up the whole story to obey his wishes, knowing what the consequences with this stern judge would be otherwise. This is the official court record entered in evidence; it is one of the most flagrant examples of a person acting both as prosecutor and judge, and leading the accused to obtain a guilty verdict with deceit and ruses. This is but another example of the severe child abuse practiced by the Puritan authorities. This verbal abuse is even worse than the physical abuse meted out in the prison against the boys.

Apparently the confessions of the two small children, Sarah Carrier and Thomas Carrier, Jr. were taken only for the purpose of adding to the weight of evidence against their mother, already condemned but not yet executed. The four imprisoned Carrier children were forced to watch their mother's execution on August 19. They did not know whether they would be next ones hanged by the neck from a tree. Cotton Mather characterized Martha Carrier as the "Queen of Hell." It is true that she had a quick temper, but that hardly qualifies her as royalty in the underworld.

With the arrest of the Carrier children, ten of the members of the so-called extended Dane family had been arrested: Nehemiah Abbot Jr. (the only one not imprisoned), Dr. Roger Toothaker, Mary (Allen) Toothaker, Margaret Toothaker, Martha (Toothaker) Emerson, Martha (Allen) Carrier and her four children, Richard, Andrew, Thomas Jr., and Sarah. All had been accused by the Salem Village complicity.

Sarah Good, we recall, was one of the first three imprisoned. Of the other two, Sarah Osborne had already died in prison on May 10, and the slave Tituba was being held as a potential witness. The Court was held again at Salem, June 30, 1692. Five women were brought upon trial: Sarah Good and Rebecca Nurse, of Salem Village; Susanna Martin of Amsbury; Elizabeth Howe of Ipswich Village; and Sarah Wildes of Topsfield. All were convicted, and were hastily executed on July 19, 1692.

Although Sarah Good was poor, and had suffered from sadness and melancholy, she was not broken in spirit. She knew she was innocent, and her indignation was roused against her persecutors. At execution, Rev. Nicholas Noyes urged Sarah Good to confess, and told her:

> "You are a witch, and you know you are a witch."

To this she replied:

> "You are a liar: I am no more a witch than you are a wizard, and if you take away my life, God will give you blood to drink."

Sarah Good's infant baby, taken to prison with her, had died before its mother was executed. Also this poor mother had to leave her four-year-old girl, little Dorothy (aka Dorcas) Good, chained in the dark jail. There is a tradition among the people of Salem, and it lasts even until today, that Sarah Good's prediction came true. Rev. Nicholas Noyes, an exceedingly corpulent person, was to die of an internal hemorrhage, bleeding profusely at the mouth.

When Rebecca Nurse came to trial, many testimonials about her Christian behavior, her extraordinary care in educating her children, and her setting good examples for them were entered in Court. She had always been a respected church member. The outcome of her trial was unexpected by the accusers. The jury brought in the verdict not guilty. The afflicted girls made a hideous outcry in the courtroom. This clamor shook up not only the spectators, but also the justices. One justice expressed himself not satisfied; another said the Court would have her indicted anew. Chief Justice William Stoughton said he would not impose upon the jury, but then he immediately brought up a technicality later shown to be false. The jury went out again. This time they found Rebecca Nurse guilty.

The Third Trial, August 5, 1692

At the next meeting of the Court of Oyer and Terminer, August 5, 1692, six more were tried, four men and two women. They were Rev. George Burroughs who was the minister at Wells, Maine; John Proctor and Elizabeth Proctor his wife; John Willard of Salem Village; George Jacobs Sr. of Salem; and Martha Carrier of Andover. They were all found guilty, condemned, and all executed August 19, except Proctor's wife, who escaped death by pleading for the life of her unborn child.

Burroughs had previously been the minister at Salem Village, but had left some enemies there, especially the Putnam family. Leaving Salem Village, Burroughs preached at Casco, and then at Wells, both towns being in the Province of Maine. In his trial he pleaded not guilty. The afflicted girls and some of the confessing witches were the main witnesses against him. They accused him of being a king in Satan's empire. They said that being a little man he had performed feats beyond the strength of a giant. They said that he could take a gun that was seven-feet long and hold it out with one hand. They said that he would take up a barrel of molasses or cider, and carry it easily from a canoe to the shore. In his self-vindication Burroughs said that there was an Indian who was there and held out the gun as he did. But the witnesses said that they did not remember any such Indian. They supposed that this unseen "Indian" must be the Black Man (the Devil), who they swore looked like an Indian.

Burroughs had been twice widowed. His second wife had been Sarah (Ruck) Hathorne, the widow of the deceased Captain William Hathorne Jr. The witnesses swore that he had treated these two wives very harshly. They also swore that Sarah had privately complained to the neighbors that their house was haunted by spirits. Cotton Mather claimed that Burroughs in his trial used many twistings and turnings, and contradicted himself in making his defense.

John Willard had been employed to take in some of the accused, but did not like the idea of capturing innocent people. He declined the service. Soon afterwards he was accused of witchcraft with great vehemence. , Willard made his escape to Nashaway, about 40 miles from Salem. The authorities sent men after him to apprehend him. Mercy Lewis, one of the afflicted girls, said she was able to tell the exact time when Willard was captured.

While John Proctor and his wife were in prison, Sheriff Corwin came to his house and seized all their goods, provision, and cattle. (The Sheriff sold some of the cattle at half price, and killed others, and put the meat up for shipment to the West Indies.) At Proctor's house, Sheriff Corwin threw away the beer out of a barrel, and carried away the barrel. He emptied a pot of broth, and took away the pot, and left nothing in the house for the support of the children. No part of these goods was ever returned to the family. Proctor earnestly requested Rev. Noyes to pray with and for him, but it was wholly denied, because Proctor would not admit to being a witch. Proctor asked for a little respite of time, saying that he was not fit to die, but it was not granted.

When George Jacobs Sr. was condemned, Sheriff Corwin and officers came and seized all he had. His wife had her wedding ring taken from her, but with great difficulty she obtained it back again. She was forced to buy provisions of Sheriff Corwin, the things that he had taken, for her own support. Still not being able to manage, she was helped by the charity of her neighbors.

Elizabeth Proctor was reprieved until the birth of her child. On August 19, 1692, the other five condemned were carried in a cart through the streets of Salem to execution. Nathaniel Hawthorne, in *Main Street*, writes about this scene.

> "Then, here comes the worshipful Captain Corwin, Sheriff of Essex, on horseback, at the head of an armed guard, escorting a company of condemned prisoners from the jail to their place of execution on Gallows Hill. The witches! There is no mistaking them! The witches! As they approach up Prison Lane, and turn into the Main-street, let us watch their faces. Listen to what the people say.
>
> "There is old George Jacobs, known hereabouts, these sixty years, as a man whom we thought upright in all his way of life, quiet, blameless, a good husband before his pious wife was summoned from the evil to come, and a good father to the children whom she left him.
>
> "There is John Willard too; a honest man we thought him, and so shrewd and active in his business, so practical, so intent on every-day affairs, so constant at his little place of trade, where he bartered English goods for Indian corn and all kinds of country produce!

> "See that aged couple—a sad sight truly—John Proctor, and his wife Elizabeth[19]. If there were two old people in all the County of Essex who seemed to have led a true Christian life, and to be treading hopefully the little remnant of their earthly path, it was this very pair.
> "Behind them comes a woman, with a dark, proud face that has been beautiful, and a figure that is still majestic. Do you know her? It is Martha Carrier.
> "Last of the miserable train comes a man clad in black, of small stature and a dark complexion, with a clerical band about his neck. Many a time, in the years gone by, that face has been uplifted heavenward from the pulpit of the East Meetinghouse [Wells, Maine], when the Reverend Mr. Burroughs seemed to worship God. What!—he? The holy man!—the learned!—the wise! Yet —to look at him—who, that had not known the proof, could believe him guilty? Who would not say, that over the dusty track of the Main-street, a Christian saint is now going to a martyr's death."

As Burroughs went to the place of death, his lips moved in prayer. It was not a petition for himself alone, but embracing all, his fellow sufferers and the frantic multitude. When he was upon the ladder, he made a speech stating his innocence with such solemn and serious expressions that all present were held in admiration. His prayer (which he concluded by repeating the Lord's Prayer) was well worded, and uttered with composedness and fervency of spirit. It was so affecting that it seemed to some that the spectators would stop the execution. As a rejoinder, the afflicted girls said the Black Man stood and dictated the prayer to him. As soon as the executioner prevented Burroughs from saying anything more, Rev. Cotton Mather who was mounted upon a horse addressed the people. He declared that Burroughs was not a properly ordained minister. To convince the people of Burroughs' guilt, Cotton Mather said that the Devil has often been transformed into an

---

[19] Actually, Elizabeth Proctor was not present with the others, as she had been reprieved until the birth of her child.

Angel of Light. Cotton Mather's speech did somewhat appease the people, and the executions went on.

After hanging, Burroughs was cut down and dragged to a grave about two feet deep between the rocks. His shirt and breeches were pulled off, and an old pair of trousers of one of the others who was executed was put on his lower parts. He was put in the grave with Willard and Carrier. One of his hands, his chin and someone else's foot were left uncovered. No prayer was said by any of the ministers present.

Fourth Trial, September 9, 1692

On September 19, Giles Corey was pressed to death. Giles Corey was the only person in New England who was ever executed in this way. Seeing the fate of those who had put themselves upon trial, Giles Corey stood mute; that is, he refused to plead either guilty or not guilty. As a result, the law said that he could not be tried by jury. The judges in their anger used an archaic law against this man. They could press him until he made a plea. Corey was adamant and chose to undergo whatever death they would put him to, but he would not enter a plea. In the pressing, his tongue was pressed out of his mouth, and the Sheriff used his cane to force it in again as he was dying.

The fourth meeting of the Court of Oyer and Terminer was held on September 9, 1692. Six women were tried and sentenced to death: Martha Corey of Salem Village, Mary Easty of Topsfield, Alice Parker of Salem, Ann Pudeator of Salem, Dorcas Hoar of Beverly, and Mary Bradbury of Salisbury.

Fifth Trials, September 17, 1692

On September 17, the fifth (and last meeting) of the Court was held. John Hathorne was one of the justices sitting for this session. Eight woman and one man were tried. The women were: Margaret Scott of Rowley, Wilmot Reed of Marblehead, Mary Parker of Andover, Abigail Faulkner of Andover, Rebecca Eames of Boxford, Mary Lacey of Andover, Ann Foster of Andover, and Abigail Hobbs of Topsfield. The man was Samuel Wardwell of Andover. All nine were sentenced to death.

At the previous session on September 9 six women had been sentenced to death. Thus at the two court meetings in September, fifteen were condemned. The magistrates intended to hang them all. However, six or seven ministers objected. In order to reject the charge that spectral evidence alone was used for conviction, these ministers had made valiant attempts to induce confessions. The killing of confessing witches at this juncture might bring further confessions to a screeching halt. The decision was made not to hang the five condemned who had confessed. Instead they would be held in prison until the time was ripe. But the ten condemned who were non-confessors would be hanged on schedule. One of the non-confessors was Mary Bradbury, but because of high connections she was able to escape.

Now there were nine who would be hanged. Among them was Dorcas Hoar of Beverly. On Wednesday September 21, magistrate Bartholomew Gedney heard her confession and consented that her execution be reprieved until further order. Because confessions were regarded as essential to encourage others to confess, the authorities deemed that only non-confessing witches should be hanged until further developments.

In these two Court meetings, 14 women and one man were convicted. Seven women and the man were hanged on September 22, a cold and rainy day. They were Martha Corey, Mary Easty, Alice Parker, Ann Pudeator, Margaret Scott, Wilmot Reed, Mary Parker, and Samuel Wardwell. One of the women, Mary Bradbury, escaped. The remaining six, all confessing witches, were continued in prison: Dorcas Hoar, Abigail Faulkner, Rebecca Eames, Mary Lacey, Ann Foster, and Abigail Hobbs. Ann Foster died in jail in December.

The Court had an unwritten policy of not sentencing to death any person who confessed witchcraft. If a person confessed, his or her life would be spared. Certainly this is why the authorities had obtained so many confessions. There were several reasons for this policy. Cotton Mather needed confessions to establish the reality of his invisible world of witches, and the civil authorities wanted to use the accusations made by confessing witches to implicate other people as witches. However this policy could be changed at any time, and it was generally believed that when the authorities had enough people in jail, they would execute them all.

Those who confessed their guilt were not executed. The case of Dorcas Hoar illustrates the privilege accorded confessing witches. Originally she had refused to confess. With her execution was imminent, she became a last-minute confessor. Rev. John Hale helped Dorcas Hoar initiate the petition that asked "that there may be granted her one month's time or more to prepare for death and eternity." She was reprieved, being given, according to the petition, "a little time of life to realize and perfect her repentance for the salvation of her soul." The question was whether such a last minute confession was based on her desire to save her soul, or just not to be hanged. Would Dorcas Hoar have confessed if she had known that they would hang her anyway? The stark fact was that execution had been reserved not for those who pleaded guilty, but for those who professed innocence. Samuel Wardwell had initially pleaded guilty by making a confession. But a few days later, he denied his confession, and was condemned.

With Dorcas Hoar plucked from the hangman, eight non-confessing convicted witches were left. These eight were Martha Corey, Mary Easty, Alice Parker, Ann Pudeator, Margaret Scott, Wilmot Redd, Mary Parker, and Samuel Wardwell. All had remained resolute in their refusals to confess. In the morning of September 22, the eight were loaded onto a cart. When the cart reached the outskirts of the town, it turned off the main road and began to climb Gallows Hill. In going up the hill, the cart became stuck in a muddy rut. The afflicted girls following close behind chanted, "The Devil hinders the cart."

Because of its dark slope and the even line of its summit, the hill from a distance resembled a green rampart. However it was less steep than its aspect threatened. Although the whole slope and summit were a peculiarly deep green, there was scarce a blade of grass visible from the base upward. All the grass has been destroyed by wood-wax, a form of weed. Its roots take over the soil and permit nothing else to grow. The cart reached the top of Gallows Hill.

1. **Martha Corey**, wife to Giles Corey, protested her innocence and concluded her life with a prayer upon the ladder. Martha Corey had been imprisoned since March 19. On September 14, Rev. Parris and a delegation from the Village church called on her to tell her that she now was under the sentence of excommunication. He entered in the parish book only the observation that she was "very obdurate, justifying herself and condemning all that had done anything to her just discovery and condemnation." He did not record his own words, except to say that they had been few, "for her imperiousness would not suffer much."

2. **Mary Easty**, sister of Rebecca Nurse took her last farewell of her husband, children and friends. It was reported by those present, that her farewell was serious, religious, distinct, and affectionate as could well be expressed.

3. **Alice Parker** of Salem, wife of a fisherman. It proved easy to find many slanderous stories to support the case against her.

4. **Ann Pudeator**, wife of fisherman, had challenged her accusers. She had asked that the testimony sworn against her by Sarah Churchill, Mary Warren, and John Best be stricken from the record as "altogether false and untrue," and that "my life not be taken away by such false evidence. Her defense did no good.

5. **Margaret Scott** of Rowley went to her death with the courage and conviction of a loving and honest woman. Margaret Stevenson was born about 1621 in England. In 1642 she married widower Benjamin Scott. They had six children. Her husband died at Rowley in 1671. In 1692 Margaret was 71 and had been a widow for 21 years. She was arrested on August 5 for witchcraft. In 1692 all kinds of deceit were used by the witch hunters in their attempts to convince the populace that certain women fitted the stereotype of witch. These efforts were made to give credibility to the witch hunt. They often chose those women whom they regarded as being particularly vulnerable to their false accusations.

Favorite targets were elderly widows. Widows were picked because, without their husbands to protect them in a male-dominated society, it was difficult for them to ward off vicious libels and slander. If the widow was left with even moderate wealth, the forces of envy were so great that any kind of attack might be made against her. The elderly widow Margaret Scott fell into this category and was one of the widows chosen for accusation. At her trial, envious and malicious people stepped forward to give false testimony. Philip Nelson and his wife Sarah testified that "for two or three years before Robert Shilleto died, we have often heard him complaining of Margaret Scott for hurting of him and often said that she was a witch and so he continued complaining of Margaret Scott saying that he should never be so well as long as Margaret Scott lived & so he complained of Margaret Scott at times until he died." Frances Wycom said "that quickly after the first court at Salem about witchcraft, Margaret Scott, whom I very well knew, or her appearance came to me and did most grievously torment me by choking and almost pressing me to death. And so she did continue afflicting me by times until the 5th August 1692 being the day of her examination. Also during the time of her examination Margaret Scott did most grievously afflict me, and also several times since, and I believe in my heart that she is a witch."

6. **Wilmot Reed** was the aging wife of a fisherman who had been accused of generally harmless sorceries, as the curdling of milk and spoiling of butter. Wilmot Reed was cried out upon by the afflicted girls. She answered "I know nothing of it." At the trial, she was condemned.

7. **Mary Parker** of Andover. On September 2, 1692, when John Hathorne asked, "How long have ye been in the snare of the Devil?" Mary Parker resolutely answered, "I know nothing of it."

8. **Samuel Wardwell,** when it was his turn, spoke to the people claiming his innocence. The executioner stood beside him, smoking. Smoke blew into Wardwell's face and interrupted his words. The afflicted girls chanted, "The Devil hinders Wardwell with smoke." Samuel Wardwell's brother Benjamin Wardwell was a seaman sailing out of Salem. Many

New England seamen were lost at sea. Benjamin Wardwell was one of them. Un-coffined and unknown, they are at rest in watery graves.

The suffering of the eight who died on September 22, 1692 is heartbreaking. The seven women had refused to fabricate confessions. The man Samuel Wardwell had renounced his false confession. The eight protested their innocence to the end and concluded their lives with prayers. Rev. Nicholas Noyes coldly watched the hangings. He refused to say prayers. The others present reported that the demeanor of the eight was devout at the time of death. After the executions, Rev. Noyes pointed to the eight bodies hanging from the great locust tree, and declared, “What a sad thing it is to see eight firebrands of hell hanging there.” Un-coffined and unknown, they are at rest in rocky graves.

Andover touch test, September 7, 1692

On Wednesday morning, September 7, 1692, the authorities called certain residents to Andover meetinghouse. Husbands accompanied their wives; some children were also invited. Those summoned were of impeccable standing in the community; some were elders of the church. The women called included.

Mary (Clement) Osgood	about 55
Deliverance (Hazeltine) Dane	about 37
Sarah (Lord) Wilson	about 44
Mary (Lovett) Tyler	about 40
Abigail (Wheeler) Barker	about 25
Hannah Tyler	14
Rebecca (Aslet) Johnson, widow	40
Rebecca Johnson Jr.	
Eunice (Potter) Frye	51

Rev. Thomas Barnard opened the meeting with prayer. This travesty was called the touch test. It was conceived and carried out by the authorities (unnamed in history, but we might reasonably infer that one was John Hathorne). These women with terror in their hearts found themselves being carted off to Salem prison. Five of the women present, Mary Osgood, Deliverance Dane, Sarah Wilson, Mary Tyler,

Abigail Barker, and one girl, Hannah Tyler, later made this statement about what followed.

> "After Mr. Barnard had been at prayer, we were blindfolded, and our hands were laid upon the afflicted persons, they being in their fits and falling into their fits at our coming into their presence, as they said. Some led us and laid our hands upon them, and then they said they were well, and that we were guilty of afflicting them; whereupon we were all seized, as prisoners, by a warrant from the justice of the peace [Dudley Bradstreet], and forthwith carried to Salem.
>
> "And by reason of that sudden surprise, we knowing ourselves altogether innocent of that crime, we were all exceedingly astonished and amazed, and consternated and affrighted even out of our reason; and our nearest and dearest relations, seeing us in that dreadful condition, and knowing our great danger, apprehending that there was no other way to save our lives, as the case was then circumstantiated, but by our confessing ourselves to be such and such persons as the afflicted represented us to be, they, out of tender love and pity, persuaded us to confess what we did confess.
>
> "And indeed that confession, that it is said we made, was no other than what was suggested to us by some gentlemen, they telling us that we were witches, and they knew it, and we knew it, and they knew that we knew it, which made us think it was so; and our understanding, our reason, our faculties almost gone, we were not capable of judging our condition; as also the hard measures they used with us rendered us incapable of making our defense, but said anything and everything which they desired, and most of what we said was but in effect a consenting to what they said. Some time after, when we were better composed, they telling us of what we had confessed, we did profess that we were innocent, and ignorant of such things; and we hearing that Samuel Wardwell had renounced his confession, and quickly after

condemned and executed, some of us were told that we were going after Wardwell."

Why were particular people singled out to come together at the meeting house in Andover to be put to the touch test? Carefully selected beforehand, all were members of the Andover elite. Mary Osgood was the second highest ranking woman in Andover, coming only after Dudley Bradstreet's wife, Ann. Eunice Frye was the deacon's wife. Abigail Barker was the daughter-in-law of proprietor Richard Barker. Deliverance Dane was Rev. Dane's daughter-in-law. Abigail Faulkner Jr. and Dorothy Faulkner were Rev. Dane's granddaughters.

Before the touch test on September 7, Dudley Bradstreet, acting in his capacity as justice of the peace, had granted arrest warrants against, and committed, some thirty Andover persons to prisons for supposed witchcrafts. On that fateful day, September 7, 1692, Dudley Bradstreet dutifully granted arrest warrants for the eighteen who were accused in the touch test. Finally, however, he realized that the leading citizens of Andover were being targeted. The controlling elite—those who gained their large land-holdings by the good fortune of being the town's first settlers—were now under attack. The Barkers, the third ranking family, and the Osgoods, the second ranking family, had been accused. The Bradstreets were the first ranking family; would they be next?

Dudley Bradstreet came to his senses. His warrants had put in jail nearly fifty Andover citizens. After the touch test, he refused to grant out any more warrants. Soon after his decision, Dudley Bradstreet and his wife, Ann, were cried out upon. The afflicted claimed he had killed nine persons by witchcraft. In response, Bradstreet and his wife found escape their safest course and in short order they fled from Massachusetts to New Hampshire. "Captain [Dudley] Bradstreet and Mr. [Ephraim] Stevens are complained of by the afflicted, have left the town, and do abscond," wrote Thomas Brattle on October 8, 1692.

On October 19, 1692 Increase Mather went to Salem and made a revealing investigation of the conditions under which the confessions had been obtained. The tide had finally turned and was ebbing. Rev.

Increase Mather interviewed Mary (Lovett) Tyler in Salem Prison by. His account, certainly colored by his own preconceived ideas, still managed to describe her terror and confusion.

> "Goodwife Tyler did say that, when she was first apprehended, she had no fears upon her, and did think that nothing could have made her confess against herself. But since, she had found, to her great grief, that she had wronged the truth, and falsely accused herself. She said that when she was brought to Salem, her brother[-in-law John] Bridges rode with her; and that, all along the way from Andover to Salem, he kept telling her that she must needs be a witch, since the afflicted accused her, and at her touch were raised out of their fits, and urging her to confess herself a witch. She as constantly told him that she was no witch, that she knew nothing of witchcraft, and begged him not to urge her to confess. However, when she came to Salem, she was carried to a room, where her brother[-in-law John Bridges] on one side, and [Rev.] Mr. John Emerson [of Gloucester], on the other side, did tell her that she was certainly a witch, and that she saw the Devil before her eyes at that time (and, accordingly, the said Emerson would attempt with his hand to beat him away from her eyes); and they so urged her to confess, that she wished herself in any dungeon, rather than be so treated. Mr. Emerson told her, once and again, 'Well, I see you will not confess! Well, I will now leave you, and then you are undone, body and soul, forever.' Her brother[-in-law John Bridges] urged her to confess, and told her that, in so doing, she could not lie. To which she answered, 'Good brother, do not say so; for I shall lie if I confess, and then who shall answer unto God for my lie?' He still asserted it, and said that God would not suffer so many good men to be in such an error about it, and that she would be hanged if she did not confess; and continued so long and so violently to urge and press her to confess, that she thought, verily, that her life would have gone from her, and became so terrified in her mind that she owned, at length, almost anything that they propounded to her. That she had wronged her conscience in so doing; she was guilty

> of a great sin in belying of herself, and desire to mourn for it so long as she lived. This she said, and a great deal more of the like nature; and all with such affection, sorrow, relenting, grief, and mourning, as that it exceeds any pen to describe and express the same."

Let us analyze the above account of Rev. Increase Mather. It relates that Mary Tyler's claim of innocence seemed to be preposterous to her brother-in-law John Bridges. He said, "God would not suffer so many good men to be in error about it." Yet his own wife, Mary (Tyler) Post Bridges was in prison, as well as two of his own daughters and three step-daughters. His remark sees inexplicable. According to Increase Mather's story, accused women who refused to confess were relentlessly pressed to do so by their next-of-kin. Was it because their husbands, to quote Thomas Brattle, "did break charity with their dear wives," aghast to find themselves mated with witches? Or was it because their kinsmen wanted them to confess, whether true or false, as the only hope of escaping the gallows?

On **October 8, 1692**, which was one month after the touch test, Thomas Brattle wrote,

> "Deacon Frye's wife, Captain Osgood's wife, and some others, remarkably pious and good people in repute, are apprehended and imprisoned [at the touch test]; and that that is more admirable, the fore-mentioned women are become a kind of confessors, being first brought thereto by the urgings of their good husbands, who having taken up that corrupt and highly pernicious opinion, that whoever were accused by the afflicted, were guilty, did break charity with their dear wives, upon their being accused, and urged them to confess their guilt; which so far prevailed with them as to make them say, they were afraid they were in the snare of the Devil; and which, through the rude and barbarous methods that were afterwards used in Salem, issued in somewhat plainer degrees of confession, and was attended with prison. The good Deacon and Captain are now sensible of their

> error they were in; do now grieve and mourn bitterly, that they should break charity with their own wives, and urge them to confess themselves witches. They now see and acknowledge their rashness and uncharitableness."

The elite of Andover had been caught off guard. Captain Osgood, Deacon Frye, and others had urged their wives to confess. Apparently these men, pillars of the church, believed the message preached by Barnard that confession was the way to eternal life. They also may have hoped that confession would save the lives of their wives. It was a grotesque and horrifying scene. "Here it was that many accused themselves of riding upon poles through the air; many parents believing their children to be witches, and many husbands their wives, etc. Not until their wives and children were in prison, did the minds of these men begin to clear. Andover's older minister, Rev. Francis Dane formed a resistance movement. Under his guidance they started to take the strong steps required to free the imprisoned members of their families. Contrast the behavior of the Andover group to that of the seventy-odd people imprisoned during the Salem Village phase of the witch hunt. Recall that only five—Abigail Hobbs, Deliverance Hobbs, Margaret Jacobs and the slaves, Tituba and Candy—had confessed. Those remaining had refused to confess under any conditions; eleven of these non-confessors were executed.

Return of Governor Phips from Maine

The mass execution on September 22, 1692 marked a turning point in the witchcraft hysteria. On the one hand, the perpetuators were going full blast, taking their spoil. Some went further and tried to bring down people in the highest echelons of society. On the other hand, the reaction against the whole thing had set in, especially by those of high social rank. Governor Phips had been away commanding the army in Maine, and when he returned on September 29, 1692 he found important people much dissatisfied at the proceedings of the Court. Nineteen persons had been hanged, and one pressed to death, and eight more convicted. Of these 28, more than a third were members of churches. Most had excellent reputations, and yet not one had been cleared. Many persons thought some or all of this number to be innocent. The prison at Salem was so full that some had to be placed in other prisons. In all there were more than 150 in prison waiting for trial, and more than 200 accused but not yet in prison. From official records, the names of most of the 150 in prison can be determined (Appendix), but only a small number of the additional 200 can be identified, except for some persons of high status who are known to have fled.

Up to October 1692, about fifty had confessed to be witches. Those who confessed and stuck to the confession were not executed in September 1692, but stayed in prison. Stoughton in the Superior Court trials held in January 1693 sentenced eight women to death, most of them confessing witches. Of the five confessing witches condemned in September, Ann Foster had died in jail and Abigail Faulkner was still pregnant. The three left, namely Abigail Hobbs, Mary (Foster) Lacey, and Rebecca Eames, plus Dorcas Hoar (the last minute confessor), plus Elizabeth Proctor, a non-confessing witch reprieved for pregnancy in August, plus the three confessing witches (Mary Post, Elizabeth Johnson, Jr., and Sarah Wardwell) condemned in January 1693, made up the eight. Fortunately, these eight death sentences were foiled by a last minute reprieve by Sir William Phips.

Spectral evidence was in a state of controversy among the New England clergy. The idea of proceeding as before dissatisfied and disturbed many people. In particular, Phips was unhappy about the use of spectral evidence. He inquired into the matter and was informed by the judges that they began with spectral evidence, but they also used human testimony. Human testimony consisted of slander about witchcraft given by various witnesses against the accused. Such unprovable slander was considered undoubted proof of a person being a witch. Despite everything, the Court, and chief judge Stoughton in particular, wanted to persist vigorously in the trying the accused by the use of spectral evidence.

A dog was afflicted by witchcraft at Salem Village. The afflicted girls were sent for to use their spectral sight. They claimed that John Bradstreet, the brother of the Andover justice of the peace, afflicted the dog. John Bradstreet made his escape into New Hampshire, and the dog was put to death. At Andover, the afflicted girls complained of another dog, one named Griff. They said that Griff afflicted them by witchcraft, and they would fall into their fits whenever the dog looked at them. The dog was put to death on the deserted Wardwell farm.

The complicity was out in the open with the accusations of people of rank such as the Bradstreet brothers, sons of the late Simon Bradstreet. The witch hunt which the very top ruling class had allowed Cotton Mather to engender had now turned upon its makers. The witch hunt proved to be a Frankenstein monster, with the highest officials being in danger, at last. Now the rich went to battle against the accusers. A worthy gentleman of Boston about this time was accused by the complicity in Andover. He sent by some particular friends a writ to arrest those accusers in a thousand pound action for defamation, with instructions to them to inform themselves of the certainty of the proof. In doing this, the deceit of the complicity was perceived, and from that time the accusations at Andover ceased. The Andover witch hunt had been given a deadly blow by this worthy gentleman. Now the whole episode had to be justified by the clergy, and those 150 in prison dealt with. Even though the tide had turned, some residual accusations still continued into October and November 1692. The town of Gloucester was the main focal point. In October some of the afflicted were sent to Gloucester. The result was that four women were sent to prison. Because Salem prison was so full that it could hold no more, two of them were sent to Ipswich prison.

In October 1692, William Stoughton, serving as chief justice for the Salem witchcraft trials, wrote a thank you letter to Rev. Cotton Mather (who was the son of Rev. Increase Mather). "Considering the place that I hold in the Court of Oyer and Terminer, still laboring and proceeding in the trial of persons accused and *convicted for witchcraft*, I express my obligation and thankfulness to you. Such is your design, your enmity to

Satan, your compassion, such your instruction and counsel, your care of truth, that all good men will greatly rejoice that the spirit of the Lord has thus enabled you to lift up a standard against the infernal enemy, that has been coming in like a flood upon us." At that point many accused witches were in jail, awaiting trial. Despite her being called a witch, the enormously rich mother-in-law of Justice Jonathan Corwin, of course, was not among the witches in jail. In fact, she was never charged as being a witch.

In November the afflicted were sent for again by Lieutenant Stephens. He had been told that his sister was bewitched. These afflicted swore that they saw three persons sitting upon Lieutenant Stephens' sister until she died. On their way the afflicted passed over Ipswich Bridge. There they met an old woman, and instantly fell into their fits. But now the validity of their accusations was questioned. Not finding encouragement, the afflicted withdrew. The witch hunt essentially had come to an end. Governor Phips felt that he was assured of the innocence of some of the accused. He believed that many important persons of un-blamable life and reputation were cried out upon as witches and wizards. Phips to his credit put an end to the Court of Oyer and Terminer on October 29, 1692. He saw many innocent persons in jail that might perish. There were at least fifty persons in prison in great misery by reason of the extreme cold and their poverty, most of them having only specter evidence against them. He caused some of them to be let out upon bail. He told the judges to find a way to relieve others and prevent them from perishing in prison.

To replace of the Court of Oyer and Terminer, the General Court passed an act constituting a Superior Court of Judicature Because some of the justices had acknowledged that their former proceedings were too violent, spectral evidence would not be used in the Superior Court. William Stoughton was chief justice, and the associate justices were Thomas Danforth, John Richards, Wait Still Winthrop, and Samuel Sewall. John Hathorne was not on the new court.

Chapter 6. Complicity of authorities

Legal process

In the winter of 1692 in Salem Village, little Betty Parris was sick, running about making strange shrieks and hiding under furniture. The contagion spread to other girls. The diagnosis was that these afflicted girls were bewitched. It was the beginning of a witch hunt to seek out the culprits. About 150 people were accused as witches and imprisoned. Twenty were executed and eight died in prison. Why did the Salem witch-hunt become widespread and out of control? Many explanations have been given. The most popular explanations claim that various disturbing political and religious factors came together and formed a perfect storm. In other words, the Salem witch trials were caused by accidental encounters of disparate events. However, this explanation is counter to history.

The witch trial of Joan of Arc took place at Rouen, Normandy in 1431. Carried out by an English-backed church court, her conviction was predetermined. She was burned at the stake. It was not an accident; it was arson. In the inquisition and in the northern European witch trials, it was arson. Salem was no exception. It was arson. The Puritan old guard (who ruled Massachusetts) seized upon the opportunity presented by witchcraft allegations in Salem Village in 1692. Instead of extinguishing the flames, the old guard fanned the flames and turned the conflagration into a firestorm. Their purpose was to affirm that they were in power in Massachusetts and that they would continue to be in power under the new royal charter. They were severe and resolute.

Let us look at the legal processes in operation. A witchcraft accusation by itself would come to nothing. In order to turn an accusation into a prosecution, the accused person has to be charged. A complainant (or plaintiff) is a person who makes a complaint, usually before justices. More exactly, an accuser officially became a *complainant* when he filed an official written document, called a *complaint,* with the magistrates. If the magistrates felt that the complaint had merit, they made out an arrest warrant against the accused. A constable or marshal would carry out the arrest. After the arrest, the accused person, now a *defendant*, was taken before the magistrates for a preliminary *examination*.

Present at the preliminary examination were the afflicted persons (i.e., the girls and others who suffered the anguish inflicted on them by the alleged witch that they had accused). The afflicted threw fits and suffered the pains of torment, claiming that the specter of the accused person was hurting them at that very time. Of course, no one could see the specter except the afflicted, but the afflictions were considered hard evidence of the witchcraft of the accused. Witnesses for the prosecution might be called to give testimony about how the accused person had practiced witchcraft in the past. Previously imprisoned persons who had confessed to witchcraft might also be present to claim that the accused person was also a witch. On the basis of the examination, the magistrates would decide whether to release the accused person or to commit her or him to prison to await trial. With the single exception of Nehemiah Abbot Jr., every accused witch in 1692 was committed to prison after the preliminary examination.

The next legal step was the grand jury inquest. The grand jury could either clear or indict the accused. If indicted, the accused person would be given a trial by jury. In the case of a guilty verdict, the death sentence would be passed. In all phases of the prosecution, the accused person was not allowed representation by a lawyer or other counsel.

Throughout the entire process, accusations of witchcraft against the accused were rife. They came from all corners: from the afflicted girls, from the girls' parents, from witnesses for the prosecution, and from confessing witches. In this overall confusion, it appears that **mass hysteria** caused an entangled morass of witchcraft allegation. However, a careful analysis shows just **the opposite**. An entangled morass of witchcraft allegations caused **mass hysteria**. The question is: What caused the entangled morass of witchcraft allegations? Was it accident or was it arson? Here we want to answer that quotation.

To establish the underlying structure of the events, we look to the extant written complaints and other documents. The written complaint filed with the magistrates consisted of three parts:

1. the accused witches,
2. the afflicted children,
3. the adults making the complaint.

The names of the accused witches and the afflicted children also appeared on the resulting arrest warrant.

The New England Puritans carefully preserved official documents. Although many of the official documents of the Salem witchcraft trials have been lost or destroyed, enough survive so that a reasonably detailed story can be reconstructed, despite some gaps. We give our main results in the form two tables; a complaint table for the Salem Village witch hunt and a complaint table for the Andover witch hunt:

The first column gives the date of the complaint or arrest.
The second column gives the name of the accused witch.
The third column gives the complainants (i.e., the accusers).
The fourth column gives the afflicted girls.

The names on the complaint or arrest warrant are used if either exists. Otherwise the names of the afflicted girls are taken from the examination document if it exists. Finally if all the preceding methods fail, the names are taken either from the indictments or from other evidence. In the last two columns, the earliest extant source is indicated, whether it be the complaint, the arrest warrant, the examination, the indictment, or an inference from ancillary information.

The Salem Village witch hunt is often attributed to the hysteria of the general public. But hysteria alone does not generate arrest warrants. There may be hysterical behavior leading up to the written complaint. However there is no hysterical behavior in the action of the authorities, who meticulously carry out their lawful duties according to their interpretation of the law. So although there are gaps in the record, a remarkably detailed story can be pieced together. Comparable legal records for the European witch hunts, on the other hand, have all but disappeared.

A complaint represents the point when an accuser took the legal step necessary to have someone arrested as a witch. This is the place where the all-inclusive general public is replaced by specific individuals, namely the people who accused the so-called witches, who then were promptly arrested. At this pivotal legal juncture the accusers could no longer remain concealed but had to expose themselves. On the legal extant complaints drawn up in 1692, the names of the accusers boldly stand forth. If the accusers represented a random sample of the general public, then it can be concluded that the witch hunt was caused by mass hysteria (i.e., by accident). However, if the accusers were members of a small interlocked group, then it can be concluded that the witch hunt was caused by design (i.e., arson). The question of whether the witch hunt was driven by accident or by arson can be answered by simply tabulating all the legal complaints filed with the official documents. In cases when a complaint is not extant, its contents in a large measure can be reconstructed from extant arrest warrants and other official documents.

Complaint Table for Salem Village

We have put together a series of thirty legal complaints that were filed from February 29, 1692 to July 1, 1692. This period represents the first half of the Salem witchcraft delusion, and is known as the Salem Village witch hunt. Accusing seventy-four people, these complaints include everyone known to have been imprisoned for witchcraft in eastern New England during this period, except for the infant child of Sarah Good and for nine people about whom very little is known by any account. The following numbered table lists the complaints in chronological order.

Complaint Table for the Salem Village witch hunt in 1692©

Date	Accused	Accusers	Afflicted

No. 1 Feb. 29	Sarah Good Sarah Osborne Tituba	Thomas Putnam Edward Putnam Joseph Hutchinson Thomas Preston	Elizabeth Parris Abigail Williams Ann Putnam Jr. Elizabeth Hubbard
No. 2 Mar. 19	Martha Corey	Edward Putnam Henry Kenny	Abigail Williams Ann Putnam Sr. Ann Putnam Jr. Mercy Lewis Elizabeth Hubbard
No. 3 Mar. 23	Rebecca Nurse	Edward Putnam Jonathan Putnam	Abigail Williams Ann Putnam Jr.
No. 4 Mar. 23	Dorcas Good	Edward Putnam Jonathan Putnam	Ann Putnam Jr. Mary Walcott Mercy Lewis
No. 5 Mar. 29	Rachel Clinton	Complaint (filed at Ipswich) not extant	Not extant
No. 6 Apr. 4	Sarah Cloyce Elizabeth Proctor	Jonathan Walcott Nathaniel Ingersoll	Abigail Williams John Indian Mary Walcott Ann Putnam Jr. Mercy Lewis
No. 7 Apr. 11	John Proctor	No formal complaint. Arrested at his wife's examination (above).	Same as for his wife
No. 8 Apr. 18	Giles Corey Bridget Bishop Abigail Hobbs Mary Warren	John Putnam Jr. Ezekiel Cheever	Abigail Williams Ann Putnam Jr. Mary Walcott Mercy Lewis Elizabeth Hubbard
No. 9 Apr. 21	William Hobbs Deliverance Hobbs Nehemiah Abbot Jr. Mary Easty Sarah Wildes Edward Bishop Jr. Sarah Bishop Mary Black Mary English	Thomas Putnam John Buxton	Ann Putnam Jr. Mary Walcott Mercy Lewis

No. 10 Apr. 30	Philip English Lydia Dustin Susannah Martin Dorcas Hoar Sarah Morrell George Burroughs	Thomas Putnam Jonathan Walcott	Abigail Williams Ann Putnam Jr. Mary Walcott Mercy Lewis Elizabeth Hubbard Susannah Sheldon
No. 11 May 7	Sarah Dustin	Thomas Putnam John Putnam Jr.	Abigail Williams Ann Putnam Jr. Mary Walcott Mercy Lewis
No. 12 May 8	Bethia Carter Bethia Carter Jr. Ann Sears	Thomas Putnam John Putnam Jr.	Ann Putnam Jr. Mary Walcott Mercy Lewis
No. 13 May 10	George Jacobs Sr. Margaret Jacobs	Thomas Putnam John Putnam Jr.	Abigail Williams Ann Putnam Jr. Mary Walcott Mercy Lewis Elizabeth Hubbard Sarah Churchill
No. 14 May 10	John Willard	Benjamin Wilkins Sr. Thomas Fuller Jr.	Bray Wilkins Daniel Wilkins
No. 15 May 12	Alice Parker Ann Pudeator	Complaint not extant	Mary Warren Parker's indictment carries the names of Ann Putnam Jr. Elizabeth Hubbard Mary Warren. Pudeator's indictment carries the names of Ann Putnam Jr. Sarah Churchill Mary Warren.
No. 16 c. May 13	Abigail Somes	Complaint not extant	Mary Warren Somes' indictment carries the names of Mary Walcott, Elizabeth Hubbard, Mary Warren.

No. 17 May 14	Daniel Andrew George Jacobs Jr. Rebecca Jacobs Sarah Buckley Mary Whittredge Elizabeth Hart Thomas Farrar Elizabeth Colson	Thomas Putnam Nathaniel Ingersoll	Ann Putnam Jr. Mary Walcott Mercy Lewis Abigail Williams
No. 18 May 15	Mehitabel Downing	Complaint and arrest warrant not extant.	Mary Warren
No. 19 May 18	Roger Toothaker	Complaint not extant	Ann Putnam Jr. Mary Walcott Elizabeth Hubbard
No. 20 May 21	Sarah Proctor Sarah Bassett Susannah Roots	Thomas Putnam John Putnam Jr.	Ann Putnam Jr. Mary Walcott Mercy Lewis Abigail Williams
No. 21 May 23	Benjamin Proctor Mary De Rich Sarah Pease	Nathaniel Ingersoll Thomas Rayment	Abigail Williams Elizabeth Hubbard
No. 22 May 28	Elizabeth Cary	Thomas Putnam Benjamin Hutchinson	Mary Walcott Mercy Lewis Abigail Williams
No. 23 May 28	John Alden John Floyd Elizabeth Fosdick Wilmot Redd Sarah Rice William Proctor Elizabeth Howe Arthur Abbot Martha Carrier Mary Toothaker Margaret Toothaker	Jonathan Walcott Joseph Houlton	Ann Putnam Jr. Mary Walcott Mercy Lewis Abigail Williams
No. 24 May 30	Elizabeth Paine Elizabeth Fosdick	Nathaniel Putnam Joseph Whipple	Mercy Lewis Mary Warren
No. 25 Jun. 2	Elizabeth Paine Elizabeth Fosdick	Peter Tufts	Tufts' slave
No. 26 Jun. 4	Mary Ireson	Edward Putnam Thomas Rayment	Abigail Williams Ann Putnam Jr. Mary Walcott Mary Warren Susannah Sheldon Elizabeth Booth

No. 27 Jun. 3	Job Tookey	Complaint and arrest warrant not extant	Ann Putnam Jr. Mary Walcott Elizabeth Hubbard Mary Warren Susannah Sheldon Elizabeth Booth Sarah Bibber
No. 28 Jun. 5	Ann Dolliver	Complaint not extant	Mary Warren Susannah Sheldon
No. 29 Jun. 28	Mary Bradbury	Complaint and arrest warrant not extant.	Ann Putnam Jr. Mary Walcott
No. 30 Jul. 1	Margaret Hawkes Candy	Thomas Putnam John Putnam Jr.	Ann Putnam Jr. Mary Walcott Mary Warren

Salem Village accuser faction (aka Putnam faction)

A faction is group of persons (as within a town) that is often antagonistic or self-seeking. A faction is usually formed for a particular purpose. Even a cursory study of the preceding table reveals a faction of a hard core of accusers belonging to the extended family of Thomas Putnam. Besides Thomas Putnam, the Putnam accuser faction included his brother Edward Putnam, his brother-in-law Jonathan Walcott, his uncle-in-law Nathaniel Ingersoll, his uncles John Putnam Sr. and Nathaniel Putnam, and his first cousins Jonathan Putnam and John Putnam Jr. This relentless faction consisted of a group of persons united for the particular purpose of filing legal complaints accusing designated people for the crime of witchcraft.

Thomas Putnam exerted complete control over the lives of the two afflicted girls living in his household. The two were his eldest daughter, Ann Putnam Jr., age twelve, and his servant Mercy Lewis, age seventeen. Jonathan Walcott had similar authority over another of the afflicted girls, his daughter Mary Walcott, age seventeen. Mary's natural mother was dead, and her step-mother was Thomas Putnam's sister, Deliverance (Putnam) Walcott. Mary's great uncle was Nathaniel Ingersoll.

The afflicted girls also include Elizabeth Parris, age nine, and Abigail Williams, age eleven. Elizabeth, called Betty, was the daughter of Rev. Samuel Parris; Abigail, called Nabby, was his niece who also lived in his household. Rev. Samuel Parris, a strict disciplinarian, would not have allowed their participation without his tacit approval. The name of Elizabeth Hubbard, age seventeen, also appears among the afflicted girls. She was the great niece of the wife of Dr. William Griggs. Elizabeth worked as a servant in his household. By necessity, Elizabeth took her cues from him. Whenever we see the names of either Elizabeth Parris or Abigail Williams on a complaint, we know that Rev. Parris was involved. Whenever we see the name Elizabeth Hubbard, we know that Dr. Griggs was involved. These men never would have permitted such exploitation otherwise. It follows that Rev. Samuel Parris and Dr. William Griggs were allied with the Putnam faction. However Parris and Griggs did not sign their names on any of the complaints. As minister and doctor, they occupied the two highest professional positions in the community, guarding the spiritual and physical health of those entrusted to them. To become involved with the actual legal mechanics of a witch hunt would have been unseemly. Rev. Samuel Parris and Dr. William Griggs make up the allied professional component of the Putnam faction.

In other ways, Parris was conspicuous. In the guise of doing his duty, he willingly acted as a witness against many of those accused. Also he acted as scribe in taking down some of the examinations and in writing them up for the official record. The Putnam faction handled all the legal documents. One or more members of this faction signed the complaints for seventy-one of the seventy-four people imprisoned in the Salem Village witch hunt. The three exceptions were accused witches Rachel Clinton, John Proctor (who was arrested with neither a formal complaint nor an arrest warrant), and John Willard.

The Putnam accuser faction include a **fringe group**. They were members of the extended family of Thomas Putnam. The Putnam fringe was made up of Joseph Hutchinson, Benjamin Hutchinson, Joseph Houlton and John Buxton. They played various roles in the witch hunt. They were allowed to put their names on some of the complaints in addition to the names of various members of the Putnam accuser faction. Except for Dr. Griggs and Rev. Parris, all were members of the extended family of Sergeant Thomas Putnam. For a few complaints, some trusted friends were also allowed to participate. In summary, the Putnam accuser faction, allied professional group and Putnam fringe group are:

Putnam accuser faction	Thomas Putnam Edward Putnam Jonathan Walcott Nathaniel Ingersoll John Putnam Sr. Nathaniel Putnam Jonathan Putnam John Putnam,Jr.
Allied professional group	Rev. Samuel Parris Dr. William Griggs
Putnam fringe group	Joseph Hutchinson Benjamin Hutchinson Joseph Houlton John Buxton

The first four girls afflicted in the witch hunt were **Elizabeth Parris** and **Abigail Williams** from Rev. Parris' household, **Ann Putnam Jr.**, the daughter of Sergeant Thomas Putnam, and **Elizabeth Hubbard**, servant in Dr. Griggs' household. These four were joined by **Mercy Lewis**, servant in Sergeant Putnam's household, and **Mary Walcott**, the daughter of Captain Jonathan Walcott. These six girls, all from the households of the four main members of the Putnam faction, comprised a select group which may be called the inner circle of the afflicted. Although there were other young girls in the families of the Putnam faction and it fringe groups, none ever appeared in any witchcraft proceeding. A depiction of the four households in which the inner circle of afflicted girls lived is:

Sergeant Thomas Putnam	Ann Putnam Jr. (daughter) Mercy Lewis (servant)
Dr. William Griggs	Elizabeth Hubbard (servant)
Rev. Samuel Parris	Elizabeth Parris (daughter) Abigail Williams (niece)
Captain Jonathan Walcott	Mary Walcott (daughter)

Soon others joined the ranks of the afflicted at Salem Village. One was **John Indian**, a slave belonging to Rev. Parris. Four other young women require special mention. The first is **Mary Warren**, age twenty, a servant in the house of John Proctor. The second is **Sarah Churchill**, also age twenty, a servant in the house of George Jacobs Jr. The third is **Susannah Sheldon**, age eighteen, who lived with her widowed mother Rebecca Sheldon. The fourth is **Elizabeth Booth**, age eighteen, who lived with her parents. These four, who were useful to the Putnam faction, made up the outer circle of the afflicted, and were recruited to work hand-in-hand with the inner circle.

The remainder of the afflicted in Salem Village consisted of several young women, and also a few older women, married and single, as well as a boy or two. These were kept at arm's length by the Putnam faction, who relegated them to a few minor and insignificant roles. The circle of afflicted girls of Salem Village is:

Inner circle of afflicted girls (the bewitched)	Ann Putnam Jr. Mercy Lewis Elizabeth Hubbard Elizabeth Parris Abigail Williams Mary Walcott
Outer circle of afflicted girls (the bewitched)	Mary Warren Sarah Churchill Susannah Sheldon Elizabeth Booth

The entries of the Complaint Table can be highlighted to clarify the work of the Putnam faction. Whenever the name of one or more members of the Putnam faction appears in an entry, the word Putnam faction is entered in its place. In a similar manner the words *Putnam fringe*, *Inner circle* and *Outer circle* are entered.

For example in the first complaint the names Thomas Putnam and Edward Putnam are replaced by *Putnam accuser faction*. The name Joseph Hutchinson is replaced by *Putnam fringe*. The names Elizabeth

Parris, Abigail Williams, Ann Putnam Jr., and Elizabeth Hubbard are replaced by *Inner circle*. If this scheme is followed for each entry, the following table is obtained.

Annotated Complaint Table for Salem Village©

Date	Accused	Accusers	Afflicted
No. 1 Feb. 29	Sarah Good Sarah Osborne Tituba	Putnam faction Putnam fringe Thomas Preston	Inner circle
No. 2 Mar. 19	Martha Corey	Putnam faction Fringe group Henry Kenny	Inner circle
No. 3 Mar. 23	Rebecca Nurse	Putnam faction	Inner circle
No. 4 Mar. 23	Dorothy (aka Dorcas) Good	Putnam faction	Inner circle
No. 5 Mar. 29	Rachel Clinton	Independent of Salem Village	
No. 6 Apr. 4	Sarah Cloyce Elizabeth Proctor	Putnam faction	Inner circle John Indian
No. 7 Apr. 11	John Proctor	Putnam faction	Inner circle John Indian
No. 8 Apr. 18	Giles Corey Bridget Bishop Abigail Hobbs Mary Warren	Putnam faction Ezekiel Cheever	Inner circle
No. 9 Apr. 21	William Hobbs Deliverance Hobbs Nehemiah Abbot Jr. Mary Easty Sarah Wildes Edward Bishop Jr. Sarah Bishop Mary Black Mary English	Putnam faction Putnam fringe	Inner circle
No. 10 Apr. 30	Philip English Lydia Dustin Susannah Martin Dorcas Hoar Sarah Morrell George Burroughs	Putnam faction	Inner circle Outer circle

No. 11 May 7	Sarah Dustin	Putnam faction	Inner circle
No. 12 May 8	Bethia Carter Bethia Carter Jr. Ann Sears	Putnam faction	Inner circle
No. 13 May 10	George Jacobs Sr. Margaret Jacobs	Putnam faction	Inner circle Outer circle
No. 14 May 10	John Willard	Benjamin Wilkins Sr. Thomas Fuller Jr.	Bray Wilkins Daniel Wilkins
No. 15 May 12	Alice Parker Ann Pudeator	Putnam faction	Inner circle Outer circle
No. 16 c. May 13	Abigail Somes	Putnam faction	Inner circle Outer circle
No. 17 May 14	Daniel Andrew George Jacobs Jr. Rebecca Jacobs Sarah Buckley Mary Whittredge Elizabeth Hart Thomas Farrar Elizabeth Colson	Putnam faction	Inner Circle
No. 18 May 15	Mehitabel Downing	Putnam faction	Outer circle
No. 19 May 18	Roger Toothaker	Putnam faction	Inner circle
No. 20 May 21	Sarah Proctor Sarah Bassett Susannah Roots	Putnam faction	Inner circle
No. 21 May 23	Benjamin Proctor Mary De Rich Sarah Pease	Putnam faction Thomas Rayment	Inner circle
No. 22 May 28	Elizabeth Cary	Putnam faction Putnam fringe	Inner circle

No. 23 May 28	John Alden John Floyd Elizabeth Fosdick Wilmot Redd Sarah Rice William Proctor Elizabeth Howe Arthur Abbot Martha Carrier Mary Toothaker Margaret Toothaker	Putnam faction	Inner circle
No. 24 May 30	Elizabeth Paine Elizabeth Fosdick	Putnam faction Joseph Whipple	Inner circle Outer circle
No. 25 Jun. 2	Elizabeth Paine Elizabeth Fosdick	Peter Tufts	Tufts' slave
No. 26 Jun. 4	Mary Ireson	Putnam faction Thomas Rayment	Inner circle Outer circle
No. 27 Jun. 3	Job Tookey	Putnam faction	Inner circle Outer circle Sarah Bibber
No. 28 Jun. 5	Ann Dolliver	Putnam faction	Inner circle Outer circle
No. 29 Jun. 28	Mary Bradbury	Putnam faction	Inner circle Outer circle
No. 30 Jul. 1	Margaret Hawkes Candy	Putnam faction	Inner circle Outer circle

In the above table, it is seen that out of thirty complaints only three were not originated by the Putnam accuser faction. Complaint No. 5 accusing Rachel Clinton is a special case involving the town of Ipswich. Complaint No. 14 accusing John Willard was filed by the Wilkins family with the complete approval and cooperation of the Putnam faction, who allowed the inner circle to act as seers as well as afflicted persons. Complaint No. 25 accusing Elizabeth Paine and Elizabeth Fosdick is especially interesting. This complaint, duplicating Complaint No. 24 filed by the Putnam faction, was filed by Peter Tufts, whose daughter-in-law was Maria (Cotton) Tufts. Because she was the first cousin of Rev. Cotton Mather, this complaint indirectly links him to the witch hunt.

Rev. Samuel Parris, age thirty-nine in 1692, was in effect the founder of the Putnam accuser faction. He lived in the Salem Village parsonage with his wife Elizabeth, age forty-four, their daughter Elizabeth Parris, called Betty, age nine, and his niece Abigail Williams, age eleven. Also he owned two slaves, Tituba and her husband, John Indian. The names of Betty and Abigail appeared on the first complaint, filed on February 29, 1692. It states that Betty and Abigail were afflicted by Sarah Good, Sarah Osborne, and Tituba. The complaint was filed by Thomas Putnam, his brother Edward Putnam, Joseph Houlton and Thomas Preston. Parris' name does not appear. Thomas Preston, in putting his name on this complaint, had been duped by the Putnam faction. The son-in-law of Rebecca Nurse, he quickly realized his folly and withdrew his support for the witchcraft proceedings.

Betty was an active participant in the courtroom until early April, when Rev. Parris withdrew her from further participation and sent her to live in Salem Town with the family of Stephen Sewall. The youngest of the afflicted girls, Betty was beginning to show preliminary symptoms of a mental breakdown. At his wife's insistence, he drew the line at the health of their daughter. His niece Abigail Williams was made of sterner stuff. After Betty left the circle, Abigail Williams and Ann Putnam Jr. continued as the most active of the group. They were now also the youngest.

In all, Abigail alleged she was afflicted by forty-four persons. She testified against many in court. Even Joseph Hutchinson, a member of the Thomas fringe, was upset by the outrageous lies of Abigail Williams. In a deposition he tried to discredit Abigail's veracity. Because Abigail was the niece of Rev. Parris, Hutchinson's deposition did little good.

Dr. William Griggs was another founding member of the accuser faction. Dr. Griggs and Rev. Parris were often brought together by their professional interests. In those days the approaches of physician and cleric in dealing with sickness were similar, converging somewhere between the occult and faith healing. The physical (sickness) and the spiritual (sin) were regarded as parts of the same whole. As already seen, Cotton Mather himself had studied medicine before entering the clergy. Originally from Boston, Dr. Griggs was the first physician to practice in Salem Village. In 1692, he was about seventy-seven years old and his wife, whose maiden name was Rachel Hubbard, was sixty-four years old. The Hubbard family was distinguished, whereas Griggs came from modest beginnings. Not particularly successful, he paid a tax of only sixteen shillings in Salem Village in 1690.

Elizabeth Hubbard, the great niece of Dr. Griggs' wife, was living with the old couple and working as their servant. Elizabeth was a good friend of Mary Walcott; both seventeen, they spent much time together. Dr. Griggs' house was only about one-half of a mile from Jonathan Walcott's house. However, on February 16, 1692, close to the start of the witch hunt, Dr. Griggs bought a better house, situated close to the Beverly line, nearly three miles from the Walcott house. Elizabeth still visited the Walcott house, but now she often spent the night. Ann Putnam Jr. and Mercy Lewis lived at Thomas Putnam's house, over a mile from the Walcott house. Ann managed to visit the Walcott house regularly to see her aunt and play with the children. Mercy Lewis often went with Ann; Mercy was the same age as Elizabeth Hubbard and Mary Walcott. Ann, only twelve, was friends with Abigail Williams, age eleven, who lived in Rev. Parris' parsonage, the nearest house to the Walcott house, just a few hundred feet away. Also at the parsonage was little Elizabeth Parris, age nine. These six girls, the two Elizabeths, Mary, Ann, Mercy, and Abigail, made up the inner circle.

As a physician, Dr. Griggs refrained from filing any legal complaints. However, we see his hand in the actions of his servant, Elizabeth Hubbard.[20] Elizabeth Hubbard maintained a spiteful and malicious role throughout the witchcraft scare. In a deposition, Clement Coldum

---

[20] At the examination of Elizabeth Proctor on April 11, 1692, "Benjamin Gould gave in his testimony that he had seen Goodman Corey and his wife, Proctor and his wife, Goody Cloyce, Goody Nurse, and Goody Griggs in his chamber last night. Elizabeth Hubbard was in a trance during the whole examination." Of course, Goodwife Griggs, being the wife of Dr. Griggs with his connection to the Putnam faction, was exempt from any possibility of being charged by the Putnam faction.

stated that on May 29, 1692 "I asked her if she was not afraid of the Devil? She answered me no, she could discourse with the Devil as well as with me." Coldum was ready to testify under oath as to his testimony. James Kettle was also willing to testify against Elizabeth and stated the "the last of May, having some discourse with Elizabeth Hubbard, I found her to speak several untruths." The records show that she was afflicted by seventeen persons, and she testified against many.

On February 10, 1693, when the witchcraft craze was coming to an end, Dr. Griggs, "being aged and infirm," conveyed his newly purchased house to his son, Jacob Griggs of Beverly. When Dr. Griggs died in 1698, his library consisted of "nine physic books," worth 30 shillings, and "bibles & other books," worth 15 shillings. His medical equipment included a case of lances, two razors, a saw, and seven instruments for chirurgeon [surgeon]. His wife survived him, living to be ninety.

Sergeant Thomas Putnam, age thirty-nine, a founding member of the accuser faction, acted as ringleader. Much can be learned by looking at events from the perspective of this man, the chief filer of the legal complaints that led to the arrest of alleged witches. Repeatedly he claimed that his eldest daughter, Ann Putnam Jr., and his servant Mercy Lewis were afflicted and tormented by a multitude of witches. Thomas Putnam demanded justice.

His wife Ann Putnam Sr.[21], age thirty, entered into this macabre witch hunt as an afflicted person on a number of occasions. In fact, Ann Putnam Sr. was in court almost as often as her daughter and her servant, all of them acting out the afflictions of witchcraft. Together, the three were responsible for the spectral evidence leading to many imprisonments, some of which resulted in death. Mother Ann and her daughter Ann were a perfect example of a particularly formidable pair

[21] Ann Putnam, Sr. was born on June 15, 1661 in Salisbury, the daughter of George Carr. In 1678 she married Thomas Putnam, born on March 12, 1653 in Salem Village. At the time of the outbreak of the Salem witchcraft in February 1692, Ann Putnam, Sr. had six children ranging from Ann, Jr., age 12, to Timothy, age ten months, and she was pregnant with Abigail.

of actors. People from miles around trooped into the courtroom to watch their performances under bewitchment. They regarded their afflictions as a matter of life and death. During the course of the witch hunt, Ann Putnam Jr. alleged that she was afflicted by a total of sixty-two persons. She testified against many people in court, and gave a number of affidavits.

In 1692 Mercy Lewis was a well-educated young woman. She was born in 1675, the daughter of Philip Lewis of Casco, Maine. The town was destroyed by the Indians in 1676. For the duration of the war, no white person ventured within this desolate locality, but after the conclusion of peace in November 1678, resettlement slowly took place. The Lewis family settled on Hogg Island as tenants of Edward Tyng. Tyng's main residence was on the Neck, the most desirable location in Casco, and the center of the present-day city of Portland. His closest neighbor was the minister, Rev. George Burroughs.

When Mercy Lewis' parents were both killed by the Indians in 1689, she was taken into the house of Rev. Burroughs. In 1690, as the only minister for all the towns between Casco and Wells, Maine, he took up residency in Wells. Because of the danger of repeated Indian attacks in Maine, Mercy was placed in the home of William and Rachel Bradford. Mercy lived a part of a year with them, during which they did "judge in the matter of conscience of speaking the truth and untruth, she would stand stiffly [following words are missing because the original document in torn]." She was finally placed as a servant in the home of Sergeant Thomas Putnam in Salem Village. According to the records she was afflicted by fifty-one persons. She testified against scores of people in court, and gave many affidavits against the accused witches. In her deposition against George Burroughs, she stated,

> "I saw the apparition of George Burroughs, whom I very well knew. He brought to me a new fashioned book, and told me I might write in that book, for that was a book that was in his study when I lived with them. But I told him, I did not believe him, for I had often been in his study, but I never saw that book there. But

> he told me that he had several books in his study which I never saw in his study, and he could raise the Devil."[22]

Although Sergeant Thomas Putnam operated mostly in the background, he did step out in the open to file legal complaints; indeed, he filed more than anyone else. In addition, he testified in a great number of cases, including those of Sarah Buckley, Rev. George Burroughs, Martha Carrier, Giles and Martha Corey, Mary Easty, Sarah Cloyce, Thomas Farrar Sr., Dorcas Hoar, George Jacobs Sr., Susannah Martin, Rebecca Nurse, Elizabeth and John Proctor, Sarah Proctor, Tituba, and John Willard. Of these people, ten were executed, and two condemned to death but reprieved at the final moment.

Sergeant Thomas Putnam's brother, Deacon Edward Putnam, age thirty-eight in 1692, was a member of the Putnam faction and the closest ally of Thomas Putnam in carrying out the witch hunt.

Another member, Captain Jonathan Walcott, was the father of Mary Walcott by his first wife. At the time of the witch hunt, he was fifty-two, and married to his second wife, Deliverance, the sister of Thomas and Edward Putnam. Not only did Captain Walcott encourage his daughter Mary Walcott to act out the role of an afflicted girl, but he testified with great effectiveness against many accused witches himself. Records show that Mary Walcott alleged that she was afflicted by fifty-nine persons. She gave many affidavits and frequently testified in court against people. Significantly, Mary Walcott and Ann Putnam Jr. were taken to Andover on June 11, 1692, to initiate a witch hunt in that area. Again, on July 26, the two girls visited that town to spur on the Andover witch hunt.

Thomas and Edward Putnam's sister Ann had been married to William Trask. Both she and William had died by 1692. Still, the Trask family helped the Putnams in the witch hunt. John Trask appeared as a

---

[22] On May 14, 1691 Priscilla Lewis, Mercy's older sister, married Henry Kenny, Jr. His father, Henry Kenny, was a signer of the complaint against Martha Corey and a witness against Rebecca Nurse.

witness against Sarah Bishop, the wife of Edward Bishop Jr. Sergeant Thomas Putnam's two uncles John Putnam Sr. and Nathaniel Putnam were eager to help. They were members of the faction, but were not as active as the younger Putnams.

John Putnam Sr. had married Rebecca Prince, step-daughter of John Gedney Sr., the wealthy owner of the Ship Tavern in Salem Town.[23] In 1692 John Putnam Sr. believed that his nephews, the two Prince boys, were being cheated out of their inheritance by Sarah Osborne. To destroy Sarah Osborne, John Putnam Sr. saw to it that she was one of the first three witches accused. Sarah Osborne died in prison a couple of months later. John Putnam Sr. also took his revenge on Rev. George Burroughs by testifying against him in the witchcraft trials.

John Putnam Sr.'s son, Constable Jonathan Putnam, was also a member of the faction. He and his first cousin, Edward Putnam, signed the complaint that put Rebecca Nurse behind bars, as well as the complaint that put four-year-old Dorothy (aka Dorcas) Good into chains.

The other uncle, Nathaniel Putnam, signed the complaint against Elizabeth Paine and Elizabeth Fosdick. His son, Constable John Putnam Jr., also a member of the faction, signed several complaints and testified against many.

Lieutenant Nathaniel Ingersoll, the innkeeper, was the final member of the faction. He was the uncle of Captain Jonathan Walcott. Lieutenant Ingersoll worked closely with Sergeant Thomas Putnam and Captain Walcott to keep the flames burning. With a wary eye toward maintaining goodwill so as not to impair the profits of his tavern, Ingersoll signed only a few complaints. However, when called as

---

[23] John Gedney, Sr., who died in 1688, was the father of John Gedney, Jr., who died in 1684, and Bartholomew Gedney, one of the witchcraft justices. After John Gedney, Jr. died, his widow moved into the house of John Gedney, Sr. and kept the tavern. Shortly thereafter, John Louder, one of the servants in the house, saw a "black thing" to which he testified in 1692 as evidence against Bridget Bishop. After John Gedney, Sr.'s death in 1688, his son's widow continued to keep the tavern, which in 1692 was known as the "Widow Gedney's."

witness he gladly testified against those accused. It was no coincidence that two of his competitors in Salem Village, tavern-owners John Proctor and Edward Bishop Jr. were both arrested for witchcraft, and that Proctor paid with his life.

Except for the departure of Elizabeth Parris, the inner circle of afflicted girls remained unchanged throughout the witch hunt. Of the six girls, only three, Elizabeth Parris, Ann Putnam Jr., and Mary Walcott, were living in their parents' homes. The other three, having lost one or both parents, had been placed in the faction's households, and, except for Abigail Williams, were servants. Since none of the four girls in the outer circle of afflicted lived in the households of the faction, they required careful control at all times.

The daughter of George and Elizabeth Booth of Salem Village, Elizabeth Booth, age eighteen, was a member of the outer circle, participating in examinations, inquests, and trials. Not a favorite of the Putnam faction, her name was only chosen for use on a couple of complaints. It appears on the warrant for the arrest of John Alden Jr. (Alden, the sea captain and trader who worked his ship along the Maine coast, had engaged in the fur trade with Indian friends before King William's War.) Elizabeth's actions as an afflicted girl were supported by her mother and younger sister, Alice, age fourteen. On October 11, 1692, nineteen days after the executions on September 22, Elizabeth Booth married Jonathan Pease, age twenty-three, and started a family of her own. Her afflictions were over; of the witches whose apparitions had hurt her, John Proctor and Wilmot Redd had been hanged, Giles Corey pressed to death, and the pregnant Elizabeth Proctor was in prison, sentenced to death, but under reprieve until the child was born.

Susannah Sheldon, age eighteen, another member of the outer circle, suffered from a deep and abiding fear of the Indians. Her parents, Rebecca (Scadlock) and William Sheldon had resided in Saco, Maine, but were driven out by the Indians in 1676 during King Philip's War. Susannah was only a baby at the time. She barely escaped death as the family fled the slaughter which ensued. Taking up residence in Salem, the family returned to Saco as soon as it was safe. With the outbreak of King William's War, the Indians again destroyed their farm. The family escaped death, but this time Susannah's father was badly wounded in trying to protect her. The family then moved to Salem Village.

Susannah's older brother, Godfrey, age twenty-four, encountered the Indians in Maine on July 3, 1690 in the service of his country. Surprised in an ambush, some of the soldiers panicked and tried to flee. Godfrey was last seen alive being pursued into the forest by a stout Indian, brightly daubed in war-paint, a gun in one hand and a hatchet in the other. Godfrey's hacked body was later found without its scalp.

Susannah's father, crippled by his wounds, fell and cut his knee. He died two weeks later, on December 2, 1691, less than three months before the witchcraft outbreak. Susannah stayed on in Salem Village with her widowed mother and remaining siblings. Having lost everything to the Indians, they were almost destitute. Cotton Mather and other divines were constantly railing that witches and Indians both were agents of the Devil. The records show that Susannah was afflicted by eleven alleged witches, and bore witness against them in examinations, inquests, and trials.

Mary Warren, age twenty, who proved to be the most faithful and dependable member of the outer circle, was an orphan. At the outset of the witch hunt she was a servant in the household of John Proctor of Salem Farms, a part of Salem Township just south of Salem Village. Both John Proctor and his wife were imprisoned on April 11, 1692. On April 18, one week later, Mary Warren herself was accused and imprisoned at Salem. The complaint was filed by Ezekiel Cheever and John Putnam Jr. for afflicting the inner circle girls. Rev. Parris' description of Mary Warren's examination on April 19 is dramatic. Mary Warren accused her master, John Proctor, and his wife Elizabeth, as well as Giles Corey. At the end of his description, Rev. Parris notes "that not one of the sufferers was afflicted during her examination after once she began to confess, though they were tormented before."

Mary Warren displeased the conspirators when she wanted to tell the truth. Imprisoned witches Mary Easty, Edward Bishop Jr. and his wife, Sarah, gave the following deposition which states how Mary Warren discredited the afflicted girls:

> "About three weeks ago today, when we were in Salem Jail, we heard Mary Warren several times say that the magistrates might as well examine Keyser's daughter, who has been distracted many years, and take notice of what she said as well as any of the afflicted persons. Mary Warren said when I was afflicted I thought I saw the apparitions of a hundred persons. She said her head was distempered; that she could not tell what she said. And Mary told us that when she was well again, she could not say that she saw any of [the] apparitions at the time aforesaid."

Early in June, however, Mary Warren was released and allowed to continue her active participation in the afflicted group. Altogether she claimed to have been afflicted by fourteen persons.

Sarah Churchill, age twenty, was the second most dependable member of the outer circle. She came from a family in Saco, Maine with considerable property and a heritage of English gentry. After her parents had been killed by the Indians, she was reduced to the position of servant in the household of George Jacobs Sr. of Salem. Soon after the outbreak of the witch hunt, she became one of the afflicted. Jacobs called the afflicted girls "bitch witches" and was otherwise very disrespectful of her. Sarah was often in court as part of the afflicted group. She was also a witness against her master.

George Jacobs Sr. was imprisoned on May 10, as was his granddaughter, Margaret Jacobs. Shortly thereafter, Sarah Churchill herself was accused and imprisoned. Her name appeared on the list of those in Salem Prison, along with Mary Warren. Sarah Churchill had angered the Putnam faction because she, too, wanted to tell the truth. Sarah Ingersoll, who worked in the tavern, gave this deposition. "Sarah Churchill after her examination came to me crying. She said she had lied in saying that she set her hand to the Devil's book. She lied because they threatened her and told her they would put her into the dungeon, along with Rev. Burroughs. She said she had undone herself in belying herself and others. She said also that if she told Mr. Noyes [assistant minister at Salem] but once that she had set her hand to the book, he would believe her, but, if she told the truth and said that she had not set her hand to the book a hundred times, he would not believe her." Sarah Ingersoll was the daughter of conspirator Nathaniel Ingersoll.

On June 1, 1692 Sarah Churchill testified that her master, George Jacobs Sr., as well as Ann Pudeator and Bridget Bishop, made her a witch. Sarah's imprisonment was of short duration, as she was in court again on July 2 to testify against Ann Pudeator.

Mary Warren and Sarah Churchill were the only two afflicted girls to be imprisoned, albeit briefly. Both were taken shortly after their masters had been incarcerated. The extant depositions show that the two were distressed with the roles they were playing in the witch hunt, and wanted to tell the truth. But naturally, being terrified in prison, they preferred to return to their acting. Each 20 years old, they were older than all the rest of the afflicted in the circle, and as servants and orphans they stood alone in a dangerous world.

John Indian, husband of Tituba, was used in court as an afflicted person. He could reliably demonstrate how grievously he was tormented by whoever was under examination. No doubt he was convinced that he would stand a better chance of survival among the afflicted than among the accused, and sensibly, he played his part well. It is most probable that others who joined the ranks of the afflicted from time to time acted from the same pragmatic standpoint. None, however, gained admittance to the favored circles, inner or outer, of the Salem Village afflicted.

In February 1692, the Putnam faction never could have guessed the extremes to which they would be allowed to go. Its members suspected that vindictive people in Salem Village and neighboring communities would support their cause of rooting out certain undesirable people as witches. They trusted that the powerful personage, John Hathorne, who gave original encouragement, would continue in his support. What they could not foresee, however, was that the highest level of government, the ruling, old-guard Puritans, would not only act in collusion to support their cause of destroying the "enemies of the church," but would give them a free hand in determining who those enemies were.

The word clergy refers to a group of people who were assigned to take care of the needs of the people of the church. Puritans were the main religious group in Massachusetts. Their views come from a Calvinistic approach to the Bible. The Puritans did not separate from the Church of England in theory, but did so in practice. They believed the Church of England had not completed its reformation and so they could not accept it in its current form. The Puritans strongly rejected Quakers and Baptists. By 1692 the Puritan clergy was more or less separated into two groups: (1) lenient pastors who accepted or tolerated different kinds of Christians, and strict pastors who demanded faithful adherence to the rules. In the same way, governmental authorities were more or less separated into two groups: (1) lenient authorities who accepted other Christian faiths (except Catholic) in the colony and strict authorities (the so-called old guard) who wanted only Puritan congregations. By 1692, England had decisively put down its heavy foot. Massachusetts would no longer be a self-governing colony with an elected governor but would be a province of the crown of England with an appointed governor. Over the previous years the strict Puritan clergy and the Puritan old-guard authorities had done everything in their power to prevent this perceived disaster. In their hearts, they believed that their cause was just. It followed that they must have been defeated by supernatural power. It was witchcraft. Witches were the agents of the devil.

We do not know the minds of men and women, and we never will. We do not know who actual believed in witchcraft, and who did not. However we do know how they lined up. Of the clergy we know that Cotton Mather was strict and was lenient. Of the authorities we know that the old guard was strict and much of the rest was lenient.

In the Salem Village witch hunt, a hierarchical structure exists. The strict Puritan clergy and the old-guard Puritan rulers were at the top. They sanctioned the agents, consisting of the Putnam faction of accusers and their afflicted circle of girls. Under them are the people who suffered, predominantly women, accused as witches. At the base is the mass of the populace who were not affected directly. Come of them were summoned on special occasions to provide malicious gossip about their accused neighbors. This structure is explained in the following table.

The Hierarchy of the Witch Hunt

Sponsor: Authoritarian clergy	A small but influential number of Puritan ministers intent on retaining tight control of their congregations. The threat of witches was a contrivance to explain things beyond their control.
Sponsor: Old guard Puritans	Key members of the upper legislative body (board of assistants or council) and various magistrates. Accustomed to ruling with an iron hand, and fearing the general franchise granted by the new charter, they sought to keep the population under their control at all costs.
Agent: The Accusers	A faction of envious and vengeful men (such as the Putnam faction) who saw in the real or imagined sicknesses of their children the means to bring down their enemies.
Agent: The Afflicted	Children caught up in the hysteria sanctioned and supervised by the accusers.
Victim: The Accused	Women, and some men and children, who were members of families that attracted the wrath of the old guard or the envy of the accusers.
Remaining population: The Unaffected	The remaining population who watched, acquiescent, until they saw that anyone was fair game.

Complaint Table for Andover

We have put together a series of legal complaints that were filed from July 15, 1692 to September 7, 1692. This period represents the second half of the Salem witchcraft delusion, and is known as the Andover witch hunt. In the case of the Andover, many documents were lost or destroyed. Still, for an event that took place more than three hundred years ago, enough survive so that a reasonably detailed story can be pieced together despite some serious gaps in the record. In the Complaint Table we have also included the May 28 entry for Andover resident Martha Carrier, which technically is part of the Salem Village witch hunt. This entry links the two witch hunts. Martha Carrier of Andover was arrested on May 28, 1692. Seven weeks later, on July 15, the second person of Andover was arrested. The chosen victim, Ann Foster, owned valuable land.

Complaint Table for the Andover witch hunt in 1692©

Date 1692	Accused Witch	Plaintiffs	Afflicted
May 28	Martha (Allen) Carrier; about 38, condemned, hanged	*complaint:* Jonathan Walcott Joseph Houlton	*complaint:* Mary Walcott Ann Putnam Jr. Abigail Williams Mercy Lewis
July 15	Ann Foster, about 72, condemned and died in prison	*inference:* Joseph Ballard	*inference:* Elizabeth (Phelps) Ballard
July 19	Mary (Foster) Lacey, 40, condemned, survived	*complaint:* Joseph Ballard	*complaint:* Elizabeth (Phelps) Ballard
July 19	Mary Lacey Jr., 18	*complaint:* Joseph Ballard	*complaint:* Elizabeth (Phelps) Ballard
July 21	Richard Carrier, 18		*warrant:* Mary Warren
July 21	Andrew Carrier, 15		*warrant:* Mary Warren
July 22	Martha (Toothaker) Emerson, 24, of Haverhill		*warrant:* Mary Warren Mary Lacey Jr.

July 28	Mary (Tyler) Post Bridges, about 50		*warrant:* Timothy Swan
About Aug. 1	Rebecca (Blake) Eames, 51, of Boxford (attended Andover Church)		*examination* Timothy Swan
Aug. 2	Mary Post, 28, condemned, survived	*complaint & warrant* Timothy Swan Mary Walcott Ann Putnam Jr.	*complaint & warrant:* Timothy Swan Mary Walcott Ann Putnam Jr.
Aug. 3	Mary (Johnson) Davis Clarke, about 52, of Haverhill (first accused of the Johnson Family)	*complaint:* Robert Swan John Swan	*complaint:* Timothy Swan Mary Walcott Ann Putnam Jr.
by Aug. 10	Daniel Eames, 29, of Boxford (attended Andover Church)		
Aug. 10	Elizabeth Johnson Jr., 22, condemned, survived		*examination:* Sarah Phelps Mary Walcott Ann Putnam Jr. Timothy Swan
Aug. 10	Thomas Carrier Jr., 10		*examination:* Sarah Phelps Ann Putnam. Jr. Mary Walcott
Aug. 10	Sarah Carrier, 7		*examination:* Sarah Phelps Ann Putnam Jr.
Aug. 11	Abigail (Dane) Faulkner, 40, condemned, survived		*examination:* Sarah Phelps
Aug. 15	Edward Farrington, 30		*indictment:* Mary Warren
Aug. 15	Sarah Parker, 22		
Aug. 15	Samuel Wardwell, 49, condemned, hanged		*indictment:* Martha Sprague
Aug. 25	Mary Bridges Jr., 13		*examination:* Martha Sprague Rose Foster
Aug. 25	Sarah Bridges, about 17		*examination:* Martha Sprague Rose Foster

Aug. 25	Hannah Post, 26		*examination:* Martha Sprague Rose Foster
Aug. 25	Susannah Post, about 31		*examination:* Martha Sprague Rose Foster
Aug. 25	William Barker Sr., about 46	*warrant:* Samuel Martin Moses Tyler	*warrant:* Abigail Martin Martha Sprague Rose Foster
Aug. 25	Mary Barker, 13	*warrant:* Samuel Martin Moses Tyler	*warrant:* Abigail Martin Martha Sprague Rose Foster
Aug. 25	Mary (Osgood) Marston, 27	*warrant:* Samuel Martin Moses Tyler	*warrant:* Abigail Martin Martha Sprague Rose Foster
Aug. 25	John Jackson Sr., about 49, of Rowley	*complaint:* Ephraim Foster Joseph Tyler	*complaint:* Rose Foster Martha Sprague
Aug. 25	John Jackson Jr., 22, of Rowley	*complaint:* Ephraim Foster Joseph Tyler	*complaint:* Rose Foster Martha Sprague
Aug. 25	John Howard, about 47, of Rowley	*complaint:* Ephraim Foster Joseph Tyler	*complaint:* Rose Foster Martha Sprague
Aug. 29	Elizabeth (Dane) Johnson, about 51	*warrant:* Samuel Martin Moses Tyler	*warrant:* Abigail Martin Martha Sprague
Aug. 29	Abigail Johnson, 10	*warrant:* Samuel Martin Moses Tyler	*warrant:* Abigail Martin Martha Sprague
Aug. 29	Stephen Johnson, 13		*examination:* Martha Sprague Rose Foster Mary Lacey Jr.
Sept. 1	William Barker Jr., 14		*examination:* Martha Sprague Rose Foster Abigail Martin

Sept. 1	Sarah (Hooper) Hawkes Wardwell, 42, condemned, survived		*examination:* Martha Sprague Abigail Martin Rose Foster
Sept. 1	Sarah Hawkes, 21		*examination:* Martha Sprague Rose Foster
Sept. 1	Mercy Wardwell, 19		*examination:* Martha Sprague Rose Foster Timothy Swan
Sept. 1	Mary (Ayer) Parker, about 55, condemned, hanged		*examination:* Martha Sprague Sarah Phelps
Sept. 7	Mary (Clement) Osgood, about 55		*touch test*
Sept. 7	Eunice (Potter) Frye, 51		*touch test*
Sept. 7	Abigail (Wheeler) Barker, 36		*touch test*
Sept. 7	Mary (Lovett) Tyler, about 40		*touch test*
Sept. 7	Hannah Tyler, 14		*touch test*
Sept. 7	Joanna Tyler, 11		*touch test*
Sept. 7	Martha Tyler, 11		*touch test*
Sept. 7	Deliverance (Haseltine) Dane, about 37		*touch test*
Sept. 7	Rebecca (Aslet) Johnson, 40		*touch test*
Sept. 7	Rebecca Johnson Jr., 17		*touch test*
Sept. 7	Abigail Faulkner Jr., 9		*touch test*
Sept. 7	Dorothy Faulkner, 12		*touch test*
Sept. 7	Sarah (Lord) Wilson, about 44		*touch test*
Sept. 7	Sarah Wilson Jr., 14		*touch test*
Sept. 7	John Sadie Jr., about 13		*touch test*
Sept. 7	Henry Salter, about 65		*touch test*
Sept. 7	Joseph Draper, 21		*touch test*
Sept. 7	Male Slave of Rev. Dane		*touch test*

The first step in identifying complicity is the elimination of the Salem Village girls Abigail Williams, Ann Putnam Jr., Mercy Lewis, Mary Walcott, and Mary Warren, as they were instruments of the Salem

Village witch hunt. Next eliminate Mary Lacey Jr., an imprisoned witch, brought into the courtroom to act as an afflicted person. Associate each Andover afflicted girl with her father, or in the case of Martha Sprague with her stepfather and stepbrother. Three married women also were afflicted; associate them with their husbands. Timothy Swan acted both as an afflicted and an accuser; his two brothers were also accusers. The men so determined were the legal accusers, the plaintiffs. The following table is the result.

Legal accuser	Afflicted circle
Joseph Ballard, 50	Elizabeth (Phelps) Ballard, 46
Samuel Phelps, 41	Sarah Phelps Jr., 10
Daniel Bigsby, 41	Hannah (Chandler) Bigsby, 35
Robert Swan Jr., 35 Timothy Swan, 29 John Swan, 24	Timothy Swan, 29
Moses Tyler, about 50 Joseph Tyler, 21	Martha Sprague, 16
Ephraim Foster, 35	Hannah (Eames) Foster, 31 Rose Foster, 14
Samuel Martin, 47	Abigail Martin Jr., 16

The table shows the names of ten legal accusers, a small group. To these add the name of Thomas Chandler, father-in-law of accusers Daniel Bigsby and Samuel Phelps. This small and interwoven group of eleven filed all the complaints in the Andover witch hunt. Thus the table plays the role of a "smoking gun" in exposing complicity. Like the Salem Village witch hunt, the Andover witch hunt was not driven by uncontrolled mass hysteria, but by the planned and deliberate actions of a mall group, called the Andover faction.

Accused witches in the Andover witch hunt

The names of the afflicted boldly standing forth in the complaint table. The next step is to associate each of the afflicted with his or her parent or guardian, the accuser. The result is the table:

Afflicted	Accuser
Martha Sprague, aged 16	Moses Tyler, aged about 50
Timothy Swan, aged 29	Timothy Swan, aged 29 Robert Swan Jr. John Swan, aged 24
Hannah (Chandler) Bigsby, aged 35	Daniel Bigsby, aged 41
Hannah (Eames) Foster, aged 31 Rose Foster, aged 14	Ephraim Foster, aged 35
Abigail Martin, aged 15	Samuel Martin, aged 47
Sarah Phelps, aged 10	Samuel Phelps, aged 41

The table shows that the accusers were members of a small group, which we call the Andover accuser faction. It can be concluded that this group acted in complicity. Like the Salem Village witch hunt, the Andover witch hunt was not driven by mass hysteria but by a faction. The Andover accuser faction consisted of the following persons:

The leader was Moses Tyler, aged about 50. He resided in Boxford near the Andover line. However, he was a member of the Andover church, as had been his first wife, Prudence (Blake) Tyler, who had died in 1689. His second wife was Sarah (Hasey) Sprague Tyler, aged about 45. She brought to this marriage her daughter, Martha Sprague, by her first husband Phineas Sprague who died in 1689. Martha Sprague, aged 16,as afflicted girl. Joseph Tyler, aged 21, son of Moses Tyler by his first wife Prudence (Blake) Tyler, was a conspirator.

Three sons of Robert Swan, an influential man in local and high government circles were in the Andover accuser faction. The first, Robert Swan Jr, resided in the north part of Andover with his wife Elizabeth (Storey) Swan, aged 27. The second, Timothy, aged 29, was a bachelor residing in the north part of Andover. Timothy Swan was an afflicted man. The third, John Swan, aged 24, was also bachelor residing in the north part of Andover.

Daniel Bigsby, aged 41, was in the Andover accuser faction. He resided in the south part of Andover with his wife Hannah (Chandler) Bigsby, aged 35. Hannah was an afflicted woman.

Ephraim Foster, aged 35, was in the Andover accuser faction. He was constable for the north part of Andover, where he resided with his wife, Hannah (Eames) Foster, aged 31. His wife Hannah and their oldest daughter, Rose Foster, aged 14, were both afflicted. Ephraim Foster had no family connection with the accused Ann Foster. Foster was a common name in New England, and Ephraim Foster was not related to the first settler Andrew Foster, the deceased husband of Ann Foster.

Samuel Martin, aged 47, was in the Andover accuser faction. He resided in the north part of Andover with his wife Abigail (Norton) Martin, aged 41. Their daughter Abigail Martin, aged 15, was afflicted.

Samuel Phelps, aged 41, was in the Andover accuser faction. He resided in the south end with his wife Sarah (Chandler) Phelps, aged 30. Their daughter Sarah Phelps, aged 10, was afflicted.

Two things stand out about the Andover accuser faction. They made vicious attacks against the family, direct and extended, of Rev. Francis Dane. Simultaneously, they viciously attacked the old proprietary families of Andover. The original settlers, the proprietors of Andover, exercised control of the town, and there was much resentment by some of the other citizens who were excluded from this privileged group. In 1692 this resentment exploded. The main purpose of the Andover accuser faction was to break the political power structure exercised by these old families in Andover, and also to obtain all land and estates that they could get. The faction picked out certain targeted people who they accused of witchcraft for bewitching the afflicted ones just named. Of course, whenever possible the faction also used the witchcraft accusations as a means of settling old grudges. In the case of Moses Tyler, he was even willing to use the witchcraft slander to bring down his own siblings.

The first families made up a small closely-knit group, most of whom were interrelated by marriage. Four or five selectmen were elected each year to run the town. (In New England, a town was governed not by a mayor but by a group of selectmen who were elected at the town meeting by the proprietors of the town.) For the 23-year period from

1670 to 1692, all these selectmen positions were filled by just 24 men representing the first families with one exception. John Marston Jr. who settled in Andover in 1664, was the only outsider ever to penetrate this exclusive group.

Over one-half of the first families, the ones who were wealthy in land and authority had members accused of witchcraft in 1692. Why? Of the 23 first families of Andover, the proprietors, the following suffered witchcraft accusations in 1692.

Mr. Simon Bradstreet
John Osgood
Joseph Parker
Richard Barker
John Stevens
John Frye
Edmond Faulkner
Nathan Parker
John Aslett
Richard Blake (related to George Blake of Gloucester)
Andrew Allen
Andrew Foster

In brief this was the sequence. The family of first settler Andrew Allen was brutally attacked by witchcraft accusations. His daughters Mary (Allen) Toothaker and Martha (Allen) Carrier were both arrested on May 28, 1692. Mary's husband, Dr. Roger Toothaker, had already been arrested on May 18, 1692. He was murdered in prison in Boston on June 16, and Martha (Allen) Carrier was hanged in August 19, 1692 in Salem. A daughter of Mary (Allen) Toothaker and four children of Martha (Allen) Carrier were also arrested and imprisoned. First settler Andrew Foster died in 1685. His widow Ann Foster, age about 65, was an easy target. She was arrested on July 15, 1692, convicted September 17 but reprieved from death, but then died in prison in December 1692. Both her daughter Mary (Foster) Lacey and her granddaughter Mary Lacey Jr. were also imprisoned for witchcraft.

On August 11, 1692, Abigail (Dane) Faulkner was arrested and imprisoned. One of the highest ranking women in Andover, she was the daughter of Rev. Francis Dane. Her husband was Francis Faulkner, the son of the first settler Edmond Faulkner. Their daughters Dorothy Faulkner, aged 12, and Abigail Faulkner Jr., aged 9, were also imprisoned. During the week of August 15, 1692, Sarah Parker, aged 22, was arrested. She was the daughter of first settler Nathan Parker. Her father Nathan was deceased, and she lived with her widowed mother, Mary (Ayer) Parker and her brother Joseph. The widow Mary Parker was then imprisoned on September 2 and hanged in Salem on September 22. The first settlers Nathan Parker and Joseph Parker were brothers.

On August 19, 1692, Rebecca (Blake) Eames, aged 51, of Boxford was imprisoned. She was convicted on September 17, but reprieved for confession. After seven months in prison she was released. Rebecca was the daughter of George Blake of Gloucester. Her father George Blake is related to first settler Richard Blake of Andover. On August 25, 1692, William Barker, aged 46, and Mary Barker, aged 13, were imprisoned. William Barker was the second son of first settler Richard Barker, and Mary Barker was a daughter of Lieut. John Barker, the oldest son of Richard. Mary Barker's mother (the wife of Lieut. John Barker) was Mary (Stevens) Barker, the daughter of first settler John Stevens. On September 1, William Barker Jr. aged 14, the son of William Barker, was imprisoned. On September 8, Abigail (Wheeler) Barker, aged 25, was imprisoned. She was the wife of Ebenezer Barker, the third son of Richard Barker.

As we have just seen, Mary (Stevens) Barker, the granddaughter of first settler John Stevens was imprisoned on August 25, 1692. On about September 8, Ephraim Stevens was accused of witchcraft (as described in Thomas Brattle's letter of October 8, 1692). First settler John Osgood was second only in rank to Simon Bradstreet in Andover. His eldest son, John Osgood Jr. was the captain of the Andover militia company. On September 8, 1692, the captain's wife, Mary (Clement) Osgood, was arrested at the Andover touch-test. Also arrested at the same time and place was Eunice (Potter) Frye. She wife of Deacon John Frye Jr., who was the son of first settler John Frye. The two women were imprisoned for 15 weeks. They were bailed out of prison on December 20 on recognizance bonds of 200 pounds sterling posted by their husbands. Because of her high status, Mary (Clement) Osgood had been interviewed by Rev. Increase Mather in prison.

Dudley Bradstreet was son of first settler Simon Bradstreet. About September 18, 1692, Dudley and his wife were accused as witches, but they managed to flee to avoid arrest. Afflicted girls produced spectral evidence that he and his wife had committed nine murders.

Enders Robinson, aged 19, Reserve Officers' Training Corps

Chapter 7. Role of confession

John Calvin on confessing sins

John Calvin (*Institutes of the Christian Religion: The First English Version of the 1541* French Edition) writes

> "As for the confession of sins, scripture teaches us thus: because it is the Lord who forgives, forgets, and wipes out sins, let us confess to Him to obtain grace and pardon. He is the Physician so let us show Him our wounds and sores. It is He who has been offended and wounded so let us ask of Him mercy and peace. It is He who knows the hearts and sees all the thoughts so let us open our hearts before Him. It is He who calls sinners so let us withdraw to Him. David says: "I have made known to you my sin and I have not hidden my iniquity. I said, `I will confess against myself, I will confess my unrighteousness to the Lord, and you have pardoned the iniquity of my heart"' (Ps. 32[5]).
>
> "To whom do we confess them? To Him certainly. That is, if with an afflicted and humbled heart we bow ourselves before Him; if in true sincerity, rebuking and condemning ourselves before His face, we ask to be absolved by His goodness and mercy. Whoever makes this confession of heart before God will also no doubt have a tongue ready to confess, when there is need to proclaim God's mercy among the people."

Confession of Hugh Stone

Hugh Stone's origins are as yet unknown, but there is a strong possibility that he is from Somerset/Devonshire area in England. He married Hannah Foster in 1667. He murdered his wife on April 20, 1689, for which he was hanged. Rev. Cotton Mather wrote the following account of the *Execution of Hugh Stone* (*Magnalia Christi Americana*, 1698). It contains the only surviving words of Rev. Thomas Barnard. Barnard's words clearly demonstrate belief in the value of confession. Cotton Mather's account reads as follows:

One Hugh Stone, upon a quarrel between himself and his wife, about selling a piece of land, having some words, as they were walking together on a certain evening, very barbarously reached a stroke at her throat, with a sharp knife; and by that one stroke fetched away the soul of her who had made him a father of several children, and would have yet brought another to him if she had lived a few weeks longer in the world.
The wretched man was too soon surprised by his neighbors to be capable of denying the fact; and so he pleaded guilty upon his trial.

There was a minister [i.e., Thomas Barnard] that walked with him to his execution; and I shall insert the principle passages of the discourses between them; in which the reader may find or make something useful to himself, whatever it were to the poor man, who was more immediately concerned in it.
Minister: I am come to give you what assistance I can in your taking of the steps, which your eternal weal or woe now depends upon the well or ill taking of.

Hugh Stone: Sir, I thank you, and beg you to do what you can for me.

M = Minister: Within a few minutes, your immortal soul must appear before God, the judge of all. I am heartily sorry you have lost so much time since your first imprisonment: you had need use a wonderful husbandry of the little piece of an inch which now remains. Are you now prepared to stand before the tribunal of God?

H = Hugh Stone: I hope I am.

M: And what reason for that hope?

H: I find all my sins made so bitter to me, that if I were to have my life given me the afternoon, to live such a life as I have lived heretofore, I would not accept of it. I had rather die.

M. That is well, if it be true. But suffer me a little to search into the condition of your soul. Are you sensible that you were born a sinner? that the guilt of the first sin committed by Adam is justly charged upon you? and that you have hereupon a wicked nature in you, full of enmity against all that is holy, and just, and good? for which you deserved to be destroyed as soon as you first came into this world?

H: I am sensible of this.

M: Are you further sensible, that you have livíd a very ungodly life? that you are guilty of thousands of actual sins, every ne which deserves the wrath and curse of God? both in this life and that which is to come?

H: I am sensible of this also.

M: But are you sensible that you have broken all the laws of God? You know the commandments. Are you sensible that you have broken every one of them?
H: I cannot answer yes to that. My answer may be liable to some exceptions.

M: Alas, that you know yourself no better than so! I do affirm to you that you have particularly broken every one of the commandments; and you must be sensible of it.

H: I cannot see it.

M: But you must remember that the commandment is exceedingly broad; it reaches to the heart as well as the life: it excludes omissions as well as commissions; and it at once both requires and forbids. **But, I pray, make an experiment upon any**

one commandment, in which you count yourself most innocent: and see whether you do not presently confess yourself guilty thereabout. I will not leave this point slightly passed over with you.

H: That commandment, "thou shalt not make to thy self any graven image:" how have I broken it?

M: Thus: you have had undue images of God in your mind a thousand times. But more than so; that commandment not only forbids our using the inventions of men in the worship of God, but it also requires our using all the institutions of God. Now, have not you many and many a time turned your back upon some of those glorious institutions?

H: Indeed, **Sir, I confess it: I see my sinfulness greater than I thought it was.**

M: You better see it. God help you to see it! there is a boundless ocean of it. And then for that sin which has now brought a shameful death upon you, tis impossible to declare the aggravations of it; hardly an age will show the like. **You have professed yourself sorry for it**.

H: I am heartily so.

M: But your sorrows must be after a godly sort. Not merely because of the miseries which it has brought on your outward man, but chiefly for the wrongs and wounds therein given to your own soul; and not only for the miseries you have brought on yourself, but chiefly for the injuries which you have done to the blessed God.

H: I hope my sorrow lies there.

M: But do you mourn without hope?

H: I thank God that I do not.

M: Where do you see a door of hope?

H: In the Lord Jesus Christ, who has died to save sinners.

M: Truly, "there is no other name by which we may be saved." The righteousness of the Lord Jesus Christ is that alone in which you may safely appear before the judgment seat of God. **And that righteousness is, by the marvelous and infinite grace of God, offered unto you.** But do you find that, as you have no righteousness, so you have no strength? that you cannot of yourself move or stir towards the Lord Jesus Christ? that it is the "grace of God" alone which must enable you to accept of salvation form the great Savior? . . . Your crime lay in blood; and your help also, that lies in blood. I am to offer you the blood of the Lord Jesus Christ, as that in which you may now have the pardon for all your sins. Well, we are now but a few paces from the place where you must breathe your last. You are going to take a most awful step, which has this most remarkable [quality] in it: that it cannot be twice taken. If you go wrong now, it cannot be recalled throughout the days of eternity. I can but commit you into the arms of a merciful Redeemer.

After this, he was, by the prayers of a minister [Rev. Thomas Barnard] then present, recommended to the divine mercy. Which being done the poor man poured out a few broken ejaculations, in the midst of which he was turned over into that eternity which we must leave him in.

Compare this with the treatment given to the victims condemned for the imaginary crime of witchcraft in 1692. The clergy present at the hangings offered no prayers.

The confessors

In Salem Village, the pastor, Rev Samuel Parris, was at great odds with about half of the parish. Salem Village was divided into two warring camps. Andover had two ministers. One was the older Francis Dane with no formal education. The other was the younger Thomas Barnard with a Harvard education. Except for the usual and expected differences, the people in Andover were united. "From all historical evidence, the two ministers served their one church without any serious friction. Indeed their personalities seemed to complement each other; and common goals, for the good of their parish, they shared." In conclusion, Salem Village has one minister and two warring groups in the town. Andover had two ministers, and appeared to have united people. As it turns out, Andover was divided into two warring camps; namely, families of the first settlors and the Johnny-come-lately families.

The first confession of witchcraft was from Tituba, the female slave of Rev. Parris, arrested on March 1, 1692. A leading question suggests the particular answer that the examiner wants confirmed. It allows the examiner to direct or influence the evidence presented. Their use of is strictly controlled in courtrooms today. However, in 1692 the accused was forbidden to have a defense lawyer and leading questions were commonplace. By leading questions, Hathorne obtained from Tituba the evidence that he wanted. Her confession contained the distinctive features of witchcraft as preached by ministers like Cotton Mather.

Only four others—Abigail Hobbs, Deliverance Hobbs, Margaret Jacobs and the slave Candy—confessed out of the more than seventy-five persons arrested in the Salem Village witch hunt. Abigail Hobbs confessed in court and said, "I hope God will forgive me." The magistrate said "The Lord give you repentance," which was a boost to confession.

Except for these five, all of the others refused to confess for any reason. Instead they suffered irons and even death. Rebecca Nurse and others went to the gallows knowing that their husbands and children supported them in their refusal to confess. The failure of the authorities to obtain a significant number of confessions weakened the credibility of the entire Salem Village witch hunt. The witchcraft persecutions in Andover represent the exact opposite. Almost all of the Andover accused confessed. The Andover confessions all follow the same script; namely, Satan's attack on the Puritan Church.

Almost immediately after the executions on August 19, 1692, Cotton Mather wrote that the five non-confessing victims of hanging [Rev. George Burroughs, John Proctor, John Willard, George Jacobs Sr., and Martha Carrier] were "imprudently demanding of God a miraculous vindication of their innocence." Instead of finding the hanging shocking, Cotton Mather found the judges' sentences "miraculously confirmed." His reason was that "immediately upon" hanging, five people from the town of Andover made "a most ample, surprising confession" of witchcraft, and declared the five newly executed of have been of their company. In other words, Cotton Mather believed that the hanging of non-confessing witches somehow induced five accused witches in Andover to confess. These five Andover confessors were

1. Ann Foster, aged 72, arrested July 15
2. Ann's daughter Mary (Foster) Lacey, aged 40, arrested July 19
3. Ann's granddaughter Mary Lacey Jr., aged 18, arrested July 21
4. Richard Carrier, aged 18, arrested July 21
5. Andrew Carrier, aged 15, arrested July 15

The European witchcraft precedent said that a confession is required to justify execution. The five executions on August 19, 1692 confirmed that the Court of Oyer and Terminer was not following precedent, which was a grave mistake according to some of the clergy. The confessions of the five Andover residents represented a turning point for Cotton Mather. Cotton Mather visited the jail in August 1692. He was oblivious to the suffering of the prisoners in the filthy conditions. He wrote that he had "lately seen, even poor children of several ages, even from seven to twenty, more or less, *confessing* their familiarity with Devils."

The confessions were obtained by the trickery and deceit of the magistrates. Their purpose was to falsity the record. For example, many of the confessions divulged the workings of the invisible world which Cotton Mather had repeatedly and consistently espoused. Some of the accused denied that devils could take the shape of innocent persons without their consent. This thesis was one of Mather's main strong points for his persecutions using spectral evidence. Virtually all the Andover confessions offered the usual account of the devil's operation. Unanimously they agreed that the Devil was a small black man. The Devil made them undo their allegiance to the church by renouncing their baptism. The Devil had them seal their covenants with him by signing his book. The Andover confessions also described the devil's methods of re-baptizing people and of giving communion. There were only minor variations as to whether the book was red or made of birch bark, and whether he dipped heads to baptize on flung initiates bodily in the water. The initial Andover confessions were obtained by mild torture or in most cases by the implied threat of torture. The contents of these extraordinary confessions were obtained by the resignation of the accused in agreeing with leading questions of the magistrates (notably John Hathorne).

The most spectacular revelations of the Andover confessions concerned a diabolic involvement. The devil was the base of Cotton Mather's paranoia. Accused witches of Andover testified to the riding of poles to meetings at Salem Village. Some meetings had as many as 500 witches plotting the ruin of New England's churches. Mary Lacey Jr. said "the Devil would set up his kingdom there and we should have happy days." Susanna Post said that she attended a witch meeting of 200 witches, where she heard there were 500 witches in the county. Mary Toothaker testified that at a Salem Village witch meeting "they did talk of 305 witches in the county. Their discourse was about pulling down the kingdom of Christ and setting up the kingdom of Satan." Many of the confessions identified the two ringleaders of the witches, Mather Carrier and the minister George Burroughs. Of course these two were first identified as Satan's leaders by Cotton Mather and these two were among the five hanged on August 19, 1692. These "most ample confessions" were the required justification of the judge's sentences described as "miraculously confirmed" by Cotton Mather. More accurately, Cotton Mather concluded the confessions confirmed the very existence of the invisible world as put forth by Cotton Mather.

Rev. Thomas Barnard, Harvard class of 1679, followed the teachings of John Calvin. Rev. Barnard believed in the power of confession for the forgiveness of sin. The authorities were able to elicit confessions from essentially all of the Andover accused witches. In hindsight, Barnard should have empathized Calvin's dictum that "we confess To Him certainly," and not to appointed magistrates.

On August 10, 1692, the Andover accusers made a direct strike at the immediate family of Rev. Francis Dane by charging his granddaughter, Elizabeth Johnson Jr., with witchcraft. In the entire Salem witchcraft affair, more members of Rev. Dane's family, both his immediate family and extended family, were accused and arrested than any other family. Apparently, the accusations against the Dane family were part of the old guard's plan to make examples of lenient Puritan clergymen (like Dane) who were deviating too far from the orthodox line.

The wife and five daughters or stepdaughters of Andover blacksmith John Bridges were imprisoned for witchcraft by August 25, 1692. Apparently John Bridges believed that their witchcraft was real; it seems that he had fallen under a spell himself—the spell of confession. What was it? Hawthorne wrote, "The complaint of the human heart, sorrow-laden, perchance guilty, to the great heart of mankind; beseeching its sympathy or forgiveness—at every moment—in each accent—and never in vain! It was this profound and continual undertone that gave the clergyman his most appropriate power."

Trials in the Superior Court in January 1693

The first meeting of the new Superior Court of Judicature was held at Salem in January 1693. This was ten months after the start of the witchcraft delusion. Fifty-six prisoners were brought to trial. Spectral testimony was not allowed as evidence in this court, which essentially left only slander and confession as evidence against the accused. All were found innocent, except for three, who received sentence of death. Two of the three, Elizabeth Johnson Jr. (called Betty) and Mary Post, were (as appeared by their behavior) the "most senseless and ignorant creatures that could be found." The third was Sarah Wardwell. It would appear then, that the other two were included in the three just so it would not be obvious that Sarah Wardwell alone had been picked. Even after the witchcraft epidemic had almost played itself out, Sarah Wardwell in January 1693 found herself singled out. No explanation has yet been given for her conviction. Calef tries to explain it as follows, "It seems that Samuel and Sarah Wardwell had both confessed themselves guilty; but he retracting his said confession, was tried and executed. It is supposed that this woman, fearing her husband's fate, was not so stiff in her denials of her former confession, such as it was."

Chief Judge Stoughton signed a warrant for the speedy execution of the three, and also of the five others who were convicted at the former Court of Oyer and Terminer but not executed then. Governor Phips was informed by the Attorney General that the three who were convicted were as innocent as the ones cleared. Phips acted quickly and sent a reprieve to stop the executions until he could get advice from England. Of course advice from England would take months. Stoughton upon this occasion was enraged and filled with passionate anger. Calef quotes him as speaking to the effect that "We were in a way to have cleared the land of these. Who it is that obstructs the course of justice I know not. The Lord be merciful to the country."

The governor, Sir William Phips, issued a general jail release in May 1693. When Sarah Wardwell came home to Andover with her baby Rebecca, she found the farm deserted, her other children gone. Eliakim, aged 5, had been bound out to Daniel Poor, one of the Andover Selectmen. William, aged 12, had been apprenticed to weaver Samuel Frye, who was associated with Christopher Osgood and Walter Wright in building mills. The oldest boy, Samuel Jr., aged 14, was with his uncle (by marriage), John Ballard. Elizabeth, aged 3, was the house of John Stevens.

After September 22, 1692, Massachusetts was never again to witness another execution for witchcraft. The people of Massachusetts had by no means all fallen victim to the mania. In fact, examination of the records shows that nearly all the hysterical and inflammatory writings were composed by Cotton Mather and his cohorts. All the utterances of the citizens, as have come to us in letters written to stop the witch hunt, were rational and well composed.

In the Salem witch trails, the old guard eagerly accepted the outmoded doctrines preached by Cotton Mather and subtly encouraged superstition and prejudice. They were willing to pervert the legal system into a judicial massacre. They urged forward the witchcraft persecutions in a desperate attempt to retain the power of their old Puritan theocracy. Ultimate responsibility for the Salem disaster of 1692, therefore, must be laid on them.

The most prominent names in the old guard were those of William Stoughton and John Hathorne. Hathorne, in carrying out most of the preliminary examinations, was especially abusive. Stoughton, as chief justice in the witchcraft trials, was the chief culprit, callous and ruthless. None of the other magistrates or judges was more fanatical than these two. Cotton Mather was the link between the conspiracies and the old guard. By calculated action and by deliberate neglect, he used his position to offer tacit if not outright encouragement to both groups. He was blinded to a bitter truth. The real threat was never Satan, but rather the glimmers of enlightened thinking among plain citizens.

Increase Mather and his son Cotton Mather were firmly identified both with the causes of the hysteria and with the political appointees who made the tragic judgments. By 1700 popular feeling had risen firmly against the Salem trials, and the blame fell upon the Mathers, especially Cotton. Most 19th-century historians place full responsibility for the trials with Cotton Mather. Brooks Adams (1848-1927), son of Charles Francis Adams, called the trials themselves the central moral issue of the 17th century. However, modern scholars, influenced by the enormous body of writings of Cotton Mather, feel that the allegations against Cotton Mather seem to overstate the case.

Appendix: About the author

The Birth of Digital Seismology at MIT

by MIT Earth Resources Laboratory, Building 54-210, 77 Massachusetts Avenue, Cambridge, MA 02139-4307, dated February 1, 2019

Led by MIT alumnus Enders Robinson, MIT's former Geophysical Analysis Group transformed the field of geophysical recording and data processing. In the late 1940s, a conversation between an MIT geologist and a mathematician led to an innovative collaboration that would revolutionize geophysics and the exploration energy industry: MIT's Geophysical Analysis Group (GAG), the precursor to the Earth Resources Laboratory (ERL) in MIT's Department of Earth, Atmospheric and Planetary Sciences (EAPS). Before the earliest computers, researchers, students, and geophysicists scrutinized seismic data—laboriously interpreting peaks and valleys on a seismic trace—to map subsurface features and find likely reservoirs of hydrocarbons. To obtain this time-series data, exploration geophysicists would trigger ground motions with explosives sending energy through the earth. The "echoes" were recorded as a waveform on a strip of photographic paper: a seismograph. As the waves traveled through layers with different porosities, they would bend, distort, reflect, and reverberate, providing information about the local geology and potential fossil fuel resources.

However, seismic data are notoriously "noisy." Seismographs pick up irrelevant motions in the earth or capture the same wave multiple times as it reflects off of underground features. In the addition model that industry used at the time, all of these wave sources combined into a single waveform trace in analog—a process called "convolution" — which scientists had to visually tease apart. The new consortium at MIT, GAG, was about to change all of that, making computation easier, quicker, and more accurate. It was during a carpool that MIT Professor George Wadsworth, a mathematician applying time-series methods to weather prediction, was discussing the use of mathematics in geology with Professors Robert R. Shrock and Patrick M. Hurley, both of whom worked in MIT's Department of Geology and Geophysics. Wadsworth needled Hurley because weather and seismic traces behaved similarly and wondered why time-series analysis had not yet been applied to seismograms. Wadsworth, now interested in geophysics, set a new graduate student, Enders Robinson1950, S.M. 1952, PhD 1954 to the task of determining if he could use time-series analysis to find wave reflections in the record that would help estimate the properties of the Earth's subsurface.

Time-series analysis fascinated Robinson. After finishing his bachelor's in mathematics at MIT, Robinson returned to MIT in the fall of 1950 and, working under Professors of Mathematics Wadsworth and Norbert Weiner, began applying time-series analysis to weather prediction and seismic exploration, using traces provided by petroleum companies. Simultaneously, Robinson pursued a master's degree in economics with Paul A. Samuelson and Robert Solow, who also worked with time-series—a move that would prove useful with his geology problem. While trying to find underlying innovations in economic data, Robinson learned that technological advances could not be predicted, so when he crafted mathematical equations to reflect this, he found that there should be a measurable prediction error in the data when one occurs. Robinson proposed applying this to geophysics—treating digitized seismic traces as economic series and carrying out prediction-error filtering, now called deconvolution. The method worked. Excited by the initial results and the technique's potential, Hurley drummed up interest from the oil and gas industry while Robinson learned to code on the Whirlwind, MIT's first digital computer.

In February of 1952, GAG was born in the Department of Geology and Geophysics, and a year later, it became a consortium—with oil and service companies, MIT researchers, and graduate students. Raytheon was contracted to help with calculations using the FERUT computer, while GAG used the Whirlwind. Despite computing setbacks, technology continued to improve and over several years, GAG consistently showed the consortium's advisory committee the promise of deconvolution using digital computing. By 1953, it became apparent that industry liked the deconvolution method, but not digital processing. They insisted on investigating the properties of noise and analog filters to boost the signal to noise ratio—the cost and inconsistency of digital processing deterred them.

Above: Dr. Enders Robinson. Image courtesy of IEEE History Center

When Robinson first started leading GAG in 1952, his objectives were to make deconvolution operable on a production basis with the Whirlwind, demonstrate that deconvolution worked on assorted seismic records, and provide a geophysical model that justified deconvolution. When he submitted his doctoral thesis "Predictive decomposition of time series with applications to seismic exploration" in the summer of 1954, GAG had achieved this. By introducing the convolutional model, GAG showed that the signal and noise are related and that the seismic trace is the sum of wavelets arriving with random strengths and arrival times. In Robinson's words, this turned the seismic world upside down.

For the remaining four years, GAG continued to perform significant research: fitting the model to the data and differentiating between different types of noise, but interest and guidance from industry petered out. By June 1957, GAG shut down and its members scattered into industry.

In the early 1960s, former GAG graduate student Sven Treitel 1953, SM 1955 PhD 1958, then working at Amoco, revived GAG's work and, with Robinson, began adapting it for the needs of the fossil fuel industry. Together, they developed Fortran software, as well as writing and republishing papers in layman's language to function as a teaching tool. By the mid-1960s digital memory improved significantly and digital processing overtook geophysics, making it the first scientific field to do so. Former GAG members, now leaders at oil and service companies, were on board, and the early 1970s saw the "Golden Era" of industry-sponsored university consortia, including MIT's ERL, which continues to this day in a similar form, to tackle geophysical challenges leveraging the latest in mathematics, machine learning and Earth sciences.

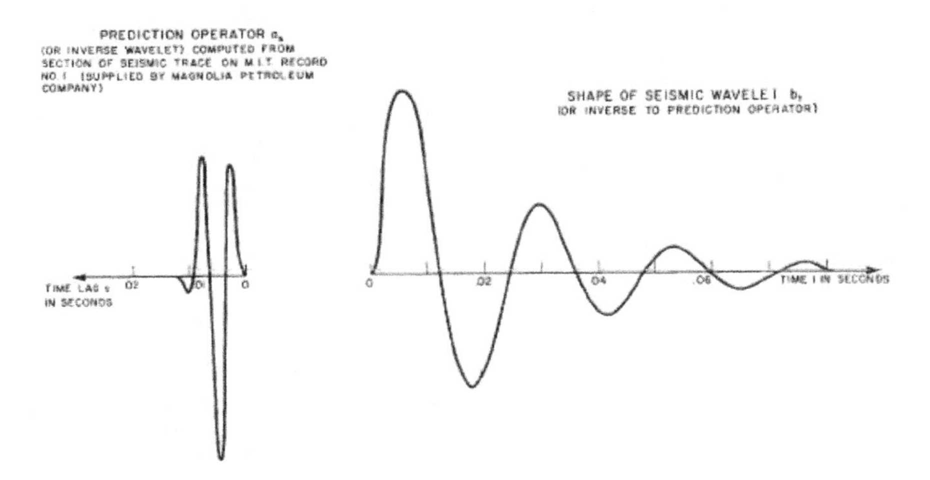

Above: The first-ever figure of a waveform computed using deconvolution, included in Enders Robinson's PhD thesis and the GAG annual report in 1954.

Columbia University

In New York City, Columbia University's **S**chool of **E**ngineering and **A**pplied **S**cience (SEAS) launched its yearlong 150th birthday celebration (1864-2014) with a full week of activities that engaged students, alumni, faculty, and staff. To cap the anniversary year, the School hosted a Founders Day Gala on the evening of Saturday, November 15, 2014 in the Cathedral of St. John the Divine. The Gala included a cocktail reception and dinner, with remarks by Dean Boyce and additional speakers, as well as a video of the School's history and milestones. This date marks the exact day in 1864 when the School first opened its doors, with 20 students and 3 teachers. In the ensuing 150 years, Columbia Engineering has grown to accommodate more than 4,300 undergraduate and graduate students and 175 faculty members.

The School of Engineering and Applied Science (SEAS) listed about 100 milestones in its history. Among them are

1786: DeWitt Clinton and the Erie Canal. Graduating with Columbia College's first class, DeWitt Clinton becomes the driving force in building the Erie Canal (1817-25), the largest American engineering project of the early 19th century.

1823. Horatio Allen graduates from Columbia. Horatio Allen graduates from Columbia, going on to assemble America's first steam locomotive, consult on the Brooklyn Bridge, and lead the American Society of Civil Engineers (ASCE).

1988: Father of Digital Seismic Data Processing. **Enders A. Robinson**, considered the father of digital seismic data processing, is appointed professor of applied geophysics, the same year he is elected to the National Academy of Engineering

1998: Stormer Wins Nobel Prize. Horst Stormer wins the 1998 Nobel Prize in Physics for the discovery of a new form of quantum fluid with fractionally charged excitations—the fractional quantum Hall effect.

References

Enders Anthony Robinson: MIT and the Birth of Digital Signal Processing, Scientist and Science series volume 4, Available from Amazon.com and other retail outlets, 2014

Enders Anthony Robinson: MIT Geophysical Analysis Group, Scientist and Science series volume 5, Available from Amazon.com and other retail outlets, 2016

Robert R. Schrock: Geology at M.I.T., 1865-1965: a history of the first hundred years of geology at Massachusetts Institute of Technology, MIT Press, 1977

Enders Anthony Robinson: Genealogy of the Barker Family of Andover, Genealogical Series volume 4, Available from Amazon.com and other retail outlets, 2019

Enders Anthony Robinson: Genealogy of the Wardwell Family of Andover, Genealogical Series volume 5, Available from Amazon.com and other retail outlets, 2019

Made in the USA
Monee, IL
22 June 2021

72038601R00125